Organising learning in the primary school classroom

Second edition

Joan Dean

London and New York

First edition published 1983 by Croom Helm Ltd
Second edition published 1992 by Routledge
11 New Fetter Lane, London EC4P 4EE

Simultaneously published in the USA and Canada
by Routledge
29 West 35th Street, New York, NY 10001

Reprinted 1993, 1994 (twice) and 1995

Laserprinted by GilCoM Ltd, Mitcham, Surrey
Printed and bound in Great Britain by
Biddles Ltd, Guildford and King's Lynn

British Library Cataloguing in Publication Data
A catalogue record for this book is available from the British Library

Library of Congress Cataloguing in Publication Data
A catalogue record for this book is available from the Library of Congress

ISBN 0–415–06249–7

Contents

Analyses

Figures

Tables

1 Introduction

Every teacher is a manager of children's learning. As a teacher you influence the children you teach in many ways. Because of you, many of them will learn things that they will remember for the rest of their lives. It is a considerable responsibility.

How you discharge this responsibility depends not only on the person you are and the relationships you are able to build with children and colleagues, important as these are. The ability to organise children's learning, the actual teaching skills you possess, your ability to observe, select and present material, lead discussion, assess, evaluate and so on, are crucial and make all the difference between the group in which most of the children come near to achieving their full potential and one in which most are under-achieving.

This book is concerned with the way you, as teacher, organise the work in your classroom. In primary schools children are normally with one teacher for the majority of the time so that he or she is able to get to know them well. Most teachers in primary school also have some freedom to plan the work as seems best to them.

Each chapter of this book deals with a particular aspect of organisation and most chapters contain suggestions for assessing your present situation preparatory to reviewing possible ways of working and selecting those which meet your needs and those of your class.

Anyone working in education at the present time is very conscious of the pressures. Public interest in education is considerable, and the *Education Reform Act* has given both governors and parents a much greater say in the way schools function. Good schools have always involved parents in the education of their children and it is now essential to demonstrate the good work the school does to the local community, because schools are in competition with each other for pupils. This is time-consuming, but it pays dividends in terms of the trust and respect which can be generated and the support which can be gained. It also helps to foster children's learning if home and school work together.

One important effect of the 1988 Act is to reduce the freedom of the school and the individual teacher in the classroom. In spite of this, teachers in the primary school still have a great deal of freedom compared with teachers at later stages and with teachers in some other countries. The National Curriculum dictates much of the content of teaching but does not dictate the process.

Schools will still need to make their own statements of policy and schemes but the way a school is managed is likely to have a considerable effect on the way the teacher in the classroom actually works. There is a considerable move in primary schools at the present time to working on a collegiate basis with all teachers involved in the decision-making process in some way. It is also becoming usual for schools to appoint teachers to lead particular aspects of curriculum. Where these ways of working are successful, the classroom teacher may lose a certain amount of autonomy in the interests of continuity for children, but will have had the benefit of being part of the agreed way of working and will be supported in different aspects of the curriculum by a colleague who has been asked to make a study of a particular area.

Different teachers have different styles of working. This provides variety which can be valuable and helps to keep the teaching dynamic in many classes. It means that there are a variety of opportunities for children to acquire, apply and practise basic skills.

Society delegates to the teacher the task of educating children. The teacher and the child come to school bringing with them a variety of talents, experiences and influences. Children also will have formed many ideas about the world around them before they come to school and these need to be taken into account by the teacher. In school the teacher's task is to see that the child experiences the curriculum, develops and learns. To achieve this the teacher creates a learning environment and organises time, space and resources to enable the child to learn.

Each chapter in this book offers you suggestions for assessing specific aspects of the situation in your own classroom. You may like to work through the book chapter by chapter, thinking out your point of view as you go along. Alternatively, you may like to select areas of your work to consider and analyse.

The profile which follows on the next few pages is designed as a starting point for your thinking and as something to come back to after you have read the book.

Every teacher organises work to suit his or her ideas, preferences and skills and for the particular group of children he or she teaches. Analysis 1.1 is designed to help you identify your own organisational preferences so that you can keep them in mind as you work through the book. You may then find it interesting to see if you change your original ideas after considering further the options open to you.

Each section of the profile represents a spectrum of possible views. There are no 'right' answers.

ANALYSIS 1.1: PROFILE OF ORGANISATIONAL PREFERENCES

Tick the statement in each section which most nearly reflects your views

Pattern of daily programme

1　Each child has an individual programme of work matched to his or her needs. I then withdraw groups for specific teaching with occasional class activity
2　My main emphasis is on group work with a good deal of individual work and some class work
3　I like to spend some time working with the whole class, some on group work and some with individuals
4　I divide work about equally between class and group work and pay attention to individuals as necessary
5　I work with the whole class for most of the time, following it up with individual and group work as necessary

Timing of daily programme

1　I like to use time flexibly, responding to ideas which occur. I am happy to have any part of the curriculum at any time of day
2　I do some core subject work in the morning and some in the afternoon but leave time to respond to ideas which occur
3　I do core subject work in the morning and other work in the afternoon, but I try to be flexible in planning each day
4　I have a timetable for core subject work in the morning and I programme all work carefully so that I cover the ground

The teacher's use of time

1　My time during the day is mostly occupied with small groups and individuals, extending their thinking and helping to plan their work

---

2 My time is mostly spent with individuals and small groups but I work with the whole class several times during the week

3 I spend about half my time in class teaching and half with small groups and individuals

4 I spend more than half my time teaching the whole class with some group teaching and follow up with individuals

5 A high proportion of my time is spent in teaching the whole class with occasional group and individual work

Children's use of time

1 I expect children to spend more than half their time on work which has been individually programmed within a framework which offers some choice in the use of time. The remaining time is spent in working in pairs or groups with occasional whole class activity

2 I believe it is important to match the needs of individuals and encourage children to plan the use of time, but this can sometimes be in the context of class or group work

3 I aim to have an even balance between work which matches the needs of individuals, with some choice in the order in which work is done, and work undertaken by the whole class or in groups

4 I expect the majority of the children to work at the pace of the class, but I try to arrange for the slower children to have extra time on aspects they find difficult. I let children choose the order of their work upon occasions

5 Almost all my children spend the same amount of time on each aspect of curriculum and do similar work, with help if necessary

Choice of activity

1 Much of the children's work allows choice within a carefully structured framework. I try to teach children to choose intelligently

2 I think it is important for children to learn to choose and I build opportunities for this into the programme

3 I like to provide a certain amount of choice as well as some compulsory activity

4 I try to provide some choice, but the majority of the work I give children is compulsory

5 I keep choice to a minimum, because I believe every child should experience a similar curriculum

Curriculum content

1 I put work in the core subjects of English, mathematics and science first, but I like to find ways in which I can integrate the concepts, knowledge and skills required by the different parts of the National Curriculum and do some work arising from current interests
2 I try to provide a mixture of work, involving planned teaching, often under subject headings and a certain amount of work arising from interests and topics
3 I use current interests when they fit into my planned programme for teaching the National Curriculum which is more or less organised under subject headings
4 My lessons are normally planned under subject headings because I believe this is the philosophy behind the National Curriculum. I cross reference when it seems appropriate

Use of competition

1 I try to avoid placing children in competitive situations, because I feel concern about the effect of competition on some children. I aim instead to foster cooperation
2 I use competition occasionally in situations where it seems unlikely to do any harm. I try to encourage cooperation
3 I use competition when I think it will motivate children. I also do some work designed to encourage cooperation
4 I find that competition is valuable providing it doesn't get out of hand. I provide occasional opportunities for cooperation
5 Competition is an important incentive in the classroom as in life and I believe children need to learn to fail as well as to win. I would like to foster cooperation but don't feel that there are many opportunities for doing so within normal classroom work

Grouping of children

1 Work in groups is usually on the basis of children's own preferences and I aim to train children to work cooperatively

2 I use group work a good deal, forming groups according to the needs of the work in hand. I aim to have children working together
3 I have some work in interest groups, some in friendship groups and some in ability groups. Children may work together if they wish
4 I normally do core subject work with children in ability groups. I also have occasional interest groups in topic work
5 I prefer to work with children in ability groups when I am not working with the whole class

Use of space

1 I use all the space I can and allow children to work in other parts of the school and move freely about the classroom. There are no fixed table/chair places for each child
2 I expect children to move freely about the classroom and adjacent space but each child has his or her own place
3 I allow children to move about the classroom to collect things and occasionally I let them work outside the classroom when this seems necessary
4 I prefer children to stay in their places except for practical work. I rarely let them work outside the classroom
5 I like children to be in their places in the classroom where I can keep an eye on them

Use of furniture

1 I set out my classroom and adjoining areas for particular activities. I aim to have these in use by groups of children for most of the day. Children sit by themselves or in groups
2 I have spaces for particular activities but other activities take place in them as well. Children normally sit in friendship groups but move to other groups when necessary
3 I rearrange the room for practical work, but I have a space for books and another for messy work. Tables are grouped and children sit in ability groups for basic work
4 I rearrange the room for practical work, but I have a space for books and another for messy work. Tables are grouped and children sit in ability groups for basic work

5 I tend to have one activity at a time. Children normally sit in ability groups. I like a formal classroom arrangement with tables in rows

Use of resources

1 I make the maximum use of resources to foster individual learning. I select and make teaching materials which can be used independently of the teacher
2 I like to have some good individual materials as well as materials to use with the whole class and I buy and make both types
3 I like to have some good individual textbooks for core subject work, but prefer to have a variety of books and materials for other subjects
4 I make a good deal of use of textbooks, supplementing them with other books and materials when necessary
5 The main resources in my classroom are my own voice, the blackboard, pictures to help children's understanding and some good textbooks.

Records and assessments

1 I keep a forecast/record of my work and aim to keep a detailed record of each child's work and progress through the National Curriculum, and in social and personal development. and I involve them in this
2 I keep a forecast/record of my work, record each child's progress in National Curriculum work and make notes about other things as necessary
3 I keep a forecast/record of my work and keep notes of children's progress in the core and foundation subjects.
4 I keep a forecast/record of my work and a check list of each child's progress in the core and foundation subjects
5 I keep a forecast/record of my work and a mark list showing each child's marks in the core and foundation subjects

Work with other teachers

1 I like to work with other teachers in a teaching team or sharing thinking and materials

2 I like to do some work with other teachers
3 I work with other teachers occasionally, usually when we take a group out
4 I discuss work with other teachers but we are each responsible for our own work and development
5 I prefer to work with my own class all the time, but I take part in staff discussion when necessary

Work with parents

1 I try to get to know all the parents of the children in my class, to take note of what they say about their children, tell them about the work we are doing and suggest ways in which they can help. I like to have parents helping in the classroom
2 I try to get to know the parents of children in my class and I suggest ways in which they can help. I like to have parents helping in the classroom
3 I try to get to know the parents of children in my class and I have carefully selected parents helping in the classroom
4 I get to know the parents of children in my class as far as I can but I am not keen to have parents in the classroom
5 I believe teaching is a professional task which should be left to professionals

Equal opportunities

1 I am conscious that it is all too easy to treat boys and girls, black and white children, middle and working class children and children with disabilities in different ways and to be prejudiced about what they can do. I am constantly checking myself to see that this is not happening and aim to teach my children not to be prejudiced
2 I am conscious that it is easy to show prejudice without being aware of it and I do my best to avoid treating any group or individual differently because of race, gender, social class or handicap. I discourage any expression of prejudice from the children
3 I try to avoid treating any individual or group differently because of race, gender, social class or handicap
4 I try to treat all children in the same way

2 The children

Education at school is about children learning. Children are different from one another and are likely to respond differently to different approaches and treatment. Any group of children, however homogeneous, is a collection of very different individuals. It is not really possible or efficient for children to be taught individually but they do need some individual attention. If as teacher you are to help them to learn and to consider and meet individual needs, you must find and create enough common strands to enable some work to take place in a group or class. This makes it possible to get the majority started and provides an opportunity to work with individuals.

The differences among children are particularly evident at the beginning of schooling, whether this is in a playgroup, a nursery class or school or a reception class. They come to school with ideas and interests and ways of looking at things and with differing experience. Children at this stage are also becoming part of a larger group than they have known previously and they need to come to terms with this.

The process of organising children's learning so that curricular aims can be achieved involves bringing together the needs, ideas, interests and characteristics of the children with the knowledge, skill, experience and personality of the teacher within a given environment. It is therefore very important to consider what children are like and how they learn.

CHILD DEVELOPMENT

Teachers of children at the primary stage of education are usually very conscious of their development, partly because the development at this stage is rapid and partly because in the past a good deal of emphasis has been placed on child development in teacher training.

The importance of this knowledge for the teacher lies in the decisions which have to be made about suitable times and methods for teaching particular things to particular children. Most teachers have encountered the child who has difficulty with some activity such as tying shoe laces or forming letters, who, six months later, performs these tasks easily. The problem is that within any given class there will be children at a variety of stages of maturity as well as varying abilities and somehow the teacher has to see that they all learn.

A child comes into the world with a legacy of inherited abilities, tendencies and characteristics. Throughout the years of schooling, each child is developing as an individual person. Home and school environments interact with these inherited abilities and tendencies and the child discovers personal talents and abilities, interests and limitations. The adults and children around provide models and a child will test out behaviour and activity in play and in everyday living, persisting with some kinds of behaviour and modifying or abandoning others in the light of the responses which come.

Children have also developed ideas about the world by the time they start school and these will be modified by their experience in and out of school. In science, in particular, the ideas children have developed may be a barrier to observation and reasoning. Wynne Harlen (1985) describes how children cling to their own ideas in science even when experience shows them to be incorrect. In a similar way Martin Hughes (1986) describes the mathematical knowledge which most children have on entry to school and suggests that problems sometimes arise because children do not relate this to the language of school mathematics. It is therefore important for you, as teacher, to be aware of children's ideas so that you can direct their observation and thinking in ways which will help them to develop further.

A child's physical attributes will have an effect on the emerging personality. A child who develops early will be at an advantage in being able to do things which others find difficult and become more confident as a result.

This is particularly relevant in relation to the time of year a child is born and the point at which he or she starts school. A child born in September is likely to be physically among the most developed in the class because he or she will be among the oldest. A child born in June, July or August is likely to be less well developed because he or she is among the youngest.

A recent piece of research, carried out in ILEA schools by a team led by Peter Mortimore and reported in *School matters* (1988), studied various aspects of classroom work, looking particularly at what makes effective teaching and an effective school. One important finding of this study is that teachers generally do not pay sufficient attention to the effects of differences in age in children. Teachers tend to regard the youngest children in the class as less able, rather than at an earlier stage of development. This could have important implications for their development since teacher expectation is known to be important in motivating children. If children begin to think of themselves as less able, this is likely to affect the effort they put into work and eventually will affect their performance. Teachers are, in any case, concerned about children who start school in the summer term and have only two years and one term in the infant school. Classes are at their most crowded in the summer and teachers work hard to try to cover work with summer entrants.

Neville Bennett and Joy Kell (1989) studied four year olds in infant classes. They found that provision for this age group was generally not very suitable and that a large amount of time was spent on basic skills and very little on play. The time spent on play was also not very profitably used and took little account of the finding that play is more effective when adults take part in it and use it for children's learning.

A child of unusual appearance may sometimes attract comment from peers, which may be damaging to confidence. A fat child, for example, has not only the problem of carrying extra weight around, but also the problem of other people's reactions to obesity.

A further point about physical development is that while children may be at varying stages in any one group, the progress through the different stages is similar for everyone. This may be very reassuring to a child who is small for his or her age. There is, of course, no guarantee that such a child will reach any particular adult size, but there is still the hope of catching up.

Physical development has a good many implications for teachers. Sight and hearing are not fully coordinated when a child starts school and coordination may pose problems which later solve themselves. It is also important for teachers of young children to be on the look out for defects not yet noticed. For example, a child may have very short or very long sight but will not realise that this is different from normal until he or she makes comparisons with what someone else can see. Much the same is true of hearing. Colour blindness is comparatively common in the population and most teachers will meet colour blind children. Children who have difficulty in distinguishing colours will have a number of difficulties to cope with and the sooner this condition is recognised the better.

A number of studies suggest that the most powerful influence on a child's life is the home and that parents are the most influential people. At the same time, the school does much to shape individuals at every stage of education and the ILEA study quoted above gives much detail which supports this view. The influence of the school has been acknowledged almost since formal education began and it is an aspect of our education service which is properly a source of professional pride among teachers.

The development of a self-image

The behaviour and response of other people towards a child helps to develop a self-image. Initially the parents start this process. A child whose parents praise and encourage him or her becomes confident in the ability to do things and is more likely to become a confident and competent adult than the child whose parents behave in a more negative way,

When the child starts school, teachers continue this process and at the primary stage much is happening that is important for the development of the self-image. The extent to which a child is praised or scolded or is acknowledged to achieve success or failure influences his or her attitudes and behaviour. All of us react positively to praise when we know it is genuine and deserved and activities in which other people tell us we have succeeded are those most likely to be repeated. Conversely, failure tends to make us want to avoid the activity in which we failed. In this sense the teacher reinforces some kinds of learning and also acts negatively by identifying behaviour to be eliminated.

There is evidence that teachers reinforce some children more effectively than others. Kelly (1989), for example, in a study which reviews research into gender differences notes that there is considerable evidence that girls get less of the teacher's attention in class than boys. This would seem to be true for all ages, ethnic groups and social classes in all subjects and with both male and female teachers. Crane and Mellon (1978) found that teachers tend to think well-behaved children have a higher academic potential than those who are less well-behaved. Galton and Delafield (1981) found that there was a tendency for children for whom the teacher had high expectations to receive more praise and more contact with the teacher than low achievers who received less praise and less feedback on their work. Tizard *et al.* (1988) found that boys generally received more criticism than girls and more praise and black boys received most criticism and disapproval and white girls least criticism and least praise.

Children also praise and criticise one another and this is an important contribution to learning. Children are building up pictures of themselves as being good at this and bad at that; able to get on well with other people or having problems in getting on with other people and so on. By the time they leave the primary school they are already confident in their ability to do some things and worried about their performance in others.

Children's self-images are also reflected in the way they relate to others. A child with a poor self-image will expect others to respond negatively and will often create this reaction by behaving provocatively.

Parsons *et al.* (1976) found that girls tended to assess their abilities as being lower than they are in actuality. Girls were also more worried about failure and more sensitive to negative information and this was evident from the age of about four.

The development of the self-image is closely related to the effect of the expectation of others for the progress of a particular child. If the child's parents or teacher demonstrate that they have high expectations of him or her, there is more likelihood that the child will, achieve and conversely. This can work for the child if the adults have high expectations which the child fulfils. He or she is then reinforced by success and starts the next task with increased confidence. There is also the complementary problem that parents and teachers can pressure children with their expectations so that they eventually give up trying, because they do not think they can live up to such expectations.

Alternatively, the expectations of others can give rise to an increasingly negative cycle in which the child fails, the teacher lowers expectation and the child's self-image is lowered correspondingly. The teacher's professional task is to get the level of expectation high enough to challenge and encourage and yet be within each child's capacity.

Edwards and Mercer in *Common knowledge* (1987) suggest that failure is too often seen as the property of pupils, whereas it may be the outcome of the communicative process. What is needed is more effective structuring of what is to be learned.

There is a good deal of research evidence to suggest that teachers under-estimate some children within the class. The study by Peter Mortimore *et al.* (1988) of Inner London schools in which the teachers studied tended to under-estimate the younger children in the class, often because they were not really aware of the differences in ages, has already been mentioned. They also tended to over-estimate the boys compared with the girls. Teachers in other studies have been found to under-estimate children from working-class homes and black children.

The development of the self-image is also closely bound up with the physical, social and emotional development of the child. Part of the self-image will concern the child's physical appearance and this may affect confidence and social development and the way in which the child learns to cope with personal feelings and reactions. You need to be very sensitive to this and try to help individuals to cope with the way others treat them and at the same time encourage children to be sensitive to each other.

Children also develop ideas about other people. Bruce Carrington and Geoffrey Short in *Race and the primary school* (1989) describe how almost half the infants in a council estate school thought that it was possible for people to change colour and that black parents did not necessarily have to have black children, and conversely. At the early stages very few children saw racism as a problem about being black, but from the second year of the junior school on almost all children recognised this. Fourth year juniors in particular were aware of racial stereotyping.

LEARNING IN THE CORE SUBJECTS

Another important set of relationships to consider is that of intelligence, experience and language. We very often under-estimate the intelligence of children and over-estimate their experience. Many of the mistakes made by children stem from their limited experience and language and from errors of generalisation from one situation to another. You need to be constantly aware of this and seek to use whatever experience a child has to help him or her to learn further.

Language development is one of the most important areas of work for the teacher and is rightly regarded as a corner stone of each child's education. The ability to use language determines not only the nature of a person's relationships with others and the ability to cooperate but to some extent also the ability to think, since language is the medium of a good deal of human thought. Vygotsky (1978) suggests that children 'undergo quite profound changes in their understanding by engaging in joint activity and conversation with other people'.

Language is also the main medium by which children learn. Edwards and Mercer (1987) describe the way in which teachers have to work to achieve common understanding in the language used in the classroom. They stress the importance of classroom talk as a means of learning and suggest that what is needed is 'sharing, comparing, contrasting and arguing perspectives against those of others'. They also stress the need for children to reflect on what is being learned.

The development of language skills is far from being a simple matter. A child starting school at five has already made tremendous progress. Most children, by this stage, have a vocabulary of about 2000 words, but, more importantly, they have acquired knowledge of the structure of the language as it is used in their home environment. They can form sentences which they have never heard spoken; they can use the past and the future tenses as well as the present; they know the meanings which lie behind word order, that *man bites dog* has a different meaning from *dog bites man,* which is conveyed by the way the words are put together. They have learned the language necessary to express needs, ideas, and thoughts to ask questions, to seek cooperation from others as well as many other things. Even where the language used at home is far from standard English, it will have a structure and consistency of its own and the child will have learned to apply its rules. This will be equally true of children with a different home language.

The intellectual achievement this represents is considerable. No one intentionally teaches pre-school children the rules of language and they do not know them as something to repeat but as something to apply. The acquisition of this knowledge requires reasoning power of a high order and it is interesting that one can sometimes see the process at work in the mistakes a child makes. The child who says 'mouses' instead of 'mice', or 'runned' instead of 'ran', for example, is demonstrating an ability to apply the rule correctly, but hasn't realised that these are exceptions.

We can conclude from this that children are capable of particular kinds of reasoning and abstraction from an early age if these are in context. We might go further and note that there is not only evidence of the motivation to communicate, but that many children appear to enjoy the challenge involved. It suggests that if we can find ways of tapping motivation of this strength, the power for learning in children is far greater than we normally see in school. It also supports the view that learning is likely to be better when children are asked to reason something through rather than just remember it.

This learning and reasoning is all related in the first instance to particular situations. Children start acquiring vocabulary and language structure in particular contexts. By the time they are five, they are already using language to refer to and discuss what is not present, but they acquired and used the language initially in particular situations and generalised from these.

This has important implications for later learning. The fact that young children's language is frequently related to a specific context means that they may use the same words as those of an adult, but give them a more limited meaning. For example, the child for whom the word 'holiday' means an air journey to foreign parts, interprets the word differently from the child whose family spend holidays at home, perhaps going out for days. The child who lives on a remote farm has a different understanding of the word 'neighbour' from the child who lives in a block of flats or in a back-to-back terrace or a council estate.

Even a teacher of older children should never assume that because a child uses particular words he or she fully understands them. Language is a way of representing the world to yourself and of talking about it to other people. Children start by talking about what is present, then develop the ability to talk about what is not present and the words used gradually become the 'inner speech' of their thoughts. It seems likely that very young children need to think aloud a good deal in the process of developing the ability to think silently in their minds.

When teachers talk of extending children's language, they normally think first about adding to vocabulary. There is also a case for emphasising language structure and considering those words which help to organise thinking. Prepositions, for example, represent relationships, between objects or people. Comparative words are also important in representing similarities and differences in relationships and a variety of pronouns, conjunctions and other words relate the parts of what we say and enable us to express increasingly complex ideas and relationships.

The programmes of study of the National Curriculum (DES 1989a) give very little attention to language structure in any direct sense, but there are references to the skill and knowledge needed in comments such as the following:

They should be taught to look for instances where
- ideas should be differently ordered or more fully expressed in order to convey their meaning
- tenses or pronouns have been used incorrectly or inconsistently
- meaning is unclear because of insufficient punctuation or omitted words
- meaning would be improved by a richer or more precise choice of vocabulary

Words also provide a convenient way of sorting our thinking into categories, much as in learning mathematics, children sort things into sets according to their attributes. Words like 'kind', 'good', 'naughty' are sorting words which are learned very early, but the process goes on right through schooling and we expect children to be able to classify in many areas of work. For example, in geography we classify soil characteristics, rocks, landscape types and so on, in science we classify plants, animals, substances, forces, etc.; and there are many other ways in which this process occurs in most aspects of curriculum. It is the basis of the ability to generalise and to reason from one premiss to the next and thus to be able to apply what is known to new situations.

This suggests that it can be useful in planning new work to start by thinking about the experience children may bring to new learning and the language they will need to express it. This process is needed in all aspects of the curriculum.

There is also a sense in which the other two core subjects, science and mathematics, may operate across the curriculum, although both need time devoted especially to them. Opportunities for using mathematical language are part of the everyday experience of young children. There are many opportunities in the infant classroom for counting and measuring and talking about shapes and size. Martin Hughes, in *Children and number* (1986) suggests that many difficulties arise from the use of the operational symbols + − × ÷. Children come across numerals in many contexts outside school, but the mathematical symbols are peculiar to the classroom and children take a long time to link them with their experience. This suggests that it might be a good idea to look for ways in which these could be used in as many practical contexts as possible. He also found that children found it helpful to use their fingers for counting and suggests that teachers should encourage this. Activities like making sets can be part of topic work of all kinds, particularly where children collect things to be studied. The classification of plants, animals, rocks and much else uses the idea of placing things in sets according to their attributes and mathematics contributes here to science and science to mathematics. Many studies can lead to the making of graphs and charts and using these to abstract information.

Opportunities for scientific investigation will arise as part of other work on many occasions. Topics will frequently provide opportunities for science. An environmental study will provide many opportunities for studying plants and animals and perhaps looking at soil and rocks. A study of a historical building could lead to an investigation of how people raised stone before modern equipment was there to help them or it could offer the opportunity to study the effects of weathering on materials.

Wynne Harlen in *Teaching and learning primary science* (1985) gives useful summaries of what may be expected by way of scientific work from children at different ages. This review of development has application in other parts of the curriculum. The following is an abbreviated version of her statements:

5–7 year olds
1   They cannot think through actions but have to carry them out in practice
2   They can only see from their own point of view. They can only see from another point of view by moving physically
3   They focus on one aspect of an object or situation at a time, e.g., their judgement of the amount of water in a container will take into account only one dimension, probably the height the liquid reaches, not height and the width of the container
4   They tend not to relate one event to another when they encounter an unfamiliar sequence of events. They are likely to remember the first and last in a sequence but not the ones in between
5   The results of actions not yet carried out cannot be anticipated

7–9 year olds
1   They begin to see a simple process as a whole, relating the individual parts to each other so that a process of change can be grasped and events put in sequence

2 They can think through a simple process in reverse, which brings awareness of the conservation of some physical quantities during changes in which there appears to be some increase or decrease
3 They may realise that two effects have to be taken into account in deciding the result of an action, e.g. if a ball of plasticine is squashed flat it gets thinner as well as wider, so it may not be any bigger overall than before
4 There is some progress towards being able to see things from someone else's point of view
5 They can relate a physical cause to its effect

All of these developments have their limitations and can only be carried out in familiar situations.

9–11 year olds
1 They can to some extent handle problems which involve more than one variable
2 They can use a wider range of logical relations and so mentally manipulate more things
3 They show less tendency to jump to conclusions and a greater appreciation that ideas should be checked against evidence
4 They can use measurement and recording as part of a more systematic and accurate approach to problems
5 They can go through the possible steps in an investigation and produce a possible plan of action

All of these skills are still only operative within simple cases where what is concerned has a concrete reality for the child. It must also be remembered that such skills will be present only if there has been good teaching at each stage.

FACTORS WHICH AFFECT LEARNING

The major task of the school and the teacher is to enable children to learn. While some of the factors affecting a child's learning can be, at best, only modified rather than changed, there is evidence (*School matters* – Mortimore *et al.* (1988), *Fifteen Thousand Hours* – Rutter *et al.* 1979) to show that the school and the teacher have an important influence. Mortimore found that the most successful school in his study of fifty schools was better than the average by 28 per cent after differences in social background and ability had been allowed for. The least successful school was 19 per cent below the average.

The teacher who is aware of the factors which cannot be changed, may be better placed to help a child. However, it is important not to regard these background factors as making it impossible for the child to make progress, and we have already noted that there is some evidence that teachers have lower expectations of children from working-class homes and from ethnic groups. Children in Mortimore's successful schools made progress in spite of background factors.

The effect of home background

In the first instance, a child is most influenced by his home background. This was most clearly demonstrated in the study by J. B. Douglas (1964) which checked the IQ of a large sample of children at eight and again at eleven years and related what happened to the children's social background. Those children who came from middle-class backgrounds increased their scores during that period, whereas children from working-class homes stood still or decreased their scores

In the first five years of life, children's learning in language and reasoning is substantial. They will also have learned something about the behaviour which brings approval and that which brings trouble, including some ideas about when to manifest different behaviours. They will have watched the activities of their parents and adopted some of their values and in play will have imitated them and other adults, trying out different kinds of behaviour to see what kind of response they get.

Children's home background may support school learning in a number of important ways which affect their ability to take what is being offered:

1   The language of home and school
    The use of language children experience at home may be very different from that used in school or very similar. It may differ, not only in vocabulary and structure, but also in the extent to which it is used to discuss ideas, respond to new experiences and talk about things. Discussion with children is therefore very important and teachers need to consider a variety of ways of stimulating children to think and talk. Merely talking is not sufficient. You need to find questions which stimulate inventiveness, use stories to introduce new ways of looking at things, encourage children to consider what a situation looks like from someone else's point of view, and so on.

2   Pre-school experience
    The experiences children have been offered in the years before school are closely related to their use of language, and what they have gained from any experience, will depend to a considerable extent on the way their parents have used the opportunities available. A child visiting the

local supermarket with a parent who knows how to use the opportunity for the child's learning, may gain more than another child taken to distant places for an expensive holiday. Experience of nursery school or play-group will also provide a background of experience for some children.

3   Adult interest
Children's readiness to learn when they first come to school will also depend on the extent to which their parents and other adults have been able to give time to them, listening to what they have to say and asking questions, extending their interests by sharing them.

4   Family background
Family size and the child's position in the family will influence the amount of adult care and conversation a child enjoys. There are now several studies of substantial numbers of children which demonstrate that the larger the family, the lower the average intelligence score for all the children in the family. This is clearly described in Ronald Davie *et al.*'s account of seven year olds in *From birth to seven* (1972) studied as part of the National Child Development Study. This study documented all the children born in one week in March 1958 and it remains one of the most important sources of information on child development.

It is also the case that the first and eldest child in a family tends to be more intelligent that the next and so on down the line. This is not to say that this is always the case. Indeed, the finding only shows up when the sample is large enough.

Social class is important in influencing various aspects of children's education. Peter Mortimore *et al.*'s study (1988) considered the social class background, defined by occupation, of both parents of each child in their study. Both were associated with achievement in reading at entry to junior school, and with achievement in mathematics. Children who had fathers in non-manual work made better progress than those with fathers in manual work, but the mother's occupation did not appear to affect progress. Father's social class was also significant in oracy.

Teachers in the study noted a higher incidence of behaviour problems from children whose parents were in manual occupations. These children were also more likely to have a poor attendance record.

The same study noted differences of ethnic background, though it is not easy to differentiate cultural from language differences. A child whose English is not fluent will find school work more difficult whatever his background. This study found that children of Carribean and Asian backgrounds made significantly poorer progress than other groups in reading but made normal progress in mathematics. There was no significant difference in writing in either quality or quantity.

Martin Hughes (1986) found that there was almost a year's difference between middle- and working-class pre-school children in their knowledge of numbers. He also found that attendance at nursery school or class appeared to make little difference to this. These are disturbing findings and one can speculate about the reasons for the difference.

Tizard *et al.* (1988) studied young children at school in the inner city looking particularly at the development of children of Afro-Carribean origin. Black in their study does not include Asians. They also studied the home backgrounds of each of these groups of children and found little to account for the differences in progress. The black parents appeared to take just as much interest in their children's schooling as the white parents and to be equally concerned to help their children.

Wells (1985) found that the strongest association with school attainment at age seven was the child's knowledge of written language at school entry. The extent of this knowledge was also related to the number of books owned by the child and to the children's and parents' interest in books.

5　The effect of parental attitudes

Parental attitudes to school, to books and to learning affect the degree of support parents give to children's schooling. We have also seen that parental expectation and attainment are related.

Gender and ethnic origin

There is now a great deal of information about the differences between boys and girls. Boys tend to be behind girls in development all the way through the primary school and they tend to get more attention from the teacher perhaps because they are more demanding. The difference in developmental level results in their being behind girls in many aspects of work, although they usually do well in mathematics and any technical subjects. Boys more often tend to be at the extremes of the ability range and most special needs groups contain more boys than girls.

The Mortimore study (1988) found that girls had a more positive attitude to school than boys and more positive self-concepts. Far more boys than girls were rated by their teachers as having behaviour problems

Tizard *et al.* (1988) found that at the end of nursery schooling there were few differences in attainment between black and white children and between boys and girls. During the infant school period black girls made more progress than white girls or boys or black boys. White boys made slightly more progress than white girls and black boys made least progress.

Security and learning

Two further aspects of children's learning may be considered here. Children, like adults, feel secure when they are able to assess a situation and predict what may happen. In school, children are likely to feel secure when they have summed up the teacher and can guess to some extent how he or she will react. They need to know:

What the teacher expects of them
How to get his/her approval
What they may or may not do
Where they may or may not go
What they may or may not use
When they may or may not do certain things

Most people placed in an insecure situation, work to achieve security. The right amount of insecurity may provide motivation for learning, but too much may be crippling. Anyone who, as a child, was taught by a teacher who appeared to be frightening will recall being preoccupied with fear and insecurity instead of learning. It is a difficult professional task for the teacher to create enough challenge for the child who is confident but to maintain security for the less confident.

On entry to school, most children feel some measure of insecurity and some feel very insecure indeed, however carefully they have been prepared for school and however welcoming the school is. Teachers of the youngest children often feel very strongly that it is important for them to relate to one adult in the beginning, although we might note that it is usual for nursery schools, nursery classes and playgroups to have several adults to whom children can relate. The reason given for this view is that security comes from having only one person to sum up.

There is also insecurity when children transfer from infant or first school to junior or middle school and from primary to secondary school. Numerous studies of primary to secondary transfer have found a large measure of anxiety on the part of children at this stage and *The Oracle study* found that progress in the first year of the secondary school was markedly less good than in the last year of the primary school (*The Oracle study* is described in four books. This point is made in Galton and Willcocks 1983.)

Motivation

Part of your task as teacher is to find ways of motivating every child in the group. This is most likely to happen when teacher, children and their parents share a common goal and can see ways of achieving it.

Most people are motivated by pleasant associations with an activity. A child who paints a picture or writes a story which is praised by the teacher and by other children will try to repeat this success and the reward it brings in approbation.

Much of our thinking about library areas in primary schools over the past twenty years or so, has involved making a space into an attractive area for reading, in the hope that this will create pleasant feelings in children's minds so that they come to associate reading with pleasant surroundings and see it as an enjoyable activity.

Young children want to please the adult. This is a great responsibility for the teacher and you need to be sure that the efforts made to please you are worth while in their own right. For example, one sometimes sees infant teachers going to considerable trouble to teach their children parts in a play. If the play and the language involved are of doubtful quality, perhaps made simple for infants, this may not be a good use of the children's time. You need to be able to justify what you do from an educational point of view as well as doing something to please the children and their parents.

The list which follows is a review of the ways in which people can be motivated. It may be useful in deciding what to do about a particular child or group to review the list, considering the possibilities in relation to the problem in question.

1   Inner need
    Human beings have a number of strong drives associated in the first instance with the need for food and shelter to survive, the need to maintain territory and to reproduce. We also need to give and receive love, gain recognition for our contributions to a group and experience responsibility. Where a child is motivated by this kind of inner need, there appears to be a greater power for learning. This is most evident in initial language learning where the need to learn is great.

2   First-hand experience
    We have already noted that children's experience is limited. Seeing and doing for oneself is motivating and it is important for children's development in all aspects of their work, that they have a good deal of experience in looking, hearing, touching, smelling and perhaps tasting, so that they begin to build images of experience to furnish their thinking.

3   A stimulating environment
    Most primary school teachers are concerned to create an attractive learning environment, but it needs to be used by the teacher and children. It may be useful to ask yourself from time to time whether

what you have on display could spark off work from different children. (Other uses of display will be discussed later.)

4   A desire for mastery or a problem which is challenging

Problem solving or mastering a skill is an enjoyable human activity, as may be seen from the popularity of crosswords and other puzzles and games of skill and particularly from children's enthusiasm for computer games. Part of your task as a teacher is to offer your children opportunities to work out ideas and tackle problems within their capacity. For example, the child who has worked out the spelling rule that the vowel before a single consonant is normally long, is much more likely to remember it than the child who is given the rule and told to learn it. Young and less able children tend to get too few opportunities for this kind of activity, partly because their reasoning power is under-estimated. They tend, as a result, to get less practice in using reasoning and less chance to improve their skill.

Computers play an important part here. There are many games which teach valuable skill and knowledge and there are also some straightforward teaching programs. All children need as much opportunity of working with computers as the school can provide.

5   Competition

Human beings are naturally competitive and most teachers use this to some extent. Even if the teacher avoids competitive situations, the children and their parents are inclined to make comparisons. The trouble about competition is that a child may place too much emphasis on winning, getting a good mark, or whatever the reward may be, and too little on the learning itself – hence the difficulty over cheating. The second difficulty is that some children tend to be losers every time and this is not good for their self-image and consequent attitude to work.

Nevertheless, competition is useful, especially if it can be a matter of beating your own previous performance or vying with someone of comparable ability. In short, competition can be motivating but needs to be used with care.

6   Self-improvement

A person who has clear goals is more likely to succeed than someone with little sense of direction. If you can help children to identify their own sets of short term targets, their natural desire for improvement will support their learning.

7   Cooperation

There is a satisfaction in working as part of a group and a degree of pressure to contribute which can motivate some children.

8   Teaching someone else

This can be a valuable way of working for everyone involved, because the 'teacher' has to learn and then get another child to learn. The child doing the teaching reinforces his or her own knowledge in the process of helping someone else.

A pair of classes differing in age might well work together on something like an environmental study with the children in the older class each having a 'pupil' from the younger class. This provides 'teachers' on a one to one basis and the achievement of the older children may be judged on how well the younger children have learned. The motivation involved in this is considerable.

9   Audio-visual equipment and computers

There is no doubt that equipment which 'does' something is motivating. At a comparatively simple level, the tape recorder and the language master are attractive to children, partly because they can control them and partly because of what they offer. The most attractive and motivating is the computer and given appropriate software children can learn a great deal with very little help from the teacher.

It seems likely that the possibilities of computers as teaching machines will develop and that many things now taught by a teacher will be learned from software programs. It is important not to think of computers entirely in terms of keyboard and VDU. Some of the best possibilities for the primary school may be in terms of a responsive environment where children's actions and answers meet with an immediate response, rather as they do in work with the turtle. Much will also change when it is possible to use the voice to interact with the computer.

THE CLASS PROFILE

Information about children

The ability to observe children and interpret their behaviour is a basic teaching skill. When you get a new group of children you need to spend time observing and finding out about them before you can teach them effectively. This will be made a good deal easier as assessment of each child's progress in the National Curriculum develops.

In the past many teachers have taken the view that they wanted to see new children with fresh eyes and they were therefore not interested in what other teachers had to say about them. While this view is understandable, it is one which is no longer tenable so far as the curriculum is concerned. A teacher who says this is usually quite properly taking the view that he or she may relate differently to a child or group of children from their previous teacher and does not want to prejudice the relationship by looking at children through someone else's eyes. Where a record is concerned with a teacher's opinion about a child and his or her potential, it makes a certain amount of sense to want to see with fresh eyes, but the papers on assessment from the School Examinations and Assessment Council (1990 a, b, c) make it clear that not only should teachers pass on full records of children's achievement to the next teacher, but that all members of a staff should work together to ensure that they are all interpreting records in a similar way.

ANALYSIS 2.1:
ASSESSING A NEW CLASS

Where children are coming into your class from another class within the school or from a feeder school, their records should be studied for factual information.

1 Look for evidence of general ability, especially standardised test results and SATs; note exceptionally high or low performance and any discrepancies between ability and attainment

2 See if there are any physical problems, such as poor sight, hearing or poor coordination; note any children who should wear glasses or hearing aids

3 Note any children with learning problems, including gaps in schooling, changes of school, non-English speaking backgrounds and so on

4 Note any other children with special needs, including any who might have been in special schools and any with exceptional ability

5 Note any children with home problems likely to affect the child in school

---

There are in any case many things you should find out in advance if you are to make the most of your first days with a new group. It is wise to prepare for a new class by getting all the factual information you can from the previous teacher about the children you will be teaching. This is different from getting opinions although all assessment has an element of subjectivity. You will be particularly concerned to find out the level each child has reached in the National Curriculum and how he or she has performed in the Standard Assessment Tasks (SATs). You also need to know such things as the books each child has read, the phonic knowledge each of the younger children possesses, the mathematical skills each has acquired and so on.

ANALYSIS 2.2:
NEW CHILDREN

You need to talk with the teacher(s) who have had the children previously:

1 Ask for any factual information abut work attempted and achieved

2 Enquire about teaching approaches and materials used and with what results

3 Ask about children who appear to have special needs of all kinds, e.g. children with exceptionally high or low ability, children with problems of various kinds, children who are under-functioning, who respond to particular approaches, who have particular skills or interests, etc.

4 Find out what children with learning difficulties can actually do and what they actually know

---

If possible visit the children you will be teaching in their own classroom during the previous term, perhaps arranging this by asking their teacher to change classes with you for a short time. Use this opportunity to get a feel for the class as a group. How do they respond to questions? Are they quick with ideas and suggestions? Do they talk enthusiastically about what they have been doing?

This is only a broad preliminary to studying further all the children, but it alerts you to those who may most need study and those whose needs are likely to be different from those of the majority. It will also colour some of your overall planning and help you to remain sensitive to the fact that your class is composed of individuals. On the other hand it is important not to let your initial summing up of children colour your expectations too much. The evidence suggests that when teachers are open about their expectations children can do very much better than when teachers' expectations are limited. It is very easy to label children but they could turn out to be very different from your preliminary ideas and you need to keep this well in mind.

ANALYSIS 2.3
CLASSROOM VISIT

During a classroom visit:

1 Identify children about whom it might be wise to know more

2 Talk with the children about what they have been doing

3 Look at the work of children who will be coming to you and make a special note of any who appear to be having difficulty or whose work seems to be outstanding

4 Look at the general level of presentation of work and at what appears to be common practice

5 Look for anything unusual, e.g. the child whose presentation of work is poor but whose ideas are good; children with unusual ideas, points of view or use of language; unusual but persistent errors

---

At this stage of planning it may be a good idea to look at children's ages. We saw earlier that the Mortimore study (1988) found that teachers were not aware of the different ages of the children in their classes and made no difference in provision for them. It was evident from this study that the younger children tended to be regarded as less able, but in reality progressed as well as older children but at a more elementary stage.

It may be helpful at this stage to start a loose-leaf ring file with a page for each child on which you can note things that happen which give you teaching information. In the first instance you will be noting points which have arisen as a result of your preliminary investigations. It is particularly important to do this for the children who have special needs or who are unusual in any way, whether exceptionally able or with particular kinds of problems. This may be the start of your record of these children, and if your school has a record keeping system which works on the basis of a sheet per child, you may start your file with the record of the previous teacher.

If you teach a reception class you have a more difficult task in getting to know the children who will be coming to you except where they come from a nursery class or school. Many schools invite new children and their mothers to visit the school on one or more occasions before they actually start and this gives you some chance to find out something about them, especially if you have a chance to talk to their parents. If you can find out something about individual children's interests and their families, you can at least start with some information which will help you to talk to them and make them feel at home. Your organisation for the first few days then needs to be very clear but very flexible so that you can adapt to the children as you go along.

Before the new school year starts you will be making preliminary plans. Try to plan your work for the first week with the need for diagnostic work in mind. Plan fairly broad topics with work at a variety of levels and some open-ended questions. Choose, where possible, areas in which all children have reasonable opportunity of success but which still provide challenges at various levels. For example, a story which provides a variety of work might be a good idea. It is likely to interest children if the level is right and it does not require complicated plans for organising work at a time when you are only just getting to know the children.

This early work may give you some opportunities for finding out about children's interests and abilities in school work and possibly related activities out of school hours. Your prior knowledge of the able children and those with problems should enable you to pitch the work at a reasonable variety of levels and it is at this stage that your class file becomes useful. Note relevant points as they arise but don't try to do too much at once.

During the first few days with a new class, you will be observing things like the way the children settle down to work, their comments and replies to questions, their first piece of writing and so on. These clues will quickly identify the problems and you will be noting the kind of response which particular work evokes from individuals. If you have a class other than reception, you will have information about each child's achievement in the National Curriculum and this will enable you to group children when you wish to work on an ability basis.

If you have a reception class, you will be noting the children who settle into school easily and those for whom it is a traumatic change from home. You will be getting to know parents as they bring and collect their children and using the opportunities this provides to learn from them about each child and the parent's view of how he or she is settling into school.

In the classroom you will be noting which children choose which activities and the level of interest and concentration shown by individuals and you will be talking with the children and finding out about them. The experience and level of understanding of each child will guide you in selecting work for them. You should get a good deal of information for your file at this stage and you need to be systematic in checking that you are observing all your children, perhaps aiming to study a few carefully each week as well as noting things which happen.

With an older group you will need to go on from your preliminary observations to check some of them. At an early stage you can check things like ability to concentrate and whether a child is right or left handed. You may hear him or her read and if you use miscue analysis (described by Elizabeth Goodacre in *Hearing children read* (1972) and also in *Extending beginning reading* by Vera Southgate *et al.* (1981) you will find out a good deal from the errors made. Collecting errors in written work may also be informative and suggestions about this may be found in *Framework for reading* by Joan Dean and Ruth Nichols (1972).

If there is not a great deal of detailed information about children's progress it may also be helpful to undertake some testing. For example, group spelling tests designed to cover all the possible phonic variations may be helpful and enable you to check for phonic knowledge. *Framework for reading* also gives suggestions for this. Tests in mathematics can similarly be designed to check on particular knowledge and skill. There is much to be said for devising diagnostic tests for a number of aspects of the National Curriculum, so that you can tell what a child needs to learn, although it is wise not to do too much testing. A group of teachers might well spend time together devising test material for different aspects of the National Curriculum. In science it may be best to observe how children tackle various tasks.

Your observation may also lead you to check sight and hearing if you see a child who seems to be peering to see or holding his or her head in a way which suggests he or she isn't hearing too well. A simple check for sight is to ask a child what he or she sees at a distance and what close to. You can check hearing by standing behind the child and asking him or her to repeat what you say. If you find a child who has difficulty with either of these two senses it will be important to refer the problem to the medical officer as soon as possible.

A very important part of this preliminary observation process is the discussion with the child and his or her parents about how they view things. This should give you some idea of what motivates a particular child and help you to identify attitudes. It will also offer you an opportunity to enlist the child's interest in meeting his or her particular needs and problems and to enlist the parents' support.

The task from then on is one of matching work to individuals and small groups. In general, studies suggest that although teachers are keen to deal with children as individuals they are not good at making provision for this. *The quality of pupil learning experiences* by Neville Bennett *et al.* (1984) describes observation of different classes. The researchers worked with individual children, giving them easier tasks if they found the original tasks given by the teacher were too difficult, and conversely. In a sample of 118 children, 45 had work which the researchers felt matched their needs, 35 had work which over-estimated their ability and 38 had work which under-estimated their ability. They found that teachers did not easily accept that some children had work which was too easy, although they were good at recognising a task which was too difficult. Another study by Neville Bennett and Joy Kell (1989) found that teachers tended to equate busy work with work that was well matched.

The main reasons for this appeared to be firstly that of poor diagnosis and secondly failure in task design. Mismatches occurred because the teacher did not check whether the child was familiar with the task content. Teachers also tended to be concerned with the product but paid too little attention to the process.

As the National Curriculum develops it will become increasingly necessary to match work to individual children if they are to make the maximum progress. It will also be rather easier to do this in that the learning to be acquired will be specified. You need to build up materials which teach or provide practice in different aspects.

Differentiating the work given to children of varying ability is not too difficult in something like topic work, although a good deal of thought needs to be given to what makes a piece of work easy or difficult for a particular child. In this type of work , the breadth of possibilities themselves offer variety. In a subject like mathematics a good deal of the work needs to be carefully built up and the teacher needs to know very clearly the point each child is at in order to match work to individual needs. The study by Neville Bennett *et al.* (1984) showed that teachers made a lot of incorrect assumptions about what children knew and could do in mathematics.

3 Effective teaching

Recent years have seen a good deal of concern with making teaching and learning more effective. There is now a substantial body of information about effective teaching and learning, coming from a number of studies here and in America. Perhaps the most straightforward of these is quoted in John Holt's book *How children fail* (1964). He quotes a study which concluded that effective schools had a number of characteristics, among them the following:

- If students did not learn, the schools did not blame them or their families, backgrounds, neighbourhoods, attitudes, nervous systems or whatever. They took full responsibility for the results or non-results of their work.
- When something they were doing with the class did not work, they stopped doing it and tried something else.

Tizard *et al.* (1988) studied young children in the inner city at home and at school and concluded that the school and teacher variables were more important than home variables in explaining differences in children's progress. They found also that curriculum coverage and teacher expectation had important implications for progress.

The ILEA junior school study, *School matters* (1988) by Peter Mortimore and his team was particularly concerned to discover the characteristics of the effective school and the effective classroom. He lists the following factors which are associated with the effective school and which the school can control:

Purposeful leadership by the headteacher
The involvement of the deputy head
Consistency among teachers
Intellectually challenging teaching
The work-centred environment

Limited focus within sessions (i.e. not more than two
subjects dealt with at one time)
Maximum communication between teacher and pupils
Record keeping
Parental involvement
Positive climate

This study also notes a number of ways in which individual teachers
were effective. There was a relationship between the teacher's enthusiasm
and the work provided for the children. The most effective teachers
frequently involved the whole class in discussion and were skilled at doing
this, which was not necessarily whole class teaching as such. They also
found that where teachers spent a high proportion of time with individuals
this had a negative effect, presumably because this results in a very small
amount of time for each child.

Effective teachers gave rewards rather than punishments because punishment
had a negative effect on learning. They spent a lot of time talking to
pupils about their work and this had a positive effect on progress. They
made good use of praise (but it was evident from this and from a number
of studies that many teachers made only a very limited use of praise and
rarely praised children for good behaviour). They created a high level of
industry within their classrooms and organised work so that there was
always plenty for children to do. Their lessons were stimulating and this
led to the formation of positive relationships between teacher and children.

The Teacher Education Project, described in *Classroom teaching skills*
by E. C. Wragg (1984) , stresses the value of high order questioning in
which children are made to think and reason. HMI confirmed this in giving
a negative view of what was actually happening by way of questioning in
Education 8–12 in combined and middle schools (1985) in which they say
that there is a weakness in questioning with teachers tending to go for
single word answers. The studies already quoted also note that there is too
little use of higher order questions and the Teacher Education Project puts
them at about 13 per cent of all questioning.

The ILEA junior school study (Mortimore *et al.* 1988), Neville
Bennett's study described in *Teaching styles and pupil progress* (1976),
The Oracle study (Galton *et al.* 1980) and some others appear to throw
doubt on some aspects of what is normally regarded as good primary
practice. Bennett found that more formal teaching in the basic skills gave
better results, although the best results of all in his study were from a
teacher who worked informally but in a structured way.

The ILEA junior school study found that children did better if lessons
were concerned with a single subject or at most two subjects and were

given only limited responsibility for their work and limited choice over a short period. They found that very high levels of pupil inter-action were negatively associated with pupil's progress. On the other hand there was a positive effect where pupils worked on the same task with others of roughly the same ability but at their own level. There was a negative result when the whole class worked on the same task.

The *Oracle study* found that children in a formal classroom spent more time on work activity and pupils in an informal classroom spent more time in distraction and other non-work activities.

These findings all suggest that more formal teaching produces better results. The picture is not as clear as this, however. The studies described above assessed progress mainly in terms of progress in the basic skills and most primary teachers would regard their task as much broader than this. The *Oracle study* also found that direct instruction was less effective where more challenging and complex cognitive skills are concerned. Two American researchers, Giaconia and Hedges (1982), found that children in 'open classrooms' developed high levels of self-esteem and better self-concepts. The HMI *Primary Survey* (1978) found that standards achieved in the basic skills were higher when the curriculum was broad.

Maurice Galton, writing in *Teaching in the primary school* (1989) suggests that many teachers who regard themselves as the kind of informal teacher described in *Plowden* (1967) do not, in the event, carry out the practice which Plowden describes. They note that there is a perception gap between what teachers think they are doing and what they are actually doing. They quote *The Oracle study*, finding that in most of the primary classes they observed children sitting in groups, but there was very little work of a cooperative nature actually taking place. A number of studies note that there is very little of the kind of extending conversation envisaged by Plowden. Vera Southgate and her fellow authors in *Extending beginning reading* (1981) note that teachers spend less time than they think on reading. In their study, the *average* time spent listening to a child read was thirty seconds.

In a study of four year olds in infant classes, Neville Bennett and Joy Kell (1989) found that although teachers often had clear ideas of what they wanted to do, the tasks children were asked to undertake often did not match the teacher's intentions. Sometimes also the task was not made clear to the child. They give an example where the teacher's intention was for a child to learn the sound of the letter 'h'. The child was given a sheet of pictures of things starting with 'h' and told to colour the pictures. Nothing was said about the sound of the letter. There would seem to be a case for making clear to children what they were expected to learn. This study also found that there was a discrepancy between the teacher's stated aims and his or her assessment of whether the work was successful. Often work was considered successful simply because the child had completed the task, irrespective of whether learning had taken place.

These studies suggest that it is not so much the methods which are less successful, than the fact that they are not fully applied in many cases. Neville Bennett's (1976) finding that the most successful teacher used informal methods suggests these can be highly successful but that some teachers using informal methods have not yet developed adequate techniques. Informal methods require much more structuring than formal methods. In particular they require clear goals although these should not be so prescriptive that they prevent children exploring avenues of interest. Detailed record keeping is important and the teacher needs to keep a good balance between work with the whole class and work with individuals and groups. It is also important to consider how children's thinking can be developed. In addition children need training to work in groups and to work independently.

It is also not altogether easy to define what is meant by good primary practice or by formal and informal methods. Various studies have found it necessary to arrive at tight definitions in order to make comparisons, but in practice there are infinite variations according to teacher preferences, personality and the particular situation. This is discussed further later in this book.

Vygotsky (1978) speaks of the 'zone of proximal development'. By this he means the distance between the stage of development the child has currently reached and his or her potential for reaching a higher level given support from an adult or more capable peer. Teachers work within this zone and need to create a structure which enables children to develop. Bruner (1985) suggests that the adult performs the critical function of 'scaffolding the learning task to make it possible for the child to internalise external knowledge and convert it into a tool for conscious control'.

We saw in the last chapter that a very important element in children's progress is teacher expectation. This was first confirmed in a study by Rosenthal and Jacobson in 1968 in which teachers in a California elementary school were told, on the basis of a spurious IQ test, that some children would make considerably more progress than others over the coming year. This was confirmed. The researchers concluded that it demonstrated that teachers acted in accordance with induced expectations. Although this study has been much criticised there remains evidence that if a teacher believes that certain standards of work and behaviour are characteristic of a certain child and treats the child accordingly there is a fair likelihood that the child will change his or her self image to accord with the view the teacher is demonstrating. Teachers tend to have higher expectations of children who have middle-class characteristics. A teacher's views about race and gender will also affect his or her expectations of boys and girls

ANALYSIS 3.1:
EFFECTIVE TEACHING AND LEARNING

1 Have I a clear idea of relevant goals for my class and for the individuals within it?

2 Have I good knowledge of the individual needs of my children and do I plan work to match these needs?

3 Do I prepare adequately?

4 Have I a good mixture of work with the whole class, work with groups and work with individuals?

5 Have I a good balance between teacher directed activity and activities arising from the children's interests?

6 How much of the time are my children working profitably?

7 How many higher order questions do I ask each day? Am I really making my children think?

8 Am I making a proper and consistent use of praise and encouragement to meet the goals I have in mind?

9 Have I trained my children to work independently and with concentration?

10 Have I trained my children to work in groups ? How much group work actually takes place?

11 Do I keep adequate records? Do I use these to decide on the programme for individual children, for groups and for the class as a whole?

12 Are my expectations for the children I teach realistic? Have I any areas of prejudice?

and children from ethnic minorities. It is therefore important to be aware of the effect of one's expectations and possible areas of prejudice.

Analysis 3.1 above identifies areas where there is known to be an association between teacher behaviour and effective learning by children and gives you a chance to assess your teaching in the context of what is known to be effective practice.

4 Teaching style

Style is the way you do things as a teacher. While there are both good and bad ways of doing things there are nearly as many good ways of teaching as there are teachers.

At the beginning of your teaching career, you tend to draw on the models you have experienced as a pupil as well as the knowledge you have gained from training, but as time goes on, you become clearer about your own strengths and limitations and your preferred way of working. It is perhaps worth noting in passing that most teachers, and especially the inexperienced, usually have too few models to draw on. It is valuable to see how other teachers teach and organise, particularly at the beginning of your career.

INFLUENCES ON STYLE

The following have influence on a teacher's style:

Personality

Your working style depends in the first place upon the kind of person you are. A person with an open and flexible personality will show this in the way he or she works.

Experience

Experience is an important factor in determining style. In particular, experience of other teachers at work gives you a choice of ways of working and those you choose become part of your style. Experience also affects your style in that you gradually become more sure of yourself and more confident.

Philosophy and values

Your beliefs about education and what constitutes good teaching and good learning situations, and your values generally, will affect the way you work, however unformed your thinking may be. Many teachers hold quite strong views which affect the way they work, without being aware that they have a philosophy as such.

Context

Your teaching style is affected by the particular group of children you are teaching and your accommodation and resources. The same teacher will work differently with a reception class and with a class of juniors. Some things which are possible in teaching in a well-resourced school, are not possible when resources are very limited.

THE DEMONSTRATION OF STYLE

Style is demonstrated in the way you work. In particular it is demonstrated in the following:

The activities you decide to undertake yourself

Your style is evident in what you decide to do as teacher. The way you present material to children is part of your style. At almost every point in the day you are making choices about how you will act and these add up to a style.

The use of time

In choosing what you do, you are also making choices about how to use time and how the children will use time.

The organisation chosen

The way you organise is part of your style. You have a wide choice of patterns of organisation, in the combination of class, group and individual work you decide to use. You also decide how much choice your children may have and the extent to which you teach them to work independently.

Methods of tackling work

The way you set about the tasks of the classroom is all part of your style. You may tell children what to do, or have a programme which they work through as they wish. You may discuss how work will be done with them and incorporate their ideas, not only into what they do but into how it is done, or you may insist that work is done as you wish.

Communication

The way you communicate with children is all part of your style. You may spend a lot of time talking about how things should be done or about the actual tasks children are doing. You may talk down to children or talk at a level which is stimulating because they have to think hard to follow what you are saying. You may also talk a great deal or give a lot of the time to getting children to talk.

Inter-personal behaviour

This is linked with communication. Teachers vary in how friendly they are with the children they teach and in how they treat children.

Michael Bassey (1978). studied how a large sample of teachers worked and described this in *Nine hundred primary school teachers.* He looked at many aspects of the teacher's work and among his findings is an account of which teaching methods predominate. The table below gives the percentages of junior teachers using the stated methods for seven hours or more during the week.

Class work	24%
Class work + group work in one subject	17%
Class work + group work in several subjects	14%
Group work in one subject	11%
Group work in several subjects	8%
Class work + self-organised individual work	8%
Self-organised individual work	6%
Other methods	4%
Variety of methods	3%
Group work in one subject + groupwork in several subjects	2%
Group work in one subject + self-organised individual work	2%
Group work in several subjects + self-organised individual work	1%

Neville Bennett's book *Teaching styles and pupil progress* (1976) defines style by identifying a number of characteristics of different forms of teaching behaviour, which are listed under the headings *traditional* and *progressive.*

Table 4.1 Characteristics of teaching behaviour

Progressive	Traditional
Integrated subject matter	Separate subject matter
Teacher as guide to educational experience	Teacher as distributor of knowledge
Active pupil role	Passive pupil role
Pupils participate in curriculum planning	Pupils have no say in curriculum planning
Learning predominantly by discovery techniques	Accent on memory, practice and rote
External rewards and punishments not necessary. Intrinsinc motivation	External rewards, e.g. grades Extrinsic motivation
Not concerned with conventional academic standards	Concerned with academic standards
Little testing	Regular testing
Accent on cooperative group work	Accent on competition
Teaching not confined to classroom base	Teaching confined to classroom base
Accent on creative expression	Little emphasis on creative expression

The Oracle study (Galton and Simon 1980) has already been mentioned. This gives a great deal of detail about teaching styles and classifies them as follows:

Individual monitors

These teachers work mainly on an individual basis and therefore spend much time in monitoring individual progress. This results in their being under pressure with a high level of interaction with individual children.

Class enquirers

This group uses a good deal of class teaching and teacher-managed learning with open and closed questions in class discussion.

Group instructors

Group instructors spend a larger amount of time than others on group interaction and less on individual attention, which allows them to engage in more questioning and making of statements.

Style changers

Fifty per cent of teachers used mixed styles to meet different demands. The group of style changers breaks down into:

- *Infrequent changers* who gradually change style according to the observed needs of the group over the year
- *Rotating changers* who work with pupils seated in groups each working at a particular aspect of curriculum and change the group activities by rotating the groups during the course of a day or week
- *Habitual changers* who make regular changes between class and individualised instruction. This group used questioning relatively little and had the lowest amount of time spent interacting with pupils.

Each style was considered in relation to children's performance in the basic skills. In language the children of *class enquirers* were much in advance of those of teachers using other styles, with the pupils of *infrequent changers* coming second. The children of *individual monitors, rotating changers* and *habitual changers* scored less well than in a pre-test.

In reading the children of *infrequent changers* did best, with those of *individual monitors* and *class enquirers* coming second. In mathematics the best score came from the children of *class enquirers* with *infrequent changers* following a considerable way behind.

This all suggests that different styles are suitable for different purposes in teaching and that the effective teacher needs to vary his or her style to match the situation.

LEARNING STYLES AND TEACHING STYLES

The Oracle study also defined pupils' styles. Four major learning styles were noted, as follows:

- *The attention seeker.* Seeks out teacher's attention more than typical class member; seeks constant feedback
- *The intermittent worker.* Avoids teacher's attention and only works when the teacher is watching
- *The solitary worker* . Spends most of the time working. Little interaction with other children and with teacher
- *The quiet collaborator.* Similar to solitary worker in that they concentrate on work. Spend more time in routine activities than others.

It is interesting to note the relationship this study discovered between teacher styles and pupil styles which are set out in Table 4.2

Table 4.2 Teacher styles and pupil styles

Pupil types	All classes	Individual monitors	Class enquirers	Group instructors	Infrequent changers	Rotating changers	Habitual changers
Attention seekers	19.5	19.0	18.4	5.4	27.5	21.7	22.8
Intermittent workers	35.7	47.6	9.2	32.1	35.3	44.9	38.6
Solitary workers	32.5	31.4	64.5	25.0	33.3	23.2	21.2
Quiet collaborators	12.3	1.9	7.9	37.5	3.9	10.1	17.5
% totals	100.0	100.0	100.0	100.0	100.0	100.0	100.0
Actual	471	105	76	56	51	69	114

DEVELOPING YOUR OWN STYLE

Wherever you place yourself in the various classifications in these studies, you have to discover the best way to work in the classroom for you. Your best way of working depends not only upon what you see as being important in curriculum terms, but also upon your strengths and limitations and, as we have seen, upon your personality, experience, philosophy and the situation in which you find yourself. Your age may also make a difference. We grow less flexible as we get older, but are usually more competent and confident and able to bring wider experience to the work in hand.

Analysis 4.1 overleaf is intended to help you to work out your personal profile as a teacher. It is closely linked to the profile given in Analysis 1.1, but is concerned with the way you work in the classroom rather than your philosophy of education. The items listed are all those where teachers tend to have personal preferences which it is sensible to take into account.

Work through the list marking your views on the statements and then look at the comments which follow. You may also like to get a colleague to mark the answers he or she thinks you would give. Sometimes the gap between your views of yourself and someone else's can be revealing. This list could also furnish useful discussion for a group of teachers highlighting areas of difference.

When you have completed the profile, you may like to consider the advantages and disadvantages of your particular preferences. The following comments may help you to do this:

Pre-planning/spontaneity

If you are a determined pre-planner, be aware that you could just miss the moment when a particular piece of teaching might be most effective

ANALYSIS 4.1 : PREFERRED TEACHING STYLE

	++	+	av	-	- -	
I like a quiet classroom for most of the time						I don't mind noise, so long as I can see that children are working
I like a tidy and well-organised room						I don't mind mess if it results in exciting work
I like to have everything well planned in advance						My best work occurs in response to something which has just happened
I like to concentrate on one thing at a time						I prefer to see my class working at a variety of things at any given time
I am normally even-tempered and patient						I get excited easily and am sometimes irritable
I like a regular timetable without too many diversions or interruptions						I like to create variety in the day and the week
I think children learn best when they are not given too much choice						I believe choice to be important in motivating children to learn
I think competition in the classroom helps children to learn						I prefer to play down competition and foster cooperation

	++	+	av	-	- -	
I tend to be a perfectionist						I am normally easy-going
I can't bear to be late for anything						I am a confirmed last-minuter
I work best with a class group						I work best with small groups and individuals
I prefer to have my classroom arranged formally with the children properly seated						I like to have children seated in groups and not always on chairs at tables

because you were too busy pursuing the goals you had planned. There is evidence in *Common knowledge* by Edwards and Mercer (1987) that teachers tend to dominate what happens in the classroom by the topics they introduce, the questions they ask and the responses they give to children's answers and comments. Up to a point this is to be expected but taken too far it prevents children from having ideas and becoming independent learners. Pre-planning is most valuable when mixed with a measure of flexibility.

If you are strong on spontaneity remember that you need to create the situations for children to achieve the learning necessary for the National Curriculum. You also need to make regular checks to see that all the children are getting relevant experiences and opportunities and that there are not substantial gaps in their learning or too much repetition of the things which interest you most. Spontaneous teachers need to keep good records of what happens.

One task/variety of tasks

If you normally have all the children doing mathematics or English or science at the same time, remember that children take differing amounts of time to learn the same things. Make sure that you are either organising so that work can be undertaken at a variety of levels or that you have plenty of interesting material for those who work quickly. Giving them more of the same simply teaches them not to work quickly! You may also need material which provides opportunities for slower children, which perhaps enables them to work through the same programme as the others but with more information and explanation available. Alternatively, you may take the kind of topic which can be studied in a variety of ways which will extend the able and provide opportunities for the weakest. Where children are at different stages of the National Curriculum, you will need different material for different groups of children.

It is worth remembering that if you don't have everyone doing the same work at the same time, you can manage with fewer similar sets of books and other materials and can use the money to buy a greater variety.

If you prefer some version of the integrated day, make sure that the children are getting enough stimulus from you and from each other. Some of the studies quoted in the previous chapter suggest that too great an amount of individual work gives poor results and that there is a limit to the range of choice which children can manage effectively. It should also be remembered that children need a good deal of training to work an integrated day effectively and you need to be very well organised if time is not to be wasted.

Patient/excitable

Patience is obviously an advantage in teaching and it can give children considerable security to know that you will treat them sympathetically and consistently. On the other hand, enthusiasm and excitement are valuable things to offer children and shared enthusiasm is infectious.

The teacher who can get children really turned on by his or her own excitement is someone whom every child needs to meet. If the other side of this valuable characteristic is that you get depressed and irritable, try to organise so that you have something to switch into when you have had enough and the children are trying you beyond endurance. For example, it is often pleasant to read them a story or get them to carry on some activity which is quiet, but interesting.

Perfectionist/easy-going

All teachers should demand high standards from children in all they do, but different teachers do it in different ways. If you tend to be perfectionist, be careful not to ask for more than your children can give and make sure you have your priorities right. A teacher who insists that every piece of writing is done in perfect handwriting with no spelling or punctuation mistakes, may find that some children write very little in order not to expose their problems. This makes it very difficult to help them.

Conversely a teacher who is easy-going needs to check that the work the children are offering is good enough and that enough attention is being paid to detail.

Never late/last minuter

If you can't bear to be late, don't be too hard on children and colleagues who find punctuality a problem. You must, of course, teach children to be punctual, but you need to recognise that for some children this is difficult, perhaps through no fault of their own. The best way of dealing with the child who is habitually late might be to make an individual chart on which he or she marks the punctual days and seeks to improve on this performance.

If you are a last minuter and often late you need to take yourself in hand so that you arrive at school sufficiently early to prepare for the children and be ready when they come in. It may help to aim at a time well before school is due to begin. A late teacher is a bad example to children and a nuisance to colleagues. He or she also risks a disorganised start to the day.

Class teaching/individual teaching

If you are a good class teacher and can hold children's attention riveted when you wish to, make the most of it. Your children will probably remember the things that you tell them for the rest of their lives However you also need to vary the approach to match the situation and the needs of individuals.

If you do most of your work with individuals and small groups, check what you and the children are actually doing in the course of a day. You could be using the time rather inefficiently.

Formal classroom organisation/informal organisation

If you do a good deal of work with the whole class, use the blackboard a lot and normally have children doing the same thing at the same time, there is much to be said for formal seating with everyone facing the front, although you will have difficulty in getting a really good discussion going and would be wise to rearrange the room from time to time to make discussion and cooperative work a possibility.

If, on the other hand, you want a good deal of discussion and cooperative work, you need a different basic arrangement. If you have children sitting in groups, remember that they need to turn their chairs when you want to work from the front or use the blackboard. Copying from the blackboard is particularly difficult if you are sitting with your back to it.

You may also need to change the way the furniture is arranged in the course of the day or week.

Tidy/creative mess

It is perhaps misleading to give these as opposites, since it is perfectly possible to be tidy and creative or untidy and uncreative. You may or may not be worried by mess, but either way you need to separate messy and noisy activities from work better done in a clean and quiet atmosphere. Quiet and noisy work need to be divided by time or place. If you are able to find spaces where a few children can carry on with concentrated quiet work, it may be reasonable for others to be discussing what they are doing or carrying out some fairly noisy activity. Conversely a few children may be undertaking noisy activities while other people are working quietly. Similarly with mess.

If you can't do this, then it may be better to have time when everyone is working silently at a clean activity and other times when the whole class is undertaking messy or noisy work.

If you are untidy, it is important not to let this interfere with the work of the class. This really means disciplining yourself to have a place for everything and checking that everything is in its place. It is important not to waste time looking for things. Your preparation for the children's work needs to ensure that they can work effectively. This is not possible if things are chaotic. Creativity is no excuse for untidiness. In any case you should be teaching your children good work habits which means that they should get into the habit of clearing up after themselves and putting things away in their proper place. Your example will be important here.

If you are tidy-minded, remember that you can take it too far and stifle creative urges by insisting that things are always done in exactly the right way (i.e. your way) It is helpful to discuss with children the best way to work to keep the room tidy and in good order and to use some of their ideas, reviewing their success after a period.

Regular timetable/variety

Teachers at the primary stage of education are usually accustomed to a good deal of freedom in the way they use time, with only the way shared facilities are used to limit them. Some teachers respond to this by creating a timetable and sticking to it for much of the time. Others use the opportunity to cash in on the educational value of what may be topical generally or for a particular child, using this as a vehicle for teaching across the curriculum. This kind of approach also provides the opportunity for children to concentrate on something for a long period if they wish to do so and you feel they are gaining from what they are doing.

The *Education Reform Act* (1988) lists subjects to be taught and although it does not prescribe the hours to be spent on each, schools should note how much time is actually being spent on each subject, whether it is being taught as part of an integrated curriculum or separately. The National Curriculum itself is having an effect on how teachers use time, because there is less time for picking up the topical and unexpected except where these contribute to some of the learning required by the National Curriculum.

Little choice/much choice

There is no doubt that the right amount of choice is motivating to children and can also have the advantage of training them in the process of making choices. On the other hand, choice can be overdone with the result that children flit from one activity to another without learning very much. We have already noted that the ILEA junior school report (Mortimore *et al.* 1988) suggests that a choice of two activities at a time provides better for effective learning than a greater number, but this may be a matter of training children to work in a choice situation. A great deal of the choice made should be a choice of when particular activities are undertaken rather than a choice of whether they are undertaken. Choice is also possible within a particular theme. In topic work, for example, there may be several ways in which children can work to acquire the learning intended by the teacher and they can have some choice of which route they pursue.

Competition/cooperation

Human beings have an ancestry which needed to be competitive to survive and we are still naturally competitive. Even in classrooms where the teacher plays down competition, the children will create competition of their own. A teacher doesn't need to introduce marks and teams and other devices to find children competing. They will do it anyway and the teacher's task is to get competition into perspective.

Some children thrive on competition and are most likely to work well when they see themselves in a competitive situation. Others fail continually and become discouraged. The task is to get the most out of competition for those who benefit with the least damage to those who fail.

An element of competition is useful under the following conditions:

- Children are encouraged to compete with themselves or others at a similar level in simple games which create interest and give practice which might otherwise seem very tedious.
- Children do not get the idea that it is the end that matters and that the means of achieving it is unimportant, or that what is learned is important only in terms of doing better than someone else, getting marks or other rewards or pleasing the teacher. One might say that if children cheat in their learning, they have gained the wrong idea of what the activity is about.

Competition may work against cooperation. There are many situations in life where cooperation is extremely valuable and school should teach children how to work effectively with other people. The researches suggest that although many teachers give lip service to this, actual examples of successful cooperative working are comparatively few.

5 The teacher's role

The teacher's task is to provide an environment and opportunities which are sufficiently challenging for children and yet not so difficult as to be outside their reach. There has to be the right mixture of the familiar and the novel, the right match to the stage of learning the child has reached.

The Plowden Report

The teacher is the most expensive and important resource in any classroom. As a teacher, you need frequently to review the way you are using your time to foster children's learning. It is very easy to spend too much time dealing with matters like finding materials for individuals or lost and broken pencils, which should be mainly taken care of by a well-organised environment.

The advent of micro-electronics and computer-assisted learning bring with them a need to reconsider the role of the teacher, since the computer could eventually take over some aspects of the teacher's present role and, in particular, would be able to match the needs of individuals very closely if the software were right.

It seems likely that technology will enhance the role of the teacher rather than usurp it, freeing the teacher to do more important educational tasks and providing more time for attending to individual children.

THE TASKS OF THE TEACHER

Society gives teachers the task of mediating the curriculum for each child. This is now a more clearly defined task than it was formerly, with the publication of *The Education Reform Act* and the National Curriculum, but a great deal is still left to teachers.

The school teachers' pay and conditions document (DES) 1988 states those professional duties which concern the children as follows:

    (1) (a) planning and preparing courses and lessons;
        (b) teaching, according to their educational needs, the pupils assigned to him, including the setting and marking of work to be carried out by the pupil in school and elsewhere;
        (c) assessing, recording and reporting on the development and progress of pupils;
    (2) (a) promoting the general progress and well-being of individual pupils and of any class or group of pupils assigned to him;

A report in the *Times Educational Supplement* (Kirkman 1990) describing the training of teachers at Exeter University suggests that there are nine dimensions to teaching. They are as follows:

– Ethos – the 'characteristic spirit of the classroom which entails mutual respect between teachers and pupils, cooperation and a shared sense of purpose'
– Direct instruction – 'the teacher's ability to tell, describe, demonstrate and explain'
– Management of materials – 'the preparation and appropriate use of teaching materials and visual aids'
– Guided practice – 'the exercises and techniques teachers must devise for the pupils to practise new skills and knowledge'
– Structured conversation – 'Teachers must be able to use a variety of aural strategies to help pupils develop concepts. These range from responding supportively to what children are saying to challenging children's ideas by drawing attention to conflicting theories'
– Monitoring – 'Teachers should use different techniques to assess children's work and use the information to plan future action'
– Management of order- the teacher should set up an established framework of rules and procedures and then try to develop an appropriate programme for disruptive pupils'
– Planning and preparation – 'the requirements for preparing successful lessons'
– Written evaluation – 'all effective teachers must analyse and evaluate their own work'

The tasks of the teacher might also be broken down as follows:

The observation of children

A teacher needs to observe children in order to match the teaching and learning programme to individual and group needs and to assess learning and progress. There is a good deal of evidence that teachers only partially succeed in this. *The Primary Survey* (HMI 1978) found teachers better at matching work to pupils in language and mathematics than in other curriculum areas and comments about not extending the most able have been made in many HMI reports. Neville Bennett *et al* in *The quality of pupil learning experiences* (1984) found that teachers often tended to under-estimate the most able children, and Bennett and Kell in *A good start* (1989) found that where the youngest children were concerned there was a tendency to over-estimate. Teachers generally were more prepared to accept that they were over-estimating than under-estimating. They also found that many teachers did not use assessments as a means of assessing needs and matching work to children. Diagnostic work was generally rather limited. The development of assessment for the National Curriculum will provide a great deal of information which could be used in matching and the SEAC booklets (1990) on assessment stress the need to do this.

Skill in observing children and in interpreting observation is basic to teaching.

The organisation of the learning programme

The learning programme needs to be organised to meet the needs identified from observation, relating each day's work broadly to a plan for the week, the term, the year or the school life of the children, using interests and experiences to provide learning opportunities and checking that the necessary ground is covered.

The good teacher is opportunist but systematic.

The selection of learning material

A teacher needs to select learning material which will enable individuals and groups to learn the part of the curriculum appropriate for their age and ability. This task involves not only considering how to teach different aspects of the National Curriculum, but looking at how they can be combined together and how the children's interests and experiences can be used for their learning.

The presentation of learning material

This is of two basic kinds. There is firstly the provision of first-hand experience through visits, exploration of the school environment or of material brought into the classroom. Such material will be selected for its interest and learning possibilities. The teacher's task will be to help children to become aware of and focus on aspects important for learning and to help them to structure what they are learning so that it fits into a developing pattern in their minds.

Secondly the teacher will provide materials within the classroom designed to foster learning. Sometimes this will involve a published scheme, a book or a radio or television programme or a computer program or the material may be provided personally by the teacher.

Children need constant interaction between first-hand experience and other learning materials if they are to be able to transfer what they have learned from one to the other.

The presentation of material by the teacher requires skill in talking about the topic under consideration. It may require the ability to describe something in a way which captures children's interest or to give explanations. It will almost certainly require skill in questioning. This is explored further in the next chapter.

Matching work to children

If children are to learn well the tasks they are asked to undertake and those they choose for themselves must match their learning needs, being difficult enough to challenge them but within their capability. This is not easy to do. Tizard *et al.* (1988) found that teachers tended to give children work which was too difficult if they had good verbal skills and to under-estimate children whose verbal skills and behaviour were less good. Boys were more likely than girls to be seen as under-achieving.

The assessment required by the National Curriculum should make it easier to match work to children if teachers use their assessments to guide them in selecting the work children should do.

The Schools Council materials *Match and mismatch* (1977) suggested that teachers should use observations from dialogue with individual children and their performance in answering questions. Information would also be gained from listening to children, watching their actions and working processes and looking at their products. These are still valid ways of assessing and matching work to children and are confirmed in many ways by suggestions in the SEAC assessment booklets (1990).

The structuring of children's learning

Learning is easiest when the material to be learned is part of an overall structure and the learner can see where the new piece of learning fits in. Children in the primary school are developing structures in their minds which will form the basis of future learning. The way they organise their thinking at this stage may govern their ability to learn in the future. They are sometimes helped by being given a structure but it is usually better to lead them to create structures of their own.

For example, at one time, it was usual to teach tables by rote, using one particular structure, which was given rather than worked out. One effect of this was that some children found difficulty in using the information except in very recognisable situations. We now tend to lead children to work out a number of different structures for tables, including the standard one.

Another example can be seen in the development of classifying skills. Children learn about sets in mathematics at quite an early stage, but very often this knowledge is not applied when, for example, children go out and come back with a collection of varied objects. These could be sorted into sets according to their attributes, which is what has happened when biologists, botanists, zoologists and geologists have classified the material they found.

The view that teachers need to lead children to create mental structures has been stressed by major studies for many years. It was stated in various ways in *The Plowden report* in *The Primary Survey* (HMI 1978) and in *The Cockcroft report* (1982). The way a teacher presents material, asks questions, summarises, points out links, encourages classifying and ordering and so on, all help children to create appropriate mental structures.

We saw in Chapter 3 that Vygotsky (1978) suggested that there is something which he calls the 'zone of proximal development' – the gap between what a child can learn and do by him or herself and what is possible with the aid of an adult, described by Bruner (1985) as a 'scaffolding' provided by the teacher for children's learning – a structure which enables them to learn. The teacher is therefore making a structure in which the children may structure their learning. The way material is presented and the discussion that goes with it are all part of these structures.

Training learning behaviour

The ability to work independently and in groups does not come automatically. A good deal of work needs to go into training these abilities throughout the primary school. With a new class you need to start with very little independent work and gradually increase the amount you expect. The ILEA junior school report, described in *School matters* (Mortimore *et al.* 1988) found that junior school children worked independently in a satisfactory way for short periods, possibly no more than a morning. This report also suggested that the choice offered should be limited.

What is not clear in this report is whether the teachers concerned trained their children in independent learning and whether training produced increased ability to work in this way.

The teacher's attitude towards making children independent is also important.

Providing inspiration and encouragement

An important part of the teacher's role is to stimulate and interest children in whatever is to be learned. This is just as important if your organisation involves much individual and small group work as it is if you do a good deal as a whole class. Individual encouragement is also needed and should be regarded as a teaching tool, since children tend to repeat what is praised and encouraged. There is some evidence that teachers praise and encourage differentially. Tizard *et al.* (1988) found that white boys were encouraged more than white girls and black boys received the least encouragement. The less able also received less encouragement.

It is very easy to think you do more encouraging than you actually do and particularly easy to encourage the able and offer little to the least able and the quiet child. It is helpful occasionally to try to check the number of encouraging comments you make in the course of a morning and note the children to whom they were addressed. It is also useful to go through the register occasionally noting when you last said something encouraging to each child.

Organising a learning environment

A learning environment might be described as one which is functional with regard to children's learning. This involves:

- An arrangement of furniture which provides the optimum conditions for the work to be done
- A layout of materials which shows clearly what is available, is arranged and marked where appropriate to show function, level of difficulty or progression and can be used by children without difficulty and without a great deal of attention from the teacher
- An organisation in which it is easy to keep materials and equipment clean, tidy and in order and easy to check over to see that everything is in the right place
- A discriminating use of display which provides standards to aim for, i.e. demonstrates what the teacher wants from the children, and offers encouragement to those who most need it, e.g. the display of less good work from time to time to encourage an individual child. It should also provide materials of all kinds which interest, stimulate and extend knowledge and thinking.

Ensuring that children develop a common understanding with the teacher

Edwards and Mercer (1987) suggest that classroom discourse depends a great deal on developing a common understanding between teacher and pupils. Much conversation depends upon the participants understanding the language they use in the same way and having the ability to make similar inferences from what is said. The teacher is inducting children into the language of education and is aiming to transfer his or her understanding to the children.

Edwards and Mercer and Neville Bennett *et al.* all found that teachers were inclined not to make clear to children their aims for the work expected. Children not only need a common understanding of the language and gestures used, but also need to know where they are expected to be going. This then puts them in a position to know what progress they are making.

Assessing and recording children's progress and development

Teachers have always been concerned to assess how well their children are doing, if only to decide what to teach them next. The National Curriculum has made this much more important because assessment is now formally required in primary schools. The task of assessment is thus an important part of the teacher's role which should inform the work selected for individuals and groups..

Assessing teaching performance and approaches

There is currently increasing concern with the performance of teachers and many schools are also involved with teacher appraisal. This involves classroom observation of all teachers as part of the appraisal process and this should make teachers generally better at self-evaluation which is a necessary part of the preparation for appraisal.

Appraisal should not be the only assessment teachers make of their work in the classroom. Any new approach, whether within a single class or introduced throughout an area of the school, should be followed after an interval by a careful evaluation to discover whether it was successful.

Teachers can also help each other to evaluate. Two teachers, both attempting a new approach, may find it helpful at some stage to exchange classes and assess how each other's class has done. If it can be arranged, it is also helpful for teachers to observe each other and try to assess how far aims are being achieved.

Children are also useful assessors of a teacher's work. Discussion with children, particularly older children, about how they feel something went and what they thought about it, is valuable as part of the evaluation process.

THE KNOWLEDGE A TEACHER NEEDS

We have already considered the tasks a teacher has to undertake; we now need to look at the knowledge and skill needed to undertake them.

When, as a new teacher, you enter the profession, you bring with you from your training a body of knowledge and the beginning of some of the skills you will need as a teacher. The school in which you find yourself at the beginning of your career is likely to provide the largest single contribution to your professional development as a teacher from then on. Even if the school you join is not a particularly good one and the head and teacher colleagues don't see it as their role to train you further, you will still learn from them – in some cases by negative example.

You will also learn a great deal on the job by observing children, by trying out ideas and selecting those which work best for you. In fact all teachers learn by interacting with their professional environment. You form and develop your own frame of reference by which you judge your own performance. You acquire new knowledge in dealing with the tasks which come your way. You develop skills in dealing with the situations you encounter as well as by reading, studying, in-service education and discussing work with colleagues.

There are a number of areas in which a teacher needs to acquire knowledge and skill. The list below outlines these and the analysis which follows suggests questions you may like to ask yourself.

Self-knowledge

To be a good teacher you need to be aware of your strengths and limitations and your preferred teaching style. This kind of self-knowledge is an essential prerequisite of good teaching, especially in the primary school where teachers are expected to teach many things and where every teacher will have some areas of strength and some weaknesses.

A thought-out philosophy

When people talk about having a philosophy of education it is sometimes assumed that what they are talking about is far from the classroom. This is not necessarily so. Having thought-out ideas does not mean having a wholly theoretical approach and, in any case, theory should support good practice. Many teachers demonstrate that they have a thought-out approach by the way they work in the classroom and the day-to-day decisions they make but would not regard this as having a philosophy.

What you need are thought-out aims and objectives which you can use for assessing your work and for deciding on approaches and materials. It is the teachers who have the clearest ideas of what they want to achieve who are likely to achieve the most.

The staff of a school also need to have some collective philosophy so that children experience a coherent programme while they are in the school and as they move from class to class. This creates a school culture in which agreed values are fostered. Staff discussion of the philosophy and the culture is not only useful in getting a school view, but it helps everyone to sort out ideas.

Child development

Initial training may have introduced you to ideas about the way children develop and learn, but knowledge in this area is constantly developing and you will be adding knowledge gained from your own observation of children as well as trying to keep up to date by reading and from in-service education.

Knowledge of how children learn

Here again initial training normally introduces students to knowledge of learning and teaching experience will add to it. Good theoretical knowledge as well as experience should guide your practice. The following points in particular are worth considering. They should be part of the background knowledge of all teachers.

1 Learning depends upon motivation
   A child's power to learn is considerable. It is evident from the extent of early language learning and from the knowledge children sometimes manifest in hobbies and out of school interests, that most children have much greater learning powers than we can yet harness for the learning we want them to achieve. Without motivation it is difficult to get them to learn. They may even use their ability to avoid learning.

2 Most people, including children, are motivated by problems which challenge but are within their capacity
   The more you can present learning as a series of interesting challenges, the more successfully your children will learn. Such learning is often more effective than memorising because the child makes the learning his or her own by working on it. We tend to forget that children lack

experience, not intelligence. Given a problem within his or her experience, a child may solve it more quickly than an adult. Many teachers will testify to the fact that children have taken to computers more quickly than they themselves.

3 Reward and praise is more effective than blame and punishment
This is well known and has been frequently demonstrated in research but the knowledge tends to be used in a very limited way. You can help children who have problems or who pose problems if you use praise and reward very specifically the behaviour you want to reinforce, doing this as soon as possible after the behaviour takes place. As far as possible the unwanted behaviour should be ignored, although this is often not possible because of the effect on the other children.

4 It is necessary to use and/or talk about a piece of learning
Learning which has not been discussed and used may remain at the rote learning level. Listening and repeating are not enough by themselves if material is to be absorbed in a way which makes it available for use.

5 Language means only as much as the experience it represents
Children learn from the words of others when they can interpret them by matching them with their own experience in a way which is reasonably similar to the understanding of the person using the words. This holds true both for speech and writing. Children are also good at disguising the limited nature of their understanding, and you may think they have understood, when in fact they are simply using the words without adequate meaning.

6 Learning needs to be made accessible and usable
The way in which learning is acquired is important in structuring it in the learner's mind. Structuring involves matching it to what the learner knows already and helping him or her to classify the knowledge into categories so that it is easy to remember and recall. Only if the structuring process is adequate will the learning be accessible and usable. It is not sufficient for the teacher to do the structuring for the children although the way the material is presented should have its own structure. What is needed is help with sorting out experiences so that the children create structures for themselves.

Group behaviour

Teaching in school depends upon the ability of the teacher to manage children in groups. In the first place you have to manage a class group. You may then choose to break up the class into smaller groups for particular work and you need to be able to manage the class in this situation. A group is sometimes essential for the activity as, for example, in dance and drama, music or team games. At other times teachers form groups for various reasons. Teaching involves keeping a delicate balance between the individual and the group and using this to further your aims.

Group behaviour varies according to the composition of the group and the extent to which any particular group contains children who serve as models for others. An individual child can set standards of work and behaviour, both positively and negatively.

Children not only use other children as models, but are themselves controlled by the group. This control is fairly minimal at the start of schooling but gradually increases as children grow older.

You can use the desire to be part of the group to get a base for the conforming behaviour which is an essential prerequisite for school learning. For example, teachers often use the device of singling out individuals to get the group to follow ('I can see that John has cleared up nicely and is ready. Come on the rest of you.') Sometimes they aim to drive a wedge between an individual and the rest of the group ('I think you'd better sit over there, Linda, where you can't disturb other people.')

These comments signal to the rest of the class that this is what is wanted if they, like John, are to gain your approval or avoid your disapproval, as shown to Linda. Research evidence suggests that teachers make far more negative than positive comments, in spite of the fact that we also know that reward is more effective than disapproval. It may be helpful to count how many of each kind of remark you make in the course of a day.

A group can be strongly supportive of its members on some occasions and highly competitive on others. Both competition and cooperation can be used to help children to learn but both can create problems. Children can cooperate to avoid work and, as we have already seen, competition can be counter-productive.

Curriculum content

The coming of the National Curriculum has changed, very radically, the task of the teacher so far as curriculum content is concerned. Initially the need to acquire enough knowledge to teach the National Curriculum in less familiar areas will put pressure on teachers, but as the material becomes known, it will be possible to concentrate on teaching methods .

The demands on a teacher at the primary stage are very considerable since he or she is expected to be able to teach virtually the whole curriculum. The development of subject coordinators who are specialists in particular areas of curriculum and are able to help colleagues is a step forward, but many staffs are too small to have coordinators in every curriculum area and since primary teachers tend to be appointed on the basis of being good general teachers, a coordinator may be asked to undertake the work simply on the basis of interest.

It is also worth noting that you need to have a good knowledge of subject matter to teach young or less able children just as much as very able children because you need to be able to select what is appropriate and this may be difficult if your own knowledge is too limited. There is also a problem when you encourage children to undertake work developing individual interests if you do not know enough in the area to identify what is worth exploring and to guide learning.

You need to be very honest with yourself over the areas in which you feel secure. You then need to consider whether there are some areas where you could learn more or less with the children and some where you simply know too little to teach at the present time. You may be able to get help from colleagues with these and there will certainly be many courses for teachers dealing with the National Curriculum. You may also find that school broadcasting offers you some useful material.

Whatever your strengths and limitations so far as the curriculum is concerned, you need to go on learning and updating your knowledge in the areas in which you are expert as well as in those where you need to know more. It may be sensible to make a long-term plan for increasing your knowledge.

In working through the questions in Analysis 5.1 below you may like to consider not only how you wish to work with children, but also to assess where you need further development of your own skill and knowledge.

THE SKILLS REQUIRED BY A TEACHER

Knowledge by itself is not sufficient to make an effective teacher; you also need teaching skills. The sections which follow explore the range of skills a teacher needs and provide an opportunity for self-assessment.

Observing and interpreting children's behaviour

The teacher's ability to observe and interpret children's behaviour is crucial, particularly at stages when children are more dependent on the teacher and limited in their ability to use language to express their needs.

The skills and strategies involved in observation and assessment might be classified as follows:

1 General observation

A teacher, over the years, develops skills in observing children at work, coming to know the signs of underfunctioning and of learning

ANALYSIS 5.1: THE TEACHER'S SKILL AND KNOWLEDGE

Self-knowledge	What are my strengths? What are my weaknesses?
Philosophy	What do I believe to be really important in educating children? What are my priorities? What would I like my children to remember of their years with me in twenty years time? Can I justify what I teach and the way I teach it? What are the implications of what I believe about education for what I do?
Child development	Do I know enough about the normal patterns of physical, intellectual, social and emotional development to recognise the norm and deviations from it? Do I consciously use this knowledge in working with children?
Children's learning	What am I doing to help children structure their learning? How well does the work I provide for children match the range of individuals in the class? Have my children the experience to understand fully the language I use? How many children in my class are not motivated for much of the time? Who are they? What interests have they? Could I use these interests to help them learn other things? Do I provide opportunities for children to talk over what they are learning? How often do I create situations in which children tackle problems which are challenging but within their capacity? Do I do this for the less able as well as the more able? How often do I use higher order questions which require thought and inventiveness? Am I helping children to learn how to learn?

Group behaviour	Am I happy with the overall behaviour of my class? How often do I praise good behaviour and how often do I comment on bad behaviour? Do I praise the same children every time? Do I make negative comments to the same children every time? What am I doing to teach children to work cooperatively? Am I satisfied with the balance I have between competition and cooperation? Do any of my children cheat in order to do better than others or to please me? Is this because there is too much competition? Would rather more competition stimulate some of the most able in the class?
Curriculum content	In which areas of curriculum do I know least? What can I do about this? When did I last update what I know in the areas of work in which I feel most at home?

problems of various kinds and what may reasonably be expected from any individual or group.

2   Systematic observation
    General observation is largely a matter of observing things as they happen. Children's performance should also be reviewed more systematically on a regular basis, working through the list of children and considering each in turn. This should be part of your assessment procedure. It is also important to work diagnostically with children, using such opportunities as hearing them read or discussing work with them to identify particular problems and difficulties.

3   Using tests and check lists
    Systematic observation may include the use of teacher-made or standardised tests and check lists. These require skills and knowledge in their interpretation. The national Standard Assessment Tasks (SATs) should add to the observations of the teacher as well as providing information about the stage each child has reached. In addition you need to have material which helps you to identify particular problems, such as inadequate phonic skills or lack of knowledge of particular mathematical operations.

In observing any individual child a teacher might look for the following:

1 Personality and learning style
There are many differences in children and the way they learn. You need to find the 'best fit' learning approaches for the particular group of children and the individuals within it.

2 Experience and interests
Communication depends upon experience shared between you as teacher and your children and the language needed to express a response to it. Any new work needs to be planned in the light of observation and conjecture about the relevant experiences that children already have and those they may need for new learning and understanding.

3 Stage of development
A child's stage of development will to some extent determine his or her thought processes and specific development within subject areas. It is therefore necessary to discover how children are thinking and what their ideas are in developing any area of work. It will also be necessary to assess specific skills as part of the assessment procedure.

4 Abilities
You need to match work to individual ability on many occasions and ensure that the most able are not marking time or under-achieving and that the least able or least interested are not doing less that they might because you have low expectations of them. There is research evidence to suggest that both these groups under-perform.

You also need to observe in order to assess the learning programme you are providing, the effects of your classroom environment and organisation and your own contribution. Much of this will be your own observation, but it can be helpful to ask a colleague to observe something you are doing and give you feedback. This is normally difficult to arrange in a primary school but is a real possibility in a team-teaching situation.

We have already noted that children will give you feedback if you discuss with the class their reactions to the various things you and they are doing.

When you ask someone else to observe you, you have to define what you are trying to do and what you want to know about it and this is a helpful activity in its own right. It can be valuable to do this for yourself, identifying what you consider to be success in different aspects of work and the clues which will tell how successful you have been.

Analysis 5.2 should help you to do this.

Skills of organisation and control

The actual process of organisation in the classroom involves selecting from a range of different ways of doing things those which fit your particular children and situation. You need to be able to anticipate likely problems and avoid them by careful planning, particularly at points of change of activity. You also need to train children to work as you think best, using the resources of time and space to full advantage. In addition you need to be able to control children in groups and individually.

ANALYSIS 5.2:
TEACHING SKILLS—OBSERVATION

1 How good were the assessments of children I made last September when they first came to me?

2 Are my records of the academic progress of each child adequate?

3 Are my records of the behaviour and development of each child adequate?

4 Do I use records and assessments to help me in my teaching?

5 Is my use of tests and check lists satisfactory as one means of observing each child's progress?

6 Do I observe individual children to find starting points for their learning?

7 Do I look for the right moment to intervene to help individuals to learn?

8 Do I discuss their progress with individual children, helping them to plan improvement in a regular and systematic way?

9 Do I observe in order to identify children's problems and deal with them?

10 Do I study children who are exceptionally able in order to help them to learn at a suitable level?

There is a good deal of more detailed material in this book about most of these skills but all the work of a teacher is dependent upon the ability to manage children in groups and as individuals. Very few teachers escape altogether from problems in the classroom and almost all beginners have to work to achieve control. Although it is certainly true that some people seem to achieve control very easily from the start, most people develop this ability over a period of time.

1 Factors involved in classroom organisation and control

There are many factors involved in good classroom organisation and control and some of these, such as grouping and the use of time and space, are dealt with in detail later in this book. The control of children is very much bound up with the organisation a teacher sets up. The following factors need to be considered:

a The quality of the classroom as a learning environment

Children learn from the environment as well as from the teacher and each other and the way the classroom is set up for learning is important. It should be attractive and welcoming but also have much available which encourages learning. Display should either be encouraging children in their work by showing it attractively or it should be stimulating material which invites questions and exploration. There should be a good deal in the classroom which supports independent learning. It is useful to ask oneself whether children left to their own devices in the classroom would be able to go on learning because of the way the room is organised.

b The use of space and resources

The way the space in the classroom is organised has a considerable effect on the way children work. If resources are easily to hand and are organised so that it is clear which materials a child should use next, it is likely that there will be better concentration on the work in hand.

It is also important to try to use resources as effectively and fully as possible. For example, you may have some major resources, such as the computer, out of use for much of the time. If so, it is worth considering whether more children could get the benefit of them if you organised their use differently.

c Grouping for learning

A good deal of primary school learning takes place in groups, although this is often a matter of children working individually within the group, at work given to the group as a whole. It is important to provide within the grouping for children who have learning difficulties and children who are exceptionally able. This need not be exceptional ability in absolute terms. What you are really concerned with is children who are a long way ahead of the rest of the class and therefore need special provision.

d The use of time

Time is the one resource which cannot be increased. You can only make better use of the time you have. There are suggestions later in this book for checking on how you and the children are using time with a view to seeing whether you are making the best possible use of it.

2 It can be frightening to find yourself not in control and inexperienced teachers need to remind themselves that not only can they learn to control children, but that the ability to do this, while an essential pre-requisite for good teaching, does not in itself guarantee it. That depends on how you use the opportunities which the control you achieve offers. There are teachers who have excellent control, but little of quality to offer children. There are also outstanding teachers who have had to work hard to achieve control in their early days.

There are a number of principles about classroom control which are useful to remember:

a Children behave badly when they don't know what to do

Think out the organisation of your work in detail, especially when you are changing activities. You also need to think carefully about how you are going to instruct children about the work you want them to do.

This is just as important when you are working with a group of children you know well as when you are working with a new group and establishing ways of doing things.

b Always get attention before giving instructions

It is a good idea to get children to look at you so that their attention is alerted and you can make eye contact with them. You may also need to find a way of attracting attention when children are doing noisy work or are absorbed in what they are doing, especially if you have a quiet voice. Establish the idea that when you clap your hands or signal in some way, you want everyone's attention.

Learn to give instructions so that each important point is reinforced and is clear to everyone. Be careful not to give too much informa-tion at once. It is often a good idea to ask particular children what the instruction was to make sure that they have grasped the message. You need to do this whatever the organisation of your classroom.

c Be ready when children come into the classroom

The way work starts is important. It can be a recipe for trouble, not to mention a waste of time, to insist that children wait quietly without anything to do for too long.

It is generally better to establish a pattern in which everyone is expected to come in and start working at something. This may be pre-planned activity which is self-explanatory or work from instruc-tions written on the board or a daily pattern of quiet work or any other regular activity. The important thing is not to leave children with nothing to do but misbehave.

This isn't nearly as easy as it seems when you see a capable and experienced teacher at work. As with so much else in teaching, you have to work to establish the behaviour you want.

d Be individual in calling children to order
It is generally more effective to pick out individuals by name when you are trying to get attention than to speak to the class generally. You can do this in two ways. You can single out children who are doing the right things 'I can see that Peter is ready' or you can comment on those who are not doing what you want 'Karen, I'm waiting for you.' By and large the first is more effective and you may find it useful to check from time to time what you are actually doing, so that you are not being too negative to particular children. It is easy to do this without realising it.

e Learn to scan the class
Good teachers are said to have eyes in the backs of their heads. Beginners often get absorbed with individuals or small groups and ignore the rest of the class. You need to look round very frequently so that you anticipate misbehaviour.

The Oracle study (Galton and Simon 1980) describes one group of children as *intermittent workers* and explains that these children work only when the teacher's eye is on them. If you scan the class regularly, very often a child about to waste time or do something unacceptable will catch your eye and settle to work again. If catching the child's eye doesn't work, move towards him or her in a determined way.

f Set rules of behaviour from the beginning
In *Classroom teaching skills* Professor Wragg (1984) describes the work done as part of the *Teacher Education Project* in looking at how experienced teachers used the first lesson with a new class. Almost without exception, they said that they would use the first few lessons to establish the rules they wanted followed. Teachers varied in the extent to which they intended to dictate the rules or discuss them or work them out with the pupils, but the areas covered tended to be fairly similar. They included rules for entering and leaving the classroom, rules about work, a rule that there should be no talking when the teacher was talking and rules about property and safety.

These were teachers in a secondary school. In a primary classroom, the teacher might wish to make rules about the movement around the room which is allowed, the numbers of children who can undertake one activity at any given time, occasions when choice is allowed, and so on.

You also need to be consistent in dealing with children, making sure you treat them in fairly similar ways and that you enforce the rules you have made or agreed with the children without too many changes.

g Work out changes in activity in careful detail

Most of the things which go wrong in the classroom do so in the process of changing from one activity to another. Even when teachers work a completely integrated day with a great deal of time for children to work as they choose, trouble can arise when individuals change activity. You can avoid problems by thinking out how to get from the first activity to the second, asking yourself what each child will be doing and listing the steps which may be needed.

Able and experienced teachers often give the impression that all you need to do when you change activities is to say 'It's time now for you to go to your number groups' for there to be a well-organised move round which leaves everyone in the right place in the least possible time. The ability to do this has usually been built up with the children and through experience over a long period. It takes time and effort to get children to work and move as you wish.

A good deal of the ability to control a class is in the confidence in your voice and manner that children will do as you wish. The trouble is that it is very difficult to have confidence when you don't know whether what you are asking will actually happen. It is possible, however, to learn to behave as if you were confident. Confident people are relaxed and speak confidently and you can learn to do this. Good teachers not only use their voices when they give an explanation of what they want, but they also reinforce their words with gesture, facial expression and tone of voice. The younger the children the greater the teacher's need for these modes of communication.

Communication skills

The ability to form good relationships with children is an essential pre-requisite of good communication and good teaching. It is difficult to communicate well or teach well if you are not on good terms with your children. The ability to form relationships depends a good deal on personality and is also partly a matter of attitudes which help you to demonstrate to children that you care about them and have confidence in their ability to learn. There is also much to be learned about the way people react to your behaviour.

Communication takes place as a result of people attending to each other. It is not simply a matter of the meaning of the words you use, but is implicit in your choice of words and language structure to match the listeners

ANALYSIS 5.3: TEACHING SKILLS—
ORGANISATION AND CONTROL

1   Is my classroom attractive and welcoming to children?

2   Is the furniture in my classroom arranged to provide the most suitable pattern for the work being undertaken?

3   Is my classroom a learning environment in which children can learn independently?

4   Are the resources of equipment, materials and books in my classroom fully used?

5   Are the resources in my classroom organised so that they are easy to find and to keep tidy?

6   Is each child in the class in appropriate groups for learning?

7   Do my plans include provision for children of different levels of ability and stages of development?

8   Is my time and the children's fully used?

9   Do children start work immediately they enter the classroom?

10   Do the children in my class discuss work in pairs and small groups when this is appropriate?

11   Am I always in control of the whole group, even when I am working with individuals?

12   Can I always get full attention from the children when I wish?

and the situation. (Think how you would say the same thing to your class and to your headteacher.) It is also implicit in your tone of voice, the inflections you use, what you say and how you say it. In addition you convey messages by movement as well as by words and you modify your message in the light of the response you get. Your view of your listeners is demonstrated in your choice of content, vocabulary and sentence structure and the variation you make in the use of pitch and pace and the use of pauses.

If it seems that children are not responding to what you say, you will, almost without noticing what you are doing, say that same thing in a different and perhaps simpler way.

Your task as teacher is to get the message over as clearly as possible in ways that draw response from children and help them to match what you are saying to what they know already. Try to tape yourself in the classroom from time to time and listen to the tape critically.

Movement is the most basic form of communication operating from birth or perhaps even earlier. Because it is so basic and automatic, its message goes over even if you actually say something different. Movement and gesture and facial expression are all the time sending messages to others. Your observation of your children involves interpreting the movement messages they are sending. Their observation of you does likewise. Very young or handicapped children often communicate with their teachers by touch.

It is often through non-verbal communication of this kind that people get across the message that they are warm and sympathetic, brisk and business-like, tired and bad-tempered, pleased or sorry, and so on.

Children learn to interpret these messages very early, since it is important for them to recognise when mother or teacher is pleased or angry.

Eye contact is an important aspect of communication in this context. We use eye contact to signal beginnings and endings of pieces of communication as well as to send messages to control children's behaviour. By making eye contact with individual children you can imply that they are being noticed and had better behave or that they are important and being cared for.

Communication through the environment is an extension of communication through movement. An experienced observer very quickly takes in the messages which a teacher's classroom is putting over. You also send messages by the way you dress and care for your appearance. These all reflect philosophy and teaching style.

Your voice is likely to be the most frequently used form of communication in the classroom. The way you use it affects children in different ways. For example, any teacher who has tried to work with a lost voice will be aware that it is possible quite quickly to have the whole class whispering. You provide an important speech model for your children and your patterns of speech will affect theirs. You need to remember, however, that children learn to use spoken language by speaking and it is not easy to orchestrate opportunities for talking for a whole class though it is now a necessary part of the National Curriculum.

Communication is a two-way process The warm and trusting relationships necessary for good communication are something built up over time, but when you start work with a new class, it is particularly important to be as responsive as you can to children's ideas and confidences. Your response at this stage to something a child volunteers may determine, not only whether this particular child will risk suggesting something again, but if other children are listening they too will be influenced by your reactions. A teacher who says 'My children never have any ideas,' needs to look at the way he or she is reacting to the ideas they offer. It is not unusual to see a group of children silent and unresponsive with one teacher but full of ideas with another.

Trust in the teacher once established brings a necessary degree of security to children. As we have seen, security depends a good deal on knowing what to do, knowing the boundaries and what is expected and how the other person will react to different kinds of behaviour. Security often stems from predictability.

What are the communication skills the teacher needs? The following need consideration:

1 Presentation skills
   Every teacher needs to be able to present material to children in ways which capture attention and help them to focus on what is important. This means making good preparation and good use of voice and gesture. It also means continually scanning the class to see how they are responding, and being aware of how long you can talk before children cease to listen.

2 Questioning skills
   Questioning is one of the most important teaching skills. You need to think out very carefully the different types of questions you want to use so that you really challenge the thinking of all the children in the class.

   Questions can be classified in a number of ways. One common classification is into open and closed questions. Another is into questions requiring recall and questions requiring thinking. Both of these are more limited than the possible range of questions but are useful for broad classification. Teachers tend to ask more closed and recall questions and not enough open and thought-provoking questions.

   It is also very easy for teachers to ask 'guess what I'm thinking' types of questions and to respond to children's answers, turning aside all answers but the one which gives the correct guess.

3 Leading discussion
   Leading a class discussion is a more difficult skill than it seems in the

hands of an expert, partly because most class groups are rather large for satisfactory discussion. It therefore requires a good deal of effort on the part of the teacher to include the whole group. A very important part of leading discussion is the ability to draw together the points that have been made and reinforce those that are important for the children's learning. This is dealt with in more detail in a later chapter. It is also important to respond positively to the responses children give. Even when a child gives a wrong answer it may be possible to say something which is encouraging. Positive reactions to responses lead children to be more ready to respond the next time.

4 Helping individuals

Whatever the organisation of the class, you will always need skill in helping individual children to move on from their present understanding. You therefore need to be good at analysing a child's thinking so that you can suggest ways forward. You also need to have the class well enough organised to be free to deal with individuals.

**ANALYSIS 5.4 : TEACHING SKILLS —
COMMUNICATION**

1 How well do I present material to the whole class?

2 Are my questioning skills good enough?

3 Do I lead discussion competently?

4 Do I get children to contribute sufficiently?

5 Is it always the same children who contribute?

6 Do I get more contributions from boys than from girls?

7 Do I get more contributions from white than from black children?

8 Am I able to draw children's contributions together to help them to learn?

9 How skilled am I at helping individual children to think on from the point they have reached?

Planning skills

Every school and every teacher needs an underlying structure for work which is constituted so that there is scope for flexibility, but also enough system behind what is done to ensure that children can progress. To some extent the National Curriculum and the associated provision for assessment will provide something of a structure, but it could also become a strait-jacket. Planning does not mean a loss of spontaneity and flexibility. It is simply that you need to be clear where you are going if you want to make the most of the opportunities which arise.

The planning of the classroom teacher must be set in a wider context. As a classroom teacher you are normally responsible for planning the work for your class. Your planning is part of the planning needed for the whole year group if your school has more than one class in each year and this in turn is part of the planning for the whole school and eventually for the whole school career of your children. It is important to see what you do in this wider context and to know where your work fits into the overall pattern. The National Curriculum makes this rather easier to do.

In planning we need to be sure that some common ground is covered by all children. This will be partly ensured by the existence of the Programmes of Study and Attainment Targets in the National Curriculum. It is important to remember that objectives can be met in a variety of ways and that one activity can meet more than one objective. There is a case with older children for a formal programme of fairly specific teaching and an informal programme which complements it by using opportunities as they occur and by making one piece of learning complementary to others.

Methods of planning will discussed later, but it should be noted here that long term planning should involve the following in some form:

1 Identifying aims and objectives
2 Making general long term plans to meet them which involve assessing the needs of children and making systematic reviews of their progress
3 Making broad outlines of curriculum plans
4 Setting dates or periods of time for completing different aspects of the work
5 Considering how you wish children to work and planning a training programme for them
6 Making plans for evaluation, including criteria by which success will be judged. Deciding on the records to be kept
7 Considering the books, equipment and materials which will be needed and taking any necessary action
8 Considering first-hand experience which will be needed and planning action to provide it

9 Considering your own development and planning the necessary action to develop your own skills and knowledge

You will also need to make short-term plans for day-to-day work which:

a will provide for children of all abilities
b are flexible enough to include interests which may arise
c pay attention to details of organisation and enable work to run smoothly
d enable you to achieve your long-term aims and objectives

ANALYSIS 5.5: TEACHING SKILLS — PLANNING

1 To what extent do I state aims and objectives in planning?

2 Do I make broad long-term plans for curriculum?

3 Do I plan evaluation and record keeping?

4 Do I work out in advance the books and materials I need and see that they will be available?

5 Do I plan adequately the first-hand experiences my children will need?

6 Do I think out how I want children to work and the training they may need?

7 Do I make short-term plans allowing for interests which may develop ?

8 Does my planning include provision for the whole range of children?

9 Do I plan organisation in sufficient detail so that things run smoothly?

10 Do I plan for my own professional development?

Problem-solving skills

Human beings develop and learn by solving the problems which face them. This is true whether one looks at problems in one's everyday life or at problems in one's place of work.

Unfortunately there is also a very human tendency to regard difficult problems as someone else's fault and something about which one can do nothing. While it is true that there are always aspects of problems which cannot be solved, the fact that there is an obstacle does not mean that the problem is insoluble.

The process of teaching and organising a class is very much a problem-solving activity for both teacher and children. For the teacher the basic problem is that of how to reconcile the heterogeneous collection of children who make up the class with what they need to learn in such a way that the optimum amount of learning takes place. The solution to this set of problems is the main subject of this book.

The term 'problem-solving' has been much in evidence recently to describe the work done with children in design and technology. Less has been said about problem-solving for the teacher but in many ways much the same activities are called for. Teachers need to introduce children to the skills of problem-solving and the suggestions which follow, while made with the teacher's problems in mind, are nevertheless also relevant for children. They need to acquire problem-solving skills and positive attitudes to problems and they acquire both skills and attitudes by working to solve problems. This is very much at the core of work in technology.

The strategies suggested below could be used by the teacher or as part of the teaching programme for children.

Many problems seem to yield to a course of action such as the following, which is a mixture of strategies from various sources.

1 Define the problem
This may sound obvious, but it is easy to miss the parts of a problem which are within your control and it helps to state what you think the problem really is. e.g. My class has a wide range of ability and I find it difficult to provide work which matches the needs of the children.

2 Examine the problem further
You then start to tackle the problem by examining it further and trying to make some more explicit statements about it. In the example given you might make some statements such as the following:
   - It is difficult to match work to individuals, particularly those at the extremes of the ability range
   - Keeping such a large range of work going means that I don't do anything properly

- I am conscious that because some children in my class will be there for two years and others for only a year, some will miss out on some aspects of curriculum and others may do some work twice over

This list could be extended very much further and each item in turn regarded as a problem to be tackled.

3 Define your objectives

For each of the statements you made as part of your definition, try to make a statement of what you want to achieve. You could set it out like this:

Table 5.1 Defined objectives

Present state	Desired state
A small group of children have work which is at about their right level. The most and least able children and some others are just occupied.	All children have a programme of work which is at their proper level.

There are probably a number of ways in which you could continue from this point. Two which seem particularly interesting are described below.

Force field analysis was devised by Kurt Lewin and involves considering the forces which are acting for and against you in solving the problem. Figure 5.1 describes this.

LEWIN'S FORCE FIELD ANALYSIS

Restraining forces

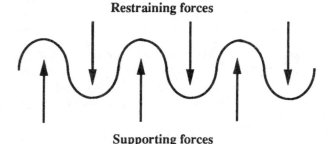

Supporting forces

Figure 5.1 Force field analysis model

Supporting forces in the situation described above might include good accommodation, a head who is prepared to let you try things and will support you financially, a class that is generally easy to handle.

Restraining forces might be the fact that the teacher who had your children last year did nothing to encourage independent working, pressure from parents to work in traditional ways with the most able children, a lack of materials for the most able children and a lack of knowledge on your part of the best way to deal with the least able.

You can then consider how you deal with each of these, looking at how you make the most of the supporting forces and what you can do to minimize the effect of the restraining forces.

Another approach, part of which fits well with the one described above, is described in Jackson's book, *The art of solving problems* (Jackson 1975) which gives a very full account of his approach. In particular, he speaks of considering the obstacles to solving a problem, which is a little like looking at the restraining forces. He suggests working through some possible ways of tackling the obstacles. You might overcome an obstacle, go round it, remove it, demolish it, neutralise it, prove it to be illusory, turn it to advantage, buy it off, alter it, find its weakest point, wait for it to go away.

If you take the restraining forces listed above as the obstacles in your situation, you might remove the first obstacles by instituting a careful programme of training your children to work more independently. The pressure from parents might be partly demolished by parents' meetings and explanation about what you are doing and why. It may also help to involve parents in the work you are doing so that they see for themselves that it is effective. Your head is supportive, so it would be possible to meet the obstacles about materials partly by buying more, but you would be wise to analyse the kind of material you need to meet the full range of your children and gradually buy and make material which fits into a framework, coding new material as you add it so that you are aware of what you have available. In practice many teachers spend a lot of time on making material but don't take enough time to sort out a structure so that new pieces fit in. If you can find time to make a structure, everything you do by way of making and buying material will fit into an overall plan.

Another possibility is to get out all the material you have which might be relevant and look to see if any of it could be made more self-contained and usable without your help. You might like to make some bridging materials to go with some material so that a child who was less able could use it .

You might also find that you could increase material to match some needs if you made the final end point of a project the creation of material which other children could use. This has many advantages. It uses the work already done; it can be an interesting incentive for the children who work on it and it creates an audience. This links with some of the recommendations of the *Bullock report* which stressed the importance of children writing and speaking for readerships and audiences other than the teacher as does the National Curriculum.

When one addresses oneself directly to an obstacle there are frequently possible ways forward. A useful strategy is to ask a series of questions such as – Can I overcome the problem by looking at it a different way, by using materials differently, by looking for time to do some basic thinking and sorting out of ideas in order to move forward, by working with colleagues, by involving parents and others, by getting children to work differently, by reorganising the situation or the use of materials, and so on? This kind of thinking is often most profitably undertaken with others. It is sometimes a useful activity for a class of children as well as for interested staff.

4 List possible solutions

The next stage is to consider solutions. You will already have a number collected from your examination of forces and obstacles and you can add to these. Write down as many ideas as you can think off, no matter how unlikely. Don't stop when you think of an idea which seems good but go on generating further ideas. Letting your mind range over ideas in this way often influences the idea you finally choose. It can sometime be useful to aim at a number of ideas; to set out, for example, to find ten ways of achieving the objective you have in mind.

If you are working with a group, one way of doing this is to pass round a piece of paper for each objective, on which each person adds an idea which could be used for that objective. It's better still if you do this with an overhead projector transparency so that the ideas can be projected for discussion.

5 Examine solutions

The next stage is to look at the solutions you have listed. It may help to draw up a page with four columns as shown below.

Idea	Advantages	Disadvantages	Points to note

Figure 5.2 Examining solutions

Now take each idea and sort it out under these headings. This will lead on to making a choice of possible solutions. You may want to use several of the ideas in this particular case.

6 Make an action plan
Include the following steps:
  – Select what seems to you to be a realistic date by which you want to have achieved your objectives.
  – Set down in detail the steps you need to take. It may be a good idea to do this in the form of a flow chart, but it depends upon the problem.
  – Consider who else is involved, including children, and note what you need to do about informing or consulting others.

7 Plan evaluation
It is very easy to try out some new idea and do nothing about evaluating its success except in a very casual way. It is much better to decide when you are planning what you will consider as success and how you will know whether you have achieved your goals. You also need to decide when you will review what has happened and be self-disciplined about carrying out an evaluation.

This is a very detailed way of tackling a problem. There will be many occasions when you will have ideas and put them into action more casually. The point about suggesting such a programme is to stress that there is always some step you can take to deal with a problem and that having some strategies for generating ideas and solutions can help. This is also a useful set of strategies for a group of teachers working together at a problem.

Make a point of periodically thinking back over what you have done, especially at the end of the year, to make sure you have learned all you can from the way you tackled particular problems.

Evaluation skills

Evaluation is dealt with in detail in Chapter 13.

6 Teaching strategies

Whenever you plan work in the classroom, you have a variety of possible ways of helping children to learn. The choices of teaching strategy you make are influenced by three factors:

- The particular group of children
- The subject matter to be learned
- Your own particular teaching style and preferences

We have already looked fairly closely at the way in which children learn and the consequences of different teaching styles for the teacher. Children's learning ability and learning style and the approaches most likely to be successful will vary within any class, but very often there are sufficient common elements to be able to select an approach likely to match the needs of the majority.

In selecting teaching methods you need to consider not only the ability of the group and the stage of development of the majority, but also their experience, their interests, their language, knowledge and skill and what is likely to motivate this particular group. The younger and less able your group, the more important it becomes to start from the first-hand and the practical, although first-hand experience continues to be important if a child's learning is to be carried over and applied in new situations.

The subject matter to be learned also dictates certains things in relation to teaching approaches. For example, it is difficult to teach young children very much about number in any effective way without a good deal of practical work. Geographical and historical concepts are unlikely to be established without some field work. You can't learn to enjoy poetry without reading it and listening to it and so on.

Edwards and Mercer (1987) stress the importance of classroom discourse in children's learning. They say:

> It is largely within the teacher/pupil discourse through which the lesson is conducted that whatever understandings are eventually created are in

the first place shaped, interpreted and made salient or peripheral, reinterpreted and so on. And it is a process which remains essentially dominated by the teacher's own aims and expectations. ...

The teacher's dilemma is to have to inculcate knowledge when apparently eliciting it. This gives rise to the general ground rule of classroom discourse, in which the pupils' task is to come up with the correct solutions to problems seemingly spontaneously while all the time trying to discern from the teacher's clues, cues, questions and presuppositions what the required solution actually is.

This may sound a somewhat cynical view to some teachers but it is firmly based in the writers' research in classrooms and reflection on the way one works in a classroom confirms that this is what happens a good deal of the time.

Edwards and Mercer (1987) and Neville Bennett and Joy Kell (1989) all found that teachers were inclined not to tell children what it was they were supposed to be learning. This was usually because the teacher did not want to limit the lesson but to use ideas which came up as well as what had been planned. They make the point, however, that this means that children are less able to focus their learning and that sharing with the children the purpose of what they are doing may be more effective.

Chapter 4 looked at teaching style and the importance of using your style to the best advantage and at the same time selecting appropriate ways of teaching for the subject matter and situation.

Children may learn and teachers may teach in the following basic ways. These should be regarded as a collection of teaching tools which can be selected according to their appropriateness for the children, the subject matter and the context.

DIRECT TEACHING

A high proportion of teaching at every level, but particularly with older children and adults, will tend to consist of exposition and questioning. It will almost certainly involve a great deal of questioning designed to elicit information from the children so that you can build on what they already know and the ideas they already have. The following would seem likely to be situations in which this approach is useful:

- It may be the most efficient and economical way of getting children to learn something and checking that they know it.
- It is a valuable way of starting and ending a piece of work. At the beginning you may want to stimulate children and interest them, or direct their attention or get work organised. At the end of a piece of work there

may be a place for drawing together what has been learned, summing up, generalising, filling gaps, questioning understanding and so on.
- It is a good approach for giving instructions on safety or organisation where it is important that every child understands the same thing. You will still need to reinforce your words more for some children than others.

The success of this method of teaching and the extent of its use depends upon the skills and the preferred style of the teacher. Direct teaching involves the following:

Good preparation

Exposition by a teacher needs to be good if it is to capture interest. Each teacher puts things over in a different way, but you need to maintain a self-critical attitude to what you do and work all the time at improving your skill. This means that some work, at least, should be prepared in considerable detail.

Making appropriate notes

This doesn't mean writing copious notes which you may not be able to use in the classroom, but finding the best way of note-making for you and selecting methods of planning which enable you to file and store lesson material and perhaps reassemble it for use in other ways on future occasions.

Preparation of notes may mean setting out activities in a flow diagram. You may put notes in a file or on small cards which can be re-shuffled for different occasions. You may also like to make a collection of overhead projector transparencies and file them by punching holes in them and placing them in a ring binder under different headings for future use.

The number of pieces of work which you can prepare thoroughly is limited, but if you prepare a few things really well each week, selecting work which you may want to repeat at some other time, you will gradually build up a stock of material.

Work which lends itself to this kind of preparation includes stories, where it is a good idea if you want to tell a story to see it in a series of scenes, thinking about what they look like in great detail so that you can create pictures in children's minds. Any topic which you want children to become involved with can be prepared in this way.

Setting the scene

When you want to present material to the whole class, try to set the scene well. Make sure children are sitting where they can see you and try to start in a way which will capture attention and will at the same time draw on their experience. It is much the same whether you are talking to five-year-olds or fifty-year-olds getting interest is something you need to do very quickly and it is always worth preparing the beginning of a piece of work extra well.

Being ready for the work to start

It is wise to look ahead to what you plan to do after introducing your topic and to make sure that books are ready, writing materials available, or whatever. It is very disappointing to create a marvellous atmosphere with a story or account of something and get the children enthusiastic and ready to go, to be brought down to earth with a bump by minor chaos resulting from not having things ready in advance.

Using questioning

We have already noted the importance of questioning as a teaching technique. It is a much more complex skill than it may seem at first. Questions are of many kinds and some are of more use than others in developing children's ability to think. The following types of questions are common in classrooms and are taken mainly from *Effective questioning* by Trevor Kerry (1980).

- *Recall questions* These are probably the most common type of teaching questions. They are undoubtedly useful and necessary but should not be used to the exclusion of other types of questions.

    Recall questions can degenerate into 'guess what I'm thinking' questions in which you see children concentrating on trying to guess what the teacher wants rather than on answering the question.
- *Reasoning questions* Questions which involve thinking things through using evidence are needed in most types of school work. A question like 'Why do you think that moss grows on this wall and not on that one? ' or 'What do you think will happen next in the story and why do you think that?' can demand reasoning from children, especially if you follow up their replies so that you take them through a sequence of reasoning.
- *Speculative questions* Many reasoning questions will also be speculative, but one can go beyond the reasoning involved in the type of questions given above and look at the reasoned speculation about hypothetical possibilities. e.g. 'What would happen if school ceased to be compulsory?' or 'What difference would it make if our school was on top of a hill or by the sea?'
- *Personal response* Questions which ask children how they feel about

something have no right answers and should help children to sort out their own thinking. e.g. 'How would you feel if someone damaged something you cared about a lot?' or 'What should happen to people who damage other people's property?' 'Why do you think they do it?'

Questioning should not be left entirely to the spur of the moment. It is wise to prepare some questions in advance so that you can give some thought to the kinds of questions you want to ask. It may be a good idea from time to time to tape a questioning session and then listen to it afterwards, perhaps with a colleague, and to consider whether the questions you used were actually making the children think. You also need to consider what evidence you need to know whether you were making children think or not and what proportion of the class this covered.

A further consideration is how you teach children to ask appropriate questions. This is particularly important in science where children need to learn to ask questions which lend themselves to investigation. Questioning might also be considered in relation to work on interviewing people and children can be asked to consider what sorts of questions get what sorts of answers. They can also be encouraged to pose questions to the class and to consider whether these were good questions for finding out what they wanted to know.

John Holt, in *How children fail* (1964) goes further than this and says:

It is not the teacher's proper task to be constantly testing and checking the understanding of the learner. That is the learner's task, and only the learner can do it. The teacher's task is to answer questions when learners ask them, or try to help learners understand better when they ask for that help.

This is something of an ideal state – something to aim for but not easy to achieve. John Holt also has a lot to say about the way children deal with teachers' questions. He believes that they are often frightened when asked a question and that they use all kinds of devices to guess the answer the teacher wants rather than seeking the answer that lies in the material under discussion.

Drama may offer something here. A group of children looking at a bridge as if they were engineers from another country studying it in order to build a similar bridge at home will ask quite different and more pertinent questions from a group who are visiting simply to study the bridge.

It is very easy for children to get the idea that the way teachers ask questions is the norm. Most people ask questions because they want to know something. Teachers are unusual in that they ask questions to which they usually already know the answer.

LEARNING BY INVESTIGATION

We all learn better the material we seek out and work o1
Primary teachers are well aware of this and work to creat
which children experiment and discover. This work is of tw\
Sometimes a teacher will set up an open-ended learning situ.
example, when a group of children is taken out of school to u.. whatever
learning situation the visit seems to offer.

On another occasion the teacher may want to get a particular piece of
learning established and may provide specific experiences and arrange for
a very specific outcome. This is most easily seen when one looks at the
development of mathematical concepts where a teacher may be providing
various kinds of practical work in order to develop conceptual thinking
based on firm understanding. We saw earlier how Edwards and Mercer
(1987) describe teachers in this situation giving children clues about what
is wanted when they don't find it out for themselves and they demonstrate
how this kind of learning can degenerate into 'guess what I'm thinking'.
They also show that teachers often miss useful comments by children
which would have helped the learning because they are so intent on seeing
that children achieve the teacher's goals. They suggest that where this
happens the learning becomes 'ritual', i.e. children can go through the
procedures and say the right words, but do not really understand the
principles underlying what they are learning. This makes it difficult to
apply in new situations and difficult also to take the learning further.

Investigatory learning needs to be part of a great deal of the work you
do with children but there are some areas of work in which it is more
important than others.

It is particularly important in the development of concepts. A concept
is, in effect, a generalisation made from a range of different experiences.
For example, children at an early age begin to acquire one aspect of the
concept of conservation when they have explored what happens when you
pour liquid into different shaped vessels. They need to do this a number of
times and to discuss their findings a good deal before they come to
appreciate that the amount of liquid doesn't change. It merely changes
shape. They then need to learn of other examples of conservation if they
are to get a full idea of the concept.

Another example might be the idea of *old*. In order to have an
understanding of the past a child needs to understand what is meant when
we say something is old. Young children use the word in several different
ways – I am six years old. My Dad has a new car. My uncle bought his old
one. Our church is very old. They need to sort out these meanings through
experience. In particular they need to begin to see that the term *old* is a

ative one. A child is *old* compared with his baby sister; his mother is *old* compared with him; the church is *old* compared with his grandparents, but the church in the next village is *old* compared with our church.

Acquiring this concept of age means experiencing and noting signs of age in people and objects and buildings, so that it becomes possible to make judgements about age. This means making generalisations from experience and discovering the clues about age which can be used.

There will inevitably be an element of telling in concept development but if there is to be true understanding and consequent ability to transfer the learning to new situations, children need to reach the point where they can formulate the concept for themselves.

The National Curriculum substantially consists of concepts. It will therefore be important to set up appropriate situations which lead to the development of the specific concepts listed in each of the subject areas. It is likely that little time will be available for completely open-ended work, but a piece of work set up to develop a specific concept will provide many opportunities for other learning, some of which will meet other curriculum requirements.

Wynne Harlen (1985) suggests that the role of the teacher in this kind of learning in science is first of all to look for questions to which to say 'Let's see if we can find out.' The question may then need to be reorganised or broken down into questions that can be investigated. In other situations the teacher's task may be as follows:

- providing problems but not instructions for solving them, then giving the children the opportunity to do the planning
- supplying a structure for the planning appropriate to the children's experience (questions to take them through the steps of thinking about variables to change to control and to measure)
- sometimes discussing plans before carrying them out and considering different ideas
- always discussing activities afterwards to consider how the method of investigation could have been improved
- providing opportunities in the form of activities where simple patterns or more general trends can be found
- enabling children to talk about their findings and how they interpret them (by questioning and listening)
- asking them to make predictions, explaining how they arrive at them and then checking them against the evidence (discussion and practical work)
- expecting them to check interpretations carefully and to draw only those conclusions for which they have evidence (discussion and practical work)
- organising for the interpretation of findings to be shared and discussed critically

This kind of learning is often particularly effective in the context of the kind of drama described earlier which requires certain learning because of the role the child has taken on.

This needs careful preparation, so that each child understands his or her role and is able to identify what is needed to help in the particular role. It is easy to see how such learning could grow in this context. If children really get inside their roles it will have tremendous motivation. There will also be a demand for information which is much more clearly defined than where the children are finding out because the teacher tells them to.

This kind of motivation is, of course, present when children investigate a real problem with an outcome to be judged on its use, but it is difficult to do this all the time and an imaginary but convincing framework can do a great deal for you and the children in terms of motivation and involvement.

Whether you use drama as part of learning or work more directly to establish a concept, your task as teacher is to draw attention to what is significant in the situation and to help children to consider outcomes in such a way that your intervention leads to the discovery of answers rather than a statement of what is to be discovered. This is difficult to do because it takes time with individuals or small groups working through questions to see where they are in their thinking.

This kind of development may also come out of direct teaching where your skill in questioning may lead to the discovery of a generalisation. This approach is far from being a soft option and it needs very careful structuring of learning if it is to succeed.

Learning by investigation also means acquiring process skills. Wynne Harlen (1985) suggests the following components of process skill development in science. These skills are also needed in most other aspects of curriculum.

- Providing the materials, time and physical arrangement for the children to study and interact with things in their environment. This involves children in having the evidence of their own senses, opportunities for them to find answers by doing things, having concrete experience as a basis of their thinking and being able to check their ideas against the behaviour of real things.
- Designing tasks that encourage discussion among small groups of children. This involves children in combining their ideas, listening to others, arguing about differences and refining their own ideas through explaining them to others.
- Discussing with children as individuals and in small groups. Children can explain how they arrive at their ideas, teachers can listen to this and find out the evidence that children have gathered and how they interpret

it and encourage children to check findings and review their activities and results critically.

- Organising whole class discussions. Children need the opportunity to explain their findings and ideas to others, to hear about others' ideas, to comment on alternative views and to defend their own; for teachers to offer ideas and direct children to sources that will extend the children's ideas.
- Teaching the techniques of using equipment and conventions of using graphs, tables, charts and symbols. Children need to have available the means to increase the accuracy of their observations and to choose appropriate forms for communication as the need arises.
- Providing books, displays, visits and access to other sources of information. Children can compare their ideas with those of others, have access to information that may help them to develop and extend their ideas and raise questions that may lead to further enquiry.

Much of what is suggested here not only leads to learning in science but also meets many of the demands of the National Curriculum for oral and other work in English as well as some work in mathematics.

Very young children may develop concepts and skills through play but only if the adult sees that this happens. Neville Bennett and Joy Kell (1989) found that teachers of infants tended to regard play as a time filler, enabling them to hear other children read. He and others stress that it is not enough to provide play activities at the reception stage, however rich. The teacher or another adult needs to interact with the children drawing out the learning possibilities. Bruner (1985), for example, notes that adult presence 'strikingly increases the richness and the length of play'. Sylva *et al.* (1980) state that children in the 3+ to 5+ age group are 'more likely to engage in complex play when in the company of adults who are interacting with them'. Tyler notes that 'learning cannot take place unless attention is directed to the relevant stimuli. Thus the adult plays a fundamental part in enabling the child to deploy its attention most effectively' – a point that refers to other learning as well as play.

Learning by investigation may enable children to follow up interests and be stimulated by an experience and respond in any way they wish. A group of children making a local study, for example, may record this in drawing or painting, model making, personal or poetic ways of writing, factual writing, music, movement, drama and so on. It may give rise to mathematical, scientific, historical, geographical exploration and in this situation the teacher may deliberately hold back from giving too much guidance in order to be guided by the children's ideas. However, it will be important to bear in mind the demands of the National Curriculum and to seek ways within the study of developing some of the concepts in the subject areas. It will also be important to see that individual children, given choice, do not always respond in the same way. A child who writes well and easily, for example, may tend to respond in writing on every occasion instead of exploring other possible responses.

This kind of activity requires a good deal of careful thought on the part of the teacher. It is not enough just to take a group of children to an interesting place, even if you direct their attention to some of the things to be seen. If they are not used to this approach they may fall back on previous successful work and miss new learning which is important. You need to help them to acquire the skills needed for studying environment and recording their observations and responses in a variety of ways.

This may sometimes involve looking for specific information and making straightforward statements about findings, sometimes using charts and diagrams. On other occasions it may involve thinking how a place made one feel and writing personally or poetically or drawing or painting, sometimes observing in detail and recording in drawing or model making; or perhaps measuring or looking for things which might be investigated further, perhaps by questioning other people or perhaps by experiment. Most visits can give rise to work in all three core subjects as well as work in art and craft, history and geography and possibly other subjects as well.

Only when children have a range of approaches and skills for making observations, do they become able to use a complex environment for learning. This doesn't mean that children need training in all the skills before you encourage responses to a new environment. Skills and approaches can be built up in the course of study and during the process children will see and suggest ideas of their own, some of which you may like to help them to develop. They will thus become independent observers who are not looking over their shoulders to see if they are doing what you want them to do, but are genuinely investigating for themselves.

This is one of the most important of the approaches to learning because it can be highly motivating and can help children to structure what they are learning and acquire concepts. It is also one of the most difficult methods to use well and creating situations in which children can make discoveries which are within their capacity but which extend their thinking is a fascinating professional task.

LEARNING THROUGH DISCUSSION

Most of us learn a great deal through talking with others and we also consolidate learning in this way. One reason why this is useful is that when you put something into words you have to think it out. The responses and questions of others to your statement may then sharpen your thinking and enlarge it. Teachers will also be very conscious that one way to learn something well is to have to teach it. Edwards and Mercer (1987) suggest that the whole process of teaching and learning is a matter of arriving at shared understandings, in particular of the meaning of the language used, through shared activity and talk. In a conversation each speaker brings his or her own experience to the interpretation of the words of the other. If the experience is very different misunderstanding is likely to follow. This can often be the case with children who may use the same words as the adult but give them a more limited meaning because of the limitations of their own experience.

Children therefore need to learn through discussion and there is much that you can do to ensure that this kind of learning takes place. It is partly a matter of organisation but also a matter of helping children to become more skilled at being members of a discussion group.

We have already seen that questioning is an important part of the teacher's role as well as being something we should help children to do. It is also a way of stimulating discussion and very often you ask questions to get the children to talk in order to draw from them material useful for the learning you have in mind.

The starting point for discussion is to think out very clearly what you hope to get from it. It may, for example, provide a series of starting points for a piece of work. It may be a way of getting children to reflect on experience and generalise from it and so it may contribute to their conceptual development. You may also be hoping to get a lot of examples to illustrate various points and ideas.

The first task in preparing discussion is to consider the function of the discussion you plan. The next stage is to identify some key questions which are likely to lead to useful conclusions. This involves thinking what experience and the language to express it your children are likely to have in relation to your key questions. You can then start in areas where you know that every child will have some experience to contribute.

There are a number of important points to remember when leading discussion.

1 Look at the way you receive children's contributions. Doing this in a sympathetic and appreciative way is particularly important if you want to get a good discussion going and it would be the same if you were working with adults instead of children.

2 Remember to scan the room looking for children who have something to say and want to get in or those who are miles away and perhaps need recalling to the present. It is easy to miss children seated at the sides of the room and those who are very near you. You need to make a deliberate attempt to look at everyone in the group every so often.

3 Every teacher becomes skilled at recognising children's body language and recognising when they are telling you that they have had enough. Class discussions should generally be short, unless the children are very absorbed.

4 Much the most important task of the discussion leader is that of summarising or pulling together the ideas and contributions that have been made, making them into a coherent whole and then possibly pushing the discussion further or moving on to some other activity. It is a vital skill for a teacher and you need to do it consciously to begin with so that you can practise the skill and improve it. It is particularly important at the end of a discussion. Many teachers build up a summary on the board as they go along but this has the disadvantage of losing eye contact with the children. An overhead projector is slightly better for this purpose, but it may be best to lead the discussion without doing any recording and then make a suitable summary at the end.

There is considerable difference between the group led by the teacher and the small group working independently. When you are leading the discussion yourself you can give it direction. If you want small groups to work on their own, you need to think very carefully about the brief you are going to give them so that they can use the opportunity really profitably.

The experience of discussion in a small group with or without the teacher, is a different experience from that of discussion in a large group. In a class discussion, however good the teacher, it is possible for some children to opt out and some may have developed considerable skill in looking involved when really far away. E. C. Wragg in *Classroom teaching skills* (1984) tells of a conversation with children in which they described how they put up their hands in answer to a question even when they had nothing to say and then put them down again if there seemed to be any danger that the teacher would pick on them!

When you are in a small group and even more when you are talking with only one or two other people, there is some pressure on you to participate and the smaller the group, the more true this becomes. This suggests that small group discussion has a particular value and when something new is being learned or some experience sorted out, a small group working with the teacher may be the best possible way of establishing learning.

There is also a case for training older children in the skills of discussion leadership, discussing with the class what is involved in leading discussion and then letting some children practise to see how well they do.

Very valuable work can be done in pairs and trios. The kind of discussion which two children might have in working out a mathematical problem together has considerable value because it requires them both to put their thinking into words and the process of communication itself helps their understanding. There is also value in one child teaching another.

LEARNING FROM MATERIALS

All teachers make some use of books and materials in their work with children. Most frequently they use books and work cards to provide practice and reinforcement of learning, so that something is taught to a group or class and then children practise what they have learned in some way using materials.

A rather different use of materials is to use them to provide work matched to individual needs. In this situation different children may be working through some kind of structured scheme, computer program or course book, each working at the level he or she has reached. Or each child may be working more independently with work which not only matches his or her stage of development and learning needs but is also related to each individual's interests.

Work cards and work sheets have been around for a long time, but we are still at a comparatively early stage of discovering how to design materials which interest children and teach them well. Desk-top publishing will gradually enable teachers to produce really good-looking material as the hardware and software reach the schools.

In making materials you need to remember the following:

1 The materials must be motivating in their own right
   They are most likely to motivate if they have an element of discovery or problem solving which is well within the child's capacity, but not so easy that there is no challenge. For example, a child learning the various ways we spell the long 'a' sound is likely to be motivated if given a list of words containing this sound and asked to work out the ways the sound can be spelled and then asked to find more examples of each. This learning is more likely to be retained than a list of words to be learned because it has demanded involvement and decision making.
2 Language is very important in teaching material
   The language level at which a child can work independently is much less complex both in vocabulary and language structure than the language level the same child can manage if the material is introduced by the teacher.
3 The layout of a work card is also important
   Good spacing between lines of writing make it more legible. The way things are arranged helps or hinders understanding. It is a good idea to study the way advertising material is set out and to apply some of the ideas to work material.
4 Good individualised learning material needs to be carefully structured

so that a child can work through it in an appropriate way
It also needs to be matched to the child.

LEARNING WITH COMPUTERS AND AUDIO-VISUAL EQUIPMENT

Computers will gradually provide more and more opportunities for children's learning. They will, in due course, provide ways of analysing the stage a child has reached, match this with appropriate programs and record his or her work on the program selected. The programs will be designed to deal with the child's problems as they occur and do many things which can only be done by the teacher at present. As computers become able to respond to voice commands they will offer even more to young children and it seems likely that, for example, a great deal of the teaching now involved in learning to read and in some early mathematics will be done effectively at the child's own pace, by a computer program. Many schools are already discovering the value of a computer for word-processing and the incentive this offers to children's writing, particularly if it involves desk-top publishing, and spelling can be checked by the computer. As small computers become cheaper and a sufficient number can be available in each class they can be built into children's learning in a way that is difficult at present. We really need a situation where every child has a lap top computer and regards it in much the same way as he or she now regards an exercise book.

Wynne Harlen (1985) suggests that in science children might use the computer as follows:

- helping in making measurements and recording data
- guiding children's thinking about identifying investigable questions and designing investigation which the children later carry out in practice
- extending the range of subject matter that can be investigated, as distinct from being observed, by simulations linked to the children's own observation
- short-circuiting time-consuming data collection by providing additional data to supplement those collected by children
- posing questions to help children to apply the ideas and methods of working they have gained from past enquiry

Excellent work has been undertaken in mathematics using the turtle and there are endless possibilities for using databases and spreadsheets for different ways of handling numbers.

Teachers already have a considerable task in selecting appropriate computer software for their children. There is a great deal of material which is simply offering a way of practising skills which might equally well be practised in other ways, although while there is an element of novelty there may be motivation in the programs. It is important to look for material which really makes children think.

It would be very easy, as computers become more available in primary schools and as software improves, to forget the importance of first-hand experience. It will be important to get this work into perspective and to marry it with other ways of working which provide different sorts of learning.

Other audio-visual equipment provides many additional opportunities for learning, since it can also in some sense duplicate the teacher. Radio and television are among the oldest of the forms of audio-visual learning available to teachers, and British teachers have access to programmes of very high quality. These can bring into the classroom experience which no child or teacher might otherwise encounter. The broadcasting authorities have access to the best of current thinking and do a good deal to consult teachers and to pilot and monitor their materials in classrooms. The video-recorder makes it possible to use just that portion of a programme which is relevant if the teacher wishes. It is now also possible to use material from non-educational programmes if your LEA has subscribed to this.

Radio and television are a comparatively cheap resource which can be of great value and are likely in the future to complement teaching of the National Curriculum very helpfully.

The great majority of programmes are made for watching with the teacher rather than as teaching material in their own right. If you wish to use radio or television as small group or individual teaching material it will be necessary to extend the materials which go with the programme or provide other material to bridge the gap between use with the teacher and independent use by the child. This isn't true for all broadcasts but it is true for the majority.

The tape recorder is among the most used pieces of classroom equipment, offering a considerable range of possibilities. It can be used for material created by the children and also for actual teaching and for various kinds of practice. It is also useful for recording interviews as part of environmental studies and, as most children have access to cassette recorders at home, a child can record discussion with members of the family and people in the neighbourhood and bring the tape into school to share with others.

The tape recorder is particularly valuable in teaching reading. It offers a child the opportunity to prepare reading by listening to a book on tape for later reading to the teacher. It can also be used for learning phonics.

At a later stage there is much to be said for putting books, stories and poetry on tape so that children who are poor readers can experience the pleasure of reading, following the reading on tape in their books. This makes available to the slower readers the benefits that better readers are getting from reading. It provides models of speech and vocabulary. It enables children to hear language structures which may be new to them. They will have the opportunity to identify with people in stories and extend their experience through the text.

Such material takes time to build up, but there are often parents with an interest in drama who might help. It could also be an activity for older children in the secondary school or good readers at the top of the primary school.

In a similar way such things as spelling, mental arithmetic and word building can be recorded for children, or a child can record the words or numbers he or she needs to learn as a personal test and then return to take the test when he or she is ready. Children might also work in pairs at a similar stage and do this for each other.

Photographic transparencies are also valuable, particularly in relation to environmental studies and it is a good idea to build a collection of slides of different buildings and objects which are likely to be used on a number of occasions. These can be used with the tape recorder and a hand viewer, or they can be used as material for the whole class, or they can be made into books with text added.

CREATIVE WORK

Creative work in whatever medium is important in its own right as a form of expression. It is also a medium for learning other things. Opportunities for both are needed. It is important as a teaching approach because children need to understand some things with their emotions and imaginations as well as in cognitive terms. Creating a picture or a model or a piece of drama may enable a child to understand what it was to be alive at a different time or to live in a different part of the world. The experience of using implements or wearing clothes from a different period or place may bring a new understanding of the people who used such implements or wore such clothes. A story may make more sense when children make a picture of it. Taking on a role may make it possible for a child to enter imaginatively into learning.

It is not easy to provide for this kind of learning in such a way that all children get this kind of understanding. You need to be on the look out for opportunities in other work to complement it with creative work. In science, for example, there is sometimes the opportunity to use creatively the materials you have been using for exploration. Mathematics may be made more real by asking children to undertake such activities as taking on the role of someone who needed to measure something but had no units of measurement, or an architect who wanted to copy some parts of a building but was unable to borrow the plans, and so on.

It is, on the other hand, important to avoid using drawing indiscriminately almost as a reward for writing. A teacher should have a purpose in asking a child to draw something or the child should have a purpose, perhaps wishing to extend what he or she is saying in writing .

You may find it useful to analyse your preferences for teaching approaches using the matrix in Analysis 6.1 below. Make a profile of the extent to which you think you use each method marking the appropriate column. Then make an analysis of what you have actually done over the course of a week using the last column and compare the two. In making the second analysis you will need to work out the percentages of time spent on each approach.

ANALYSIS 6.1: TEACHING METHODS

Teaching methods	++	+	av	-	- -	Actual
Direct teaching using exposition and questioning						
Open-ended investigation						
Planned investigation						
Individualised learning from books and work cards						
Individualised learning with computers and other audio-visual equipment						
Class discussion						
Discussion in pairs and small groups						
Creative work						
Practice work						

CONCLUSION

The intention of the last three chapters was to help you to analyse your role as teacher and to look at alternative strategies which can be used in working with children.

The information about your style and preferences forms a background for your decisions about how to organise your teaching.

7 The curriculum

The main concern of this book is classroom organisation but we need to consider what we want to organise before we can consider how to do it. Many studies suggest that *how* children learn is probably as important as *what* they learn. The way work is organised affects the extent of each child's contact with the teacher, the opportunities and resources available and the actual learning which takes place, both by conscious intent on the part of the teacher and also as a hidden curriculum with its own values and assumptions.

There are many definitions of the word curriculum. The National Curriculum, for example, might be defined as the intended content of children's learning. However, children learn a great deal in school which is not intended directly or even not intended at all. The definition discussed in this chapter is that of all the learning a child does in any aspect of his or her school life. This might be seen to include at least three kinds of activity.

THE TAUGHT CURRICULUM

This is the usual meaning of the word curriculum. It covers all the teaching and learning which goes on intentionally and deliberately within the classroom and elsewhere during the school day. It is the work which those outside the school recognise as what the school is in business to do and is largely covered by the National Curriculum.

THE INSTITUTIONAL CURRICULUM

Any organisation teaches those who work in it about its way of life, its values and codes of behaviour, *the way we do things here.* Sometimes this is done explicitly, as when a teacher actually trains children to run an assembly or talks about school rules. Sometimes it is implicit, as when children are praised for behaviour which accords with the views and values of the head and staff or scolded for behaviour which is not in accord.

Schools are usually very clear about the patterns of behaviour required from teachers and children, partly because the immaturity of the majority of the school population requires the support that this offers. These patterns teach children many things and probably should be discussed much more by teachers so that shared values are reinforced and differences recognised. This learning is often less effective than it might be because of inconsistencies in what is demanded by different teachers. Children also find themselves unwittingly behaving in ways which teachers dislike, but which may be acceptable at home. For the child, school life can be fraught with problems in working out the demands of the institutional curriculum.

The institutional curriculum also includes opportunities for taking responsibility and for leadership and for working with others. It includes the social learning that goes on in the playground and the classroom; the learning which takes place at lunch and in assembly and all the attitudes developed as a result of the way a child is treated in school by teachers and by peers.

THE HIDDEN CURRICULUM

Some parts of the curriculum are hidden, not only from the children, but from the teachers. Much which we might now list under the institutional curriculum was once part of the hidden curriculum. As soon as we become conscious of it, it is no longer part of the hidden curriculum, which is, by definition, hidden. Since it is hidden, a school cannot control it.

It is therefore possible that there is learning going on which you don't know about. Is the child who is able, for example, learning to work slowly because finishing first brings more of the same? Are children learning to give you the answers they think you want rather than seeking the right answer? Do some children get the impression that they are unimportant because they are, for example, not good at games or craft or writing? Do some children get the impression that reading, writing and mathematics and possibly science, are the only things that matter? Do girls feel inferior to boys and conversely? Do children get the impression that it is better to be white than black?

FACTORS AFFECTING THE CURRICULUM

The curriculum a school offers is determined by government in the National Curriculum. However, it is affected by the views of the LEA ,the governors, head and teachers. Thus although the National Curriculum is laid down in some detail, it is very far from dictating all that an individual teacher or school does.

Teachers affect the curriculum because each teacher has a particular personality, teaching style and a particular set of skills and knowledge to offer and is free to select material to teach the National Curriculum and anything else which he or she thinks will be appropriate for the particular group of children. Teachers work with three sets of variables:

Variables which are pre-determined

- Current educational thinking
- Current national policies and needs
- The National Curriculum
- Location of the school
- Children and parents
    Social and educational background
    Ability levels
- School building and facilities
- Head and staff of the school
    Background and experience
    Ability
- Staffing ratio

Variables which can be influenced but not determined

- Parental expectations of the school and the child
- Support from parents
- Support from governors
- Behaviour of children
- Attitude of head and colleagues
- School organisation
- Interpretation of the National Curriculum
- School schemes of work
- Use of building, facilities and resources
- Money available

Areas of self-determination by teachers

- Vehicles for curriculum
    e.g. choice of books, materials, approaches, some subject matter
- Use of time within the classroom
- Use of learning space
- Use of resources
- Teaching skills and knowledge

– Teaching behaviour and methods
– Children's learning

These areas are not separated very clearly, but you are most likely to be using time effectively if you concentrate most attention on the last section.

AIMS AND OBJECTIVES

The National Curriculum Council paper *A framework for the primary curriculum* (1989a) suggests that in planning frameworks for the curriculum the school should:

– be flexible enough to allow for a range of approaches to the planning of the whole curriculum and the organisation of learning and teaching in the primary school
– ensure a whole school approach to implement the National Curriculum
– recognise the entitlement of all pupils to a broad curriculum as embodied in the core and other foundation subjects; this being regardless of race, gender, disability or geographical location
– improve communication between schools, governors, parents and LEAs
– inform all aspects of planning and the efficient use of resources, both human and material
– ensure that the monitoring of pupils' progress takes place, together with consistent, informative record keeping

The National Curriculum Council's publication *The whole curriculum (1990a)* includes the following:

– the core subjects of English, mathematics and science
– the foundation subjects of geography, history, music, physical education, art and craft, technology and, at the secondary stage, a modern foreign language
– religious education
– skills which go across the curriculum i.e. communication, numeracy, study, problem solving, personal and social skills, information technology
– five themes – economic and industrial understanding, careers education and guidance, health education, education for citizenship and environmental education
– four dimensions – equal opportunities, educational for a multicultural society, provision for pupils with special needs and preparation for adult life

The core subjects, plus the foundation subjects and the dimensions, skills and themes identified by *The whole curriculum* may at first seem a tall order but in practice many of these aspects of learning are part of the everyday life of the classroom.

The National Curriculum is set out as a series of subjects, but many of the documents make it clear that it is not intended that primary schools should revert to a subject-based curriculum. It is normal at the primary stage for children to move from work which is not subject-based at all, except perhaps for mathematics and reading and now science, towards the kind of structuring of experience which subjects represent. The task for the teacher is to introduce learning in such a way that it builds the necessary subject-related knowledge, concepts and skills without losing the value of looking across subjects and seeing where one fits into another.

It has been normal practice in the primary school to do a good deal of work which crosses subject barriers. There are many advantages in this. In the first place it echoes the natural way of learning of young children. Pre-school children do not study separate subjects. The whole of their everyday experience is part of their learning and they probably learn more and more effectively at this stage than they ever learn again. It can also be more efficient to work across the curriculum in that the same piece of work provides experience for work in a number of different subjects. Cross-curricular work also shows how subjects are related to each other and children gradually come to understand what the subject labels actually mean. However, it is also necessary to do some work in most subjects which is subject specific, particularly as children grow older, so that the nature of the subject itself can be studied.

One breakdown which can be applied to some extent to most subjects is a division into underlying ideas or concepts, knowledge or information, language, skills and creative work. The National Curriculum is very helpful here because it identifies knowledge, concepts and skills in each subject area. It does not include very much on language within subject areas, however, except in English, and creative work is implicit rather than explicit in the suggestions given. When this breakdown is used for a particular piece of teaching, you will need to add *outcomes* to the list.

Each subject discipline has its own language, its linguistic register, and even where subjects use the same words, they may not be using them with the same meaning. For example, at an early stage, children discover that when they paint, the primary colours are red, blue and yellow and they learn how to mix these colours together to make other colours. At a later stage in science, however, they learn about the colour of light, where the primary colours are different and they have to adjust to the difference in meaning.

We tend not to think very much about this kind of problem and yet it is relevant from the earliest stages. A child at home will learn that the postman brings a letter. At school the same child has to learn that a letter is something else as well.

There are many such linguistic traps for children and it is often valuable to list the words and language you want to use for any piece of work and ask yourself what experience the children will need to understand them fully. This would be a useful thing to do with each item in the National Curriculum.

If you teach very young children you are more likely to be aware of this than if you teach older children because young children force you to recognise the inadequacies in their understanding. They often give you clues to their thinking in the mistakes they make or in what seem to be amusing sayings. For example, the child who defined less as 'downer' partly understood the word, but one could not be certain that her understanding would be sufficient for a phrase like 'less space' or a more abstract phrase like 'less hope'.

If you teach older children the problem is still with you and possibly increased by the fact that children learn to disguise their lack of understanding. It is important to ask questions to see if language is really understood.

Thought about language as part of the framework in major areas of knowledge must also include thought about the use of symbols in mathematics and science, the language of movement in dance and drama, the language of shapes and forms in art, sounds in music and so on. Each subject area not only has its own linguistic register or way of using language, but also has its own forms of expression which need to be studied and understood so that they can be used.

Each subject discipline also has a set of techniques and skills required for its study and these too can be listed although they are best acquired in the context of their use. If emphasis is placed on concepts, the skills often come in naturally. For example, children acquiring the concept of area by counting the squares that are covered by a leaf are not only practising counting in whole numbers, but are also likely to find ways of adding fractions to account for the parts of squares covered. In writing children are most likely to persist in practising if they want to express something on paper and this motivation has to be reconciled with the need for appropriate teaching and practice of letter formation.

THE CORE SUBJECTS

English

HMI in their study of the implementation of the National Curriculum (1989) found that the main characteristics of successful English teaching were as follows:

- a wide range of suitable language activities covering speaking and listening, reading and writing

- well-timed and thorough teaching of the basic skills of literacy
- a good range of different purposes and audiences for developing the use of English so that the children received, for example, a rich experience of fictional material and similar good-quality non-fictional material, within the teaching of English and across the curriculum as a whole
- agreed strategies for helping children to refine their work, for example by re-drafting and by marking which gives consistent attention to standards of correctness in sentence construction, spelling and presentation

Over the past twenty years or so, some important developments have taken place in our knowledge of language. In particular the tape recorder has made it possible to study language as people actually use it, giving us valuable insights which have implications for teachers. We have become aware that we use language in different ways according to background, the particular situation, the person(s) to whom we are speaking, the subject matter and so on. This is reflected in the *English programme of study* (DES 1989b) which starts with the statement

> Through the programme of study pupils should encounter a range of situations, audiences and activities which are designed to develop their competence, precision and confidence in speaking and listening, irrespective of their initial competence or home language.

The *Non-statutory guidance* (NCC 1989) balso stresses the idea of audience, situation and activity.

We each use language in ways which are personal to us. Your language initially developed from your background, upbringing and education and most of us retain traces of the speech of the area in which we grew up, sometimes as accent, sometimes in the tunes of our speech and the language structures we employ. Children starting school may find that their teachers and other children speak in much the same way as their parents or they may find that language is used in a different way at school from the way it is used at home – so different in some cases that some children have difficulty in coming to terms with it.

Everything that happens to children may affect their language development. They add words and phrases to their store of language with each new experience. They imitate. They adopt language habits from people they admire. They pick up what is currently fashionable in language and develop their language skills through reading, conversation and listening to others.

Each group of people – the family, the friendship group, the class, the professional work group, the nation – has certain uses of language which are peculiar to it. We also use language differently in different social classes and in Britain this is very marked. The use of language in this way is a mark of membership and a way of excluding those outside the group – which is why is can be very difficult to persuade children from working-class backgrounds to use language in a middle-class way. Their use of language identifies them with the home and their peer group and pressure to change language may be seen as a threat to personal identity.

The National Curriculum for English makes it very clear that teachers should work towards all children acquiring standard English, not with the idea that there is something wrong with whatever variety of English a child may use at home, but because this is the most widely used and widely understood form of the language. Using standard English does not mean acquiring a middle-class accent. It refers to a standard use of grammatical constructions and use of words.

We need to stress in school that adopting standard forms of English is necessary and appropriate for some purposes, but does not mean abandoning other ways of talking at home or with friends. The individuals who are in this sense bi-lingual in the different ways they can use language have an advantage. They can feel at home and be accepted by a much wider variety of social groups than would be the case if they were unwilling to extend their language in this way.

Appropriateness of language use is a very useful concept for teachers. If we want to help children to use language in ways which match situations and purposes, we need not appear threatening or apparently condemning of the language they already possess if we ask them to extend their language knowledge and skill and to learn to select the language behaviour they need for a particular situation. The importance of this is stressed in the *English programme of Study* (1989b) for speaking and listening which says:

> by informal and indirect means, develop the pupils' ability to adjust the language they use and its delivery to suit particular audiences, purposes and contexts and when listening to others, to respond to different ways of talking in different contexts and for different purposes.

An important element in learning here is the opportunity to match language to real circumstances upon occasion. The teacher is a very particular kind of audience or readership since it is his or her task to read what children write and listen to what they say. Teachers usually read or listen in the classroom not because they want to know, in the sense that the reader of a book or article may want to know about its content but in order to assess a child's ability or progress, to see what help is needed or what has been learned. The child reading or writing for the teacher is thus in a different position from the adult speaking or writing with a particular purpose which affects the nature of the communication.

When we speak or write, we try to match the language we use to our purpose, situation and its recipient. We use language differently in speaking to children as distinct from speaking to adults and try to find language we think they will understand. We use language differently in writing to apply for a job from the way we use it in writing to a friend. Talking to a group is different from talking to an individual. Giving instructions is different from persuading, and so on.

These variations are reflected in our choice of content, vocabulary, language structure and form, in the way we speak, in our body language of gesture and facial expression. In writing we have fewer variables but still match language to likely readership. It can be useful to look at language work with these variations in mind and consider where children have the opportunity to practise the variety of language this suggests.

Children growing up are both adding to their language store and also learning the language behaviour required of them by different people in different situations. They learn this best when they are called upon to use language for a genuine purpose and are helped to match language with the situation.

Language work in school thus needs to involve work which adds to each child's store of available language. It also needs to provide children with opportunities to use language for a wide range of purposes and a wide range of audiences. This is difficult to do and it is easy to feel that the need is being fully met by such activities as writing letters for practice or writing as if one were someone else. This kind of work has a necessary and valuable place, but children really need the discipline of working from time to time with a real audience or readership, who will read or listen only if the material is right. Many opportunities for this will be found as part of other aspects of the curriculum. For example, children may plan to interview adults in connection with local study and may need to write letters to arrange this and also to plan and undertake the interviews. Inviting a visitor who has valuable information to give into the classroom offers similar opportunities, plus a need to think about how you make a visitor welcome. Some topic work can be planned for presentation for another group of children, perhaps much younger, whose understanding of language will need to be taken into account. Making books for younger or less able children is also a useful task.

The *Non-statutory guidance* (NCC 1989b) has some useful advice about the teacher's role where speaking and listening are concerned. The teacher may be:

- helping to sustain what children are trying to do by showing interest

- an exploratory user of language
- supportive and encouraging to children in their use of language
- prepared to intervene only when it is appropriate
- aware of the special needs of speaking impaired and/or hearing impaired children
- sensitive to individual needs, especially when the child is shy and lacking confidence
- aware of the need to make the verbally aggressive or dominating child sensitive to others
- aware of the need for bilingual children to work with others in their home language and in English, to strengthen their capacity to use English for a range of purposes
- prepared to monitor and evaluate the child's use of spoken language

In reading the teacher should be:

- a responsive and interested listener to children's reading of their own writing and chosen books
- an organiser of opportunities to read with other adults and children
- a partner/guide in the discussion of reading experience
- a reader of books and children's own stories, in order to provide an example and encourage interest
- a support, helping children to use all the available clues to make sense of their reading
- a monitor of reading development
- a recorder of progress

In writing the teacher may be:

- an organiser of adults other than teachers who can work alongside children 'scribing' for them, or using a keyboard and enabling them to compose at greater length than they could on their own
- an editorial consultant
- an appraiser of achievement
- an example of adult writing behaviour
- a setter of procedures
- a setter of standards
- a recorder of progress
- a monitor of language development

The *Non-statutory guidance* places drama as part of English. This is not altogether an appropriate placing, since drama might be regarded as cross-curricular, with something to contribute to virtually every subject. However, there are some aspects of drama which are particular to English. For example, children may learn to use spoken language through their work in drama. They may also, at a later stage, study written plays and perform some of them. Drama is also a means of solving social problems. A group can tackle a problem such as what to do about a friend stealing from the supermarket or problems of children left out of the group for one reason or another. It can be a means of tackling gender or race problems, with children seeking to understand how it feels to be a different gender or a different colour.

Drama also offers a chance to identify with people in other times and other places. Such work should be firmly based on careful study of what is involved, however, and is more effective if those involved have a task to do within the historical or geographical roles they are adopting. For example, a group might take on the roles of different members of a society in the Third World which has to make very difficult choices about how to get enough food to stay alive.

The *Non-statutory guidance* also includes media education as part of English. This means learning to look critically at all the media. Children can study newspapers, looking at how they are laid out and the way in which headlines are designed to attract our attention. They can look at television programmes, studying the effect different kinds of images have on us. Advertisements are particularly interesting to study, because they often use very subtle means to give us messages about the products. Radio is also an interesting medium to study. Children can consider such issues as how you know when you turn on the radio whether you are listening to a play or to spontaneous talk. They can also make radio programmes themselves using what they have discovered about what makes good radio. If a video camera is available, they can also make television programmes.

Mathematics

HMI in their study *The implementation of the National Curriculum in primary schools* (1989) identified the characteristics of successful mathematics classes as follows. There was:

- effective teaching to ensure that the children had a sure grasp of the basic skills of number and the ability to calculate accurately
- a range of mathematical activities, frequently related to the children's everyday experiences and covering the broad areas of mathematics which are widely agreed as appropriate to this age group and are reflected in the statutory orders: number, algebra, measurement, shape and data handling
- a good mix of practical work and expository teaching engaging the children in mathematical discussion, problem solving, investigatory

work and sufficient practice to secure competence in the mathematical operations and skills

The *Non-statutory guidance in mathematics* (NCC 1989c) suggests that

> mathematics provides a way of viewing and making sense of the world. It is used to analyse and communicate information and ideas and to tackle a range of practical tasks and real life problems.
> Both in tackling problems and in exploring within the subject itself, mathematics has the capacity not just to describe and explain but also to predict. This gives mathematics the power and persuasiveness that accounts for its importance in the school curriculum. ...
> Mathematics is not only taught because it is useful. It should also be a source of delight and wonder, offering pupils intellectual excitement and an appreciation of its essential creativity.

The *Non-statutory guidance* also stresses the importance of organising so that children within the same class are able to work at different levels, possibly on the same topic. There should not be a situation where everyone is doing the same thing.

Children have never found mathematics an easy subject and criticism of mathematics teaching has been common for many years. Most adults still find mathematics difficult except for the particular calculations they happen to use in their daily lives. Some of the reasons for this problem are summed up in *The Cockcroft Report* (1982):

> Mathematics is only 'useful' to the extent to which it can be applied to a particular situation and it is the ability to apply mathematics to a variety of situations that we give the name 'problem solving'. However, the solution of a mathematical problem cannot begin until the problem has been translated into the appropriate mathematical terms. This first and essential step presents very great difficulty to many pupils – a fact which is often too little appreciated.

This problem is also present in reverse, when pupils have to translate a written problem into mathematical language. Cockcroft saw the solution as giving more attention to applying mathematical skills to real situations, with much more discussion of mathematical problems, both between teacher and pupils and between pupils themselves, and a greater emphasis on practical work. Calculators have made it possible to use real situations much more than formerly when the untidiness of the calculations needed in real problems made them too difficult for children.

There is a lot of evidence to suggest that teachers do not do enough practical work. In the *First School Survey* (HMI 1982), for example, HMI found only a fifth of the classes with 'a good balance between learning how to perform a calculation and using it in a practical setting'.

Hughes (1986) found that children appeared to have considerable difficulty in translating between their everyday language and mathematical language, and that this difficulty persisted well into the junior school. He makes the point that mathematics provides a means of communication which is 'powerful, concise and unambiguous'. The trouble is that for children the phrasing of mathematical problems can be ambiguous. Hughes gives as an example of the kind of difficulty which some children encounter the child who was asked 'What is the difference between 11 and 6' and gave as an answer '11 has two numbers'. When this was marked wrong, she answered that 6 was curly and 11 straight. This exemplifies the kind of problem children meet over language. The child in question was giving everyday meanings to the mathematical questions when what was wanted was a mathematical interpretation. Her answers are correct and reasonable given the way she interpreted the question.

The ability to use calculating skills in a practical setting depends to some extent on the acquisition of concepts. A concept is acquired when a child has met a range of examples and non-examples and can use and apply the underlying idea. Bruner and Kenney (1974), studying competent eight year olds, make the point:

> what struck us about the children, as we observed them, is that they had not only understood the abstractions they had learned, but also had a store of concrete images that served to exemplify the abstractions. When they searched for a way to deal with new problems, the task was usually carried out not simply by abstract means but by matching up images.

James Heibert (1984) makes the reverse of this point:

> Many of the children's observed difficulties can be described as a failure to link the understandings they already have with the symbols and rules they are expected to learn. Even though teachers illustrated the symbols and operations with pictures and objects, many children still have trouble establishing important links.

This would seem to be another argument for practical work and real problems. This is made clear in the first points made in the *English programme of study* (DES 1989b):

> To achieve level 1 within the Attainment Targets pupils should be:
> using materials for a practical task
> talking about own work and asking questions
> making predictions based on experience

Hughes' evidence suggests that this process needs to go on for a long time and be the standard way of introducing new work. He suggests that there is need for continuing emphasis on linking the concrete and the formal. He found that children started school with more knowledge of mathematics in practical situations than most reception class teachers were aware of and he suggests that teachers should talk to parents about what their children seem to know and can do. He believes that schools should build on children's own strategies and encourage them to discover their own ways of writing mathematical statements so that they gradually move to more formal ways of writing. This is rather similar to the way most teachers introduce length, by first getting children to measure using their own hands and feet and then gradually moving to standard measures.

There is, at the same time, a need to explore mathematics for its own sake. It is here that the 'delight' mentioned above is likely to come in. There needs to be a balance between practical and purely mathematical activities, with both involving a good deal of personal investigation. The exploration of mathematics for its own sake involves open-ended questions which can be dealt with at a variety of levels. For example, younger children might explore how many ways they can find of making the number twelve. Rather older children might explore square and triangular numbers. The *Non-statutory guidance* (NCC 1989c) gives as example: Make a model with the largest possible surface area from six linking cubes.

Mathematics also provides opportunities for learning across the curriculum as well as needing its own opportunities for study. The need to count, calculate and measure is present in the everyday life of the classroom as well as in most subject areas. Teachers of young children are usually very aware of the possibilities of such activities as laying tables and counting out materials and equipment for children to use. There should also be opportunities in play with sand and water for developing ideas about volume and capacity, although observation of what happens in play at the early stages suggests that not enough attention is given to helping children to use these opportunities (Bennett and Kell 1989). Most infant classes make use of shopping activities. Cooking provides scope for weighing and measuring. As children's skills increase they are able to undertake such activities as measuring growing things and animals, checking their own height and weight and making graphs of this information. Understanding of maps brings with it ideas of scale and measurement of distance. Discussion in history offers opportunities for considering how long ago something happened. The possibilities are endless if you are aware of the skills you need to develop.

Science

Wynne Harlen (1985) states that: 'Science is essentially about understanding things through interacting with them, finding out by enquiring of the things themselves.' This links with the statement at the beginning of the *Science programme of study* (DES 1989c) which states: 'The abilities to communicate, to relate science to everyday life and explore are essential elements of an initial experience of science.'

A statement from UNESCO (Harlen 1983) includes the following among the reasons why science should be taught at the primary stage:

- science can help children to think in a logical way about everyday events and to solve simple practical problems. Such intellectual skills will be valuable to them wherever they live and whatever job they do;
- science and its applications in technology, can help to improve the quality of people's lives. Science and technology are socially useful activities with which we would expect young children to become familiar;
- as the world becomes increasingly more scientifically and technologically oriented, it is important that future citizens should be equipped to live in it;
- science, well taught, can promote children's intellectual development;
- science can positively assist children in other subject areas, especially mathematics and language.

The *Non-statutory guidance in science* (NCC 1989d) echoes other writers in stressing the importance of taking children's initial ideas into account in working with them. Children develop ideas about why things are as they are from a very young age and if they do not have opportunities to investigate these ideas errors may persist and will be very difficult to overcome later. It is also important that they understand from an early stage that scientific knowledge is continually subject to modification as more becomes known through investigation. The question 'Will it always happen like that?' following an investigation should gradually lead children to the idea that there can never be a certain answer to this question.

HMI in their study of the implementation of the National Curriculum (1989) found that classes which achieved a satisfactory or better standard in science had the following characteristics:

Practical work in these classes was well-organised with a reasonable balance between exploratory work, in which the children learned to observe, question, record, plan and carry out investigations, often through direct teaching or information seeking from books and other sources. Much of the work stemmed from environmental starting points and often called upon and reinforced knowledge, skills and understanding in the other core subjects. Through their science activities the children were nearly always motivated to discuss and write about their observations, not similarities, compare differences and observe changes.

Science requires a way of thinking about evidence which is relevant in other areas as well. For example, evidence is very important in learning history and the idea that the likelihood of something being the case increases as more evidence is gained applies here as well as in science. Work in geography on the nature of the earth has very strong links with science – in fact the boundary between science and geography is not a clear one. Home economics is also related to science and provides the opportunity for considering why foods behave as they do, what happens when we cook them, what happens when they decay, what our bodies need for nourishment and growth, and so on. Technology is perhaps more involved with science than any other subject and much work within it will be the practical outcomes of the applications of science.

The making and testing of hypotheses is also a way of working which can be applied in any area of curriculum. Considering and predicting what happens if you take particular actions and then acting and checking to see if the prediction was right is relevant in many aspects of daily life and is something which may often be the subject of classroom discussion.

THE FOUNDATION SUBJECTS

Music, physical education and art and craft have played an important part in primary education for many years. History and geography have also had a place, usually as part of topic work. Technology is a completely new area for most schools and one where the thinking may be influential for other subjects.

Geography and history

School geography and history have been the subject of a good deal of disagreement in arriving at the Programmes of Study and Attainment Targets for the National Curriculum. This is mainly a matter of how far schools should be concerned with knowledge and how far with the interpretation of evidence and empathy with people who live in other places or lived at other times. The outcomes place some emphasis on both.

Primary schools have tended to incorporate these subjects into topic work and will no doubt continue to do so, but whereas in the past, the actual history and geography chosen was often subservient to the main subject of the topic, it will be necessary in future to see that certain elements are included.

Both history and geography require an act of imagination to understand the way different people have lived and do live in the world today. It is very easy to give children the impression that people who live differently from them are in some way odd and a variation from the norm. Since children's experience is limited, it will be important to provide as much first-hand experience as possible and to complement this with video tape and television programmes. Field work is an essential part of these subjects, particularly at primary level. Drama may also help in enabling children to imagine what life at another time or in another place might be like and a visit to one of the museums where children are incorporated into a drama about a particular period in history will be immensely valuable.

Physical education

Physical education should serve two important purposes in school. It is concerned with achieving and maintaining fitness and it is also concerned with helping children to be able to move in a controlled way. It also aims to teach the beginnings of games skills which may form the foundation for activity in adult life, when there is a need for people to take exercise since, for many now, work is sedentary. Young children are naturally active so that their need for physical education lessons is probably more a matter of extending their movement skill and developing games skills than of keeping fit.

There is a tendency to regard physical education lessons as separate from the rest of the curriculum. There is a need to make links in many ways. In physical activity a teacher can see whether children are understanding the language he or she is using in a way which is more difficult elsewhere, because they have to respond directly to instructions. Many mathematical words come into physical education – fast, slow, circle, line, shape, and so on. It is also important to observe children's movement in the classroom and about the school and to consider the implications of the way children move at other times for work in physical education.

Art and craft

Art and craft has tended to be used mainly as an adjunct to other work, usually in topics. It is important that it is also explored in its own right. Children need to work in three major areas. They need experience of drawing at first-hand and this can usefully be part of work in other subjects, although encouragement to draw anything and everything is also necessary. Secondly they need to explore what different media will do, in both two and three dimensions. Thirdly they need the opportunity to think about putting these skills together to make compositions of one sort or another, again in both two and three dimensions.

The teacher's role in the exploration of media is initially to provide the opportunities. It is then to set problems which encourage exploration. For example, you may ask children to make a pattern or a picture using as many different reds as possible, making the colours by mixing red with every other colour in differing amounts. You might ask for a pattern or picture using as many different textures as possible. With clay you might ask children to move in particular ways and then make figures doing the same thing. Or you might ask children to explore surface textures in clay, making them by impressing objects and in any other way they can think of.

The teacher also has an important role where composition is concerned. You can encourage children to look at the relationships of the things they put into their pictures or creations. You can encourage them to make first-hand observations of the objects and people they draw or make, or feel how a person might look by moving themselves in similar ways.

Technology

The development of technology in schools is an exciting prospect. It is not only a new subject in the curriculum, but it is also likely to affect the way we teach other subjects, since it demands a learning methodology which is widely applicable.

Technology has a very close relationship with science, but whereas science is concerned with the pursuit of knowledge through investigation, technology is concerned with meeting human needs and with making things and requires children to apply their knowledge and skill to solving practical problems. The *Non-statutory guidance* (NCC 1990b) suggests that it is about 'identifying needs, generating ideas, planning, making and testing to find the best solutions'. It also involves the need to work with others cooperatively in a team.

Three categories of work are envisaged – artefacts, systems and environments. This allows the design process to be applied in a wide variety of contexts, many of which can be part of the study in other subjects. It is fundamentally about problem-solving. Details of the processes of problem-solving were given in Chapter 5 in the context of the teacher's need to be a problem-solver. The headings given there are also appropriate for problem-solving with children. The following process is needed:

1 Define the problem
   This is a necessary starting point whether the problem is one in any of the three areas given above. It might be the problem of how to make a

bird-table which squirrels cannot reach or a problem in the classroom, such as difficulty in keeping some areas tidy or a problem of everyone wanting the same things at the same time, or the problem of how to present material to the best advantage. You need to work with the children to help them to make statements about what the problem really is. It is often helpful at this stage to consider what you wish the outcome to be.

2 Examine the problem further

This is a matter of discussing the nature of the problem and the needs which the solution must be designed to fit. It might be a matter of defining the social setting of a problem or discussing the range of materials which might be used or discussion of why the problem arises. In some cases a good deal of research may be needed to find out about the needs and the situation which the design must meet. At later stages it will be important to introduce the constraints within which the problem has to be solved. These may be a matter of the time available, the materials, the costs, the equipment needed, and so on.

3 Define your objectives

It is very helpful in problem-solving to know exactly what it is you are trying to do in as much detail as possible. If we take the problem of presenting material, objectives would include the reasons for making the presentation, for whom it was intended and what they were supposed to gain from it.

These three items provide the design specification.

4 Consider possible solutions

Here children need to be encouraged to find a number of alternative solutions before settling on one. It may be a good idea at this stage for them to work in groups, each group trying to make as many suggestions as possible.

5 Examine solutions

Here children need to examine the possibilities and problems of each solution. They need to look at such things as practicality, ease of making or doing and the extent to which each solution meets the criteria set out in the design specification. This kind of approach has the advantage that each solution is carefully considered against similar criteria. It can sometimes be useful to set this out as a table so that each solution is considered against each of the criteria.

6 Select a solution

If this is a group decision it will need a good deal of discussion and the final decision might be made by voting or by discussing to the point where there is a consensus. Whether it is a group or an individual decision it will involve careful weighing of the points arising out of the consideration of the possible solutions.

7 Make an action plan

It is valuable to get children into the habit of making action plans for work in hand and this is particularly relevant where problem-solving is concerned.

8 Plan evaluation

Evaluation should be part of the planning with any problem-solving activity and should take into account the criteria which were part of the design specification.

9 Carry out the project

10 Evaluate against the criteria defined

Part of the work in technology will involve evaluating one's own work and that of other people; the other people may be other children in the class. Or an artefact may be discussed, looking at what it was designed to do and considering how effectively it does it.

The teacher's role in technology will be to define the parameters within which work takes place. In many cases it will be the teacher who identifies the problems to be tackled, although children should be encouraged to identify their own problems as well. It will be important to define tasks in such a way that there is ample scope for children to solve them in their own way, selecting materials and tools as seems best to them. The teacher will also need to help children at every stage of the process so that they gradually become able to work independently.

Music

Music has changed very radically in the past few years, partly as a result of the introduction of electronic music-making, but also because of relatively cheap pitched percussion instruments. While it is still important that children get the opportunity to perform the works of others by singing and on instruments, there is now a much greater emphasis on composition.

Learning to read music is still important and it is probably best approached by asking children to invent methods of writing down the music they make up, then gradually introducing more formal ways of writing.

It is also important for children to listen to a wide range of music and discuss their reactions to it. Some of this may be played as part of the morning assembly but they also need opportunities to listen and discuss in class, where they can be asked to listen for particular things and can be introduced to the instruments of the orchestra.

RELIGIOUS EDUCATION

Religious education is not an easy subject to teach in a plural society. On the other hand, the presence of children of many faiths in a school gives the study of religion a reality which is difficult to achieve in schools where all the children are either at least nominally of Christian background or of no faith at all.

Religious teaching in schools other than Church schools is teaching about religion and the part it plays in human history. An understanding of Christianity is essential for an understanding of British history and customs. An understanding of Judaism, Islam, Sikhism and Hinduism is necessary to understand present-day British society and also to understand some of what is happening in different parts of the world, as well as for understanding world history.

Religious education is governed by Agreed Syllabuses devised by local Standing Committees for Religious Education. They should therefore reflect local needs.

Religious education is also concerned with moral education although this needs to be pursued in other contexts as well. Children need to know the moral basis of Christianity, since it is the moral basis of much in our society. At a later stage in education they may learn about the moral ideas of other religions.

SKILLS

Communication

Communication skills are clearly an important part of the National Curriculum, running through all the subjects.

A child should learn to communicate and receive communication using movement, language, mathematics and graphics, adequately and appropriately for different people, situations, purposes and topics. The development of communication skills is highly relevant when one looks at organisation since children cannot learn unless they and the teacher can communicate with each other. All aspects of living and learning involve communication and the teacher who is clear about what the children might learn incidentally will find opportunities at all times of the day for using the ordinary work of the classroom to foster learning in this area.

The word *communication* tends to be used in schools in relation to the language skills. It can be looked at much more widely, however, and this will be particularly important in technology, where communication is often through drawings and diagrams. All the higher forms of animal life have sophisticated forms of communication and human beings are no exception. We differ from other animals, however, in the primacy accorded to language, particularly as a way of representing experience to ourselves and others and we use language as an important and integral part of our thinking. It also enables us to cooperate and achieve collectively more than any individual can achieve alone.

This stress on language tends to make us less aware of other kinds of communication, particularly that transmitted by movement. Movement communication is present before language and indeed, in some senses, before birth and it continues to be an essential part of the way we relate to other people and communicate with them.

Teachers of young children, in particular, need to be aware of the importance of body language for communication, since they both read this kind of communication made by their children and themselves use it to help the children understand what they are saying. Facial expression, gesture, movement of the body and extensions of this, such as the way you dress and organise your environment, all communicate something to other people about the kind of person you are, the mood you are in, the kind of relationship you see yourself having with them, and so on.

Children explore a great deal of this in play, and school can take this further as children grow older in work in drama and in talking about how people behave in different situations.

Children are also discovering how other people react to them and part of the response will be demonstrated by movement and facial expression which the children learn how to read. This learning is already well advanced by the time a child starts school and it goes on all the time.

A further extension of this is graphic communication. One might argue that the way people dress and organise their environment is a form of graphic communication. Teachers of younger children will be aware that children not infrequently use drawing, painting and modelling to express feelings and reactions.

At the other end of the age range, graphic communication also involves the use of maps, graphs, diagrams, tables, charts, and so on. It is particularly relevant to work in technology where drawing is often needed to explain ideas. These are all part of the communication process, complementing language and sometimes communicating more effectively than language, since graphic communication can show more easily than words how things relate to one another. For example, a map shows more than a verbal account of how to get somewhere. It can also be seen all at once, whereas verbal instructions have to be heard or read in sequence.

Certain kinds of organisation within the school will give children better opportunities for practising this kind of learning than others. For example, if children are expected to work jointly on something, a good deal will be learned about communication within the group and this will be complementary to the language learning taking place.

The advent of information technology has reinforced the need to acquire skills in organising material and ideas. We are also affected with the growing internationalism of the world and the need for forms of communication which are not language dependent. The signs one sees on roads and in airports are good examples of this.

Mathematics can also be described as a form of communication. So can music.

Numeracy

Much that has already been said about mathematics applies to the skills of numeracy. Being numerate requires us to have the skills which are widely needed in everyday life. The basis of those skills is acquired at the primary stage.

In recent years calculators have changed our needs. Most jobs which require calculation now involve the use of calculators or computers and children need to know how to use both for calculation. Neither can be used intelligently without understanding, however, and it is important for children to develop understanding as they develop the use of these aids.

The calculator and the computer enable a child to perform many calculations quickly so that patterns can be seen which might not be evident if all the calculations had to be done manually. This enables children to reach a level of understanding which it was difficult to achieve before calculators were available.

Study

Today's children will need to go on learning all their lives and it is therefore important for them to acquire the skills of study. New technology makes study skills important, because if you have a world of knowledge to choose from, how you seek it and what you actually do with it becomes as important as remembering parts of it. There is much to be said for regarding the ability to learn without a teacher as a major aim for education to be achieved by almost all children by the time they leave school. Very few children would pass a test in this at the present time, because we are not really geared to this idea. We generally pay too little attention to the process of learning and give children too little help with it. In one way the National Curriculum should help us to concentrate more on process because content is decided for us. In another sense, however, teachers will be hesitant about giving children opportunities for learning independently because of the need to cover the content.

We use the word *learn* for several different activities. Sometimes we are asking children to memorise something, e.g. 'Learn those spellings'; sometimes we are describing a more complex process involving different kinds of learning, e.g. 'We are learning about conservation' and sometimes we are talking about doing something, e.g. 'John is learning to turn a back somersault'.

These are three rather different activities which need different approaches and children need to know how to tackle all three when required.

The extent to which your children are able to work independently has implications for the way you organise your work. If you want time to work with small groups and individuals, you need to do all you can to train children to work profitably without constant reference to you.

Although the information explosion makes learning by heart less necessary, there is still a great deal which we all need to remember and children need to memorise some things. They need help with this process, although it is often easier to memorise when young than it is later. Most people remember best when things make sense or can be grouped or classified in some way or associated with something else. Learning to spell correctly also depends on teaching children to group things which have to be memorised, to look for associations and write as well as say. One may remember the feel of writing something.

Where understanding is involved, the business of grouping and seeking patterns and rearranging the material becomes essential. We understand something only when we make it our own by working with it and using it. Children need a great deal of help in learning how to structure things for themselves. Work which asks children to put things in groups or order of priority or to select out things which go together or contrast with one another, all work involving sets, work which looks for patterns in numbers or spelling or involves the use of flow charts or other forms of graphic layout all contribute to the ability to learn and understand.

Doing also has an important place in understanding. Physical activity is often more easily remembered than mere words. It is interesting, for example, that a hairdresser, who, in the course of a week may work on eighty or ninety customers, rarely forgets the way each customer likes her hair done. This is a quite remarkable feat of memory and illustrates well the way in which the memory of movement helps other forms of memory. The more you can get children to associate movement with things to remember, the more likely it is that they will learn them successfully.

There is a need to learn movement skills in work such as art, craft, needlework, cookery, physical education, science, technology and handwriting. We normally teach most of the skills involved by demonstration. It seems likely that the computer will eventually be helpful here, but we should certainly teach children to work out practical tasks from written instructions from an early age, since this is a very necessary skill for adult life.

With older children, in particular, there is much to be said for setting out for them what needs to be learned in some context and discussing with them their ideas for setting about learning it. Children not only need the skills for independent learning, but also need to have some idea of how to set about the learning process. This needs frequent discussion in many different contexts.

This stress on process makes classroom management a very complex business and the pressure to complete what is in the National Curriculum could make teachers feel that there is too little time to be concerned with how children learn, as long as they do learn. This would be a great pity and in the long run works against helping children to achieve their maximum potential. When children are involved in considering the learning process as well as the learning content, teaching becomes a much more exciting business because they will come up with ideas you haven't thought of and the detective work of finding out how they view things can be very challenging.

The skills involved in study are numerous and complex, but it is possible to identify some of them and to look for ways in which children can acquire and practise them. They include the following, although the list is by no means exhaustive:

1 Investigating

You can find out from your own observation and experiment, by asking other people, by turning to books and printed material, using a computer or perhaps using television or video tape. Most people use observation and questioning more than they use other sources and we need to take this source of information seriously and teach children to use it well.

An analysis of these skills can be found in *The literacy schedule* (Dean 1977) obtainable from the Reading and Language Information Centre at Reading University.

Children need to learn to make observations of various kinds. This involves learning to use the tools which extend the senses, such as lenses and microscopes, and the tools which help us to measure, such as rulers, clocks, weights, and so on. These are all extensions of observation. They also need to learn to use the tools of analysis, from simple graphs to databases.

Asking questions to get information is also a skill to be learned. Field study work is important in providing such opportunities and this has implications for organisation since it is difficult to develop questioning skills if you don't have the opportunity for asking questions of anyone except the teacher. Children need to learn that some questions bring more information than others and that you need to ask the right person i.e. someone likely to know the answer. Children may also need to learn to ask questions in a polite and tactful way.

2 Sorting, classifying, ordering, generalising, making and testing hypotheses, problem solving

When material has been collected, learning may involve sorting and classifying it and putting it into some sort of order for presentation or to see if there are generalisations which could be made or further questions which could be explored. It may be possible to find ways of applying what has been learned, perhaps to deal with a situation or to do or make something. As a result of sorting material, patterns may emerge which could be tested as hypotheses or problems could present themselves which could be investigated.

This again has implications for the way you teach and the way you organise. If you do not provide children with opportunities to do their own sorting and classifying with help from you, they will not acquire these skills.

3 Evaluation

A further very important learning skill is the ability to evaluate your own and other people's work and behaviour. Young children starting school will depend very much on the adults in their world for views on what is good or bad, right or wrong.

Parents tell them that this is good and this is naughty and they gradually internalise this view. When they start school their teachers do much the same thing and the children internalise the teachers' views also, occasionally finding some conflict between what is good or naughty at home and what is good or naughty at school.

As they grow older, however, children learn to set their own standards and to make judgements using both the standards they have been given by adults and their own emerging judgement. The teacher can do a great deal to help this development by discussing work and trying to help children to identify criteria for making judgements and then matching work and behaviour to them.

This is an important part of the process of learning how to learn without a teacher as well as part of the process of developing a moral framework for life.

4 Creativity

A further pattern of skills might be summed up roughly by the word *creativity.* This involves the ability to be inventive, to make new relation-ships whether with words, sounds, colours, shapes, symbols, movements or anything else. It is an attitude of mind which goes across the curriculum and which can be encouraged in many aspects of work.

One might describe creative thinking as thinking in which the mind ranges over experiences, selecting from them and relating objects, ideas and thoughts in new ways. The relationships discovered and the form of the expression will be part of the creative process, perhaps changing the relationships which were in the person's mind at the beginning. Further ideas may come to a writer, for example, in the process of seeking words to express an idea.

If the ability to think creatively, to make and express new relation-ships, depends upon ranging over experience, the first requirement is enough images of experience to range over. This brings us back to the need for first-hand experience of many things at this stage of education. The teacher not only needs to see that many experiences are available, but also needs to help children to focus on each experience, so that gradually their minds become furnished with images of experience which they can recall.

They also need opportunities to explore the various forms of expres-sion such as paint, clay, wood, metal, plastic and other three-dimensional work, collage, movement, drama as well as words and information technology and explore the many ways in which constructions can be made to move and meet specific criteria.

Part of the process of running over possibilities involves running over possible forms of expression. This means that one has to be able to imagine what a given form of expression can do if one is able to work creatively with it. Exploring a material such as paint may mean discovering effects by chance and then trying to get them again by intention, and some of the creative process will be thought through in paint. Much the same goes for other materials and for words and sounds and movement. Choosing the best form of expression for a particular response is an important part of learning.

You may need to help children to realise that a person can be creative in mathematics or science in the ideas he or she has and pursues as well as in the more obviously creative areas of work. Creativity will be particularly important in technology.

5 Planning skills

You will also need to teach some planning skills. Initially this may be a matter of discussing the order in which work might be done. You can go on from there and encourage children to anticipate how long a piece of work may take and then check how long it actually does take. The next step is to plan for increasing lengths of time, so that older children are eventually planning some of their work for a week or so ahead or even longer for some work and pacing themselves in doing it.

This does not mean that all the time should be used in this way. There is an important place for teacher-directed work and for whole class and group work. What it does mean, however, is that you need to give some time to work planned by children in which they have an increasing degree of choice in how they set about things, though not necessarily choice in the actual work that they do.

The discussion about the order in which children do things should include some consideration of thinking which takes account of children's own knowledge of their ability to concentrate. One child might, for example, be saying after half an hour, 'I would be sensible to change what I am doing and come back to it later. That way I'll get more work done.' Another may have a much longer concentration period.

Planning involves organising time. Human beings have different body rhythms which enable some people to work best in the morning and others at other times of the day. School does not do very much to help children find their own rhythms, particularly at the secondary stage when the timetable tends to govern things fairly strictly because of the size and complexity of the school community.

In a primary school it is much easier to provide some opportunities for recognising natural differences in rhythm. Children can be encouraged to consider whether they work best at a long stretch or more easily in short bursts and to think about the time of day which suits them best.

We used to think young children could not concentrate for more than twenty minutes. What we really meant is that they cannot concentrate on something which someone else wants for very long. Many teachers will testify, however, that some quite young children will concentrate for very long periods given the chance and given a piece of work which absorbs and interests them.

This has important implications for the way you organise. If you are to train children to use their time you need opportunities for them to plan work with a certain amount of choice in how they do it.

Problem-solving

Problem-solving, like language, is a skill which can be practised right across the curriculum and problem-solving strategies can be applied to many aspects of the daily life of the classroom. This has already been discussed in detail in the section on technology.

Personal and social

There are many skills involved in personal and social development and you are concerned with them throughout all your work in the classroom.

1 Self-knowledge

We have already looked at the way children develop and at the importance of the development of a good self-image. Throughout the years of schooling each child is developing a view of him or herself which is made up from the reactions of those around, both adults and children.

Initially a child's parents are very influential in forming an early self-image, but teachers are also very powerful at the primary stage and the peer group plays an increasing part as the child grows and develops. It is very important for the teacher to recognise that this is happening and that his or her recognition of progress and success counts. It is also essential that the teacher sees that there are opportunities for every child to succeed in some way and for every child to take responsibility and contribute to the class community.

A child also needs to know and come to terms with his or her own strengths and limitations. Children need a range of opportunities, encouragement to try new things and help and support in overcoming difficulties. It may be helpful to recognise and discuss a difficulty frankly with an individual child and make a plan to overcome it so that you can genuinely praise each step taken.

The development of self-confidence is closely related to the development of the self-image. Children need to be confident in themselves as people, in their ability to learn and tackle tasks successfully and in their relationships with others.

You need to help all children to develop a confident attitude to at least some part of their activity. The secret of this is to match tasks to the level at which a child who tries can succeed. This is not easy, but it is more important for some children than for others and you can see very quickly those who lack confidence and need success. In the first days with a new group it is worth concentrating rather more attention on these children so that they achieve fairly early and gain confidence in you and in themselves and become ready to try new things. Your reaction to their ideas and contributions is crucial at the early stages.

Children are influenced not only by the example, teaching and behaviour of teachers, but also by their peer group. We tend to forget the learning which goes on between child and child. Parents often have this in mind when they choose to send a child to one school rather than another. This is not necessarily because they think the teaching is any better, but because they want their child to be with children from similar families rather than learning a way of life from other children which they see as alien.

2 Ability to live and work with others

Learning to work with others is an important part of the National Curriculum which is noted in various Programmes of Study. The ability to do this and also to get on with other people involves a number of sub-skills.

We want all children to be socially competent, knowing what to do in different situations. There is also a case for seeing that all children learn the conventions of normal social behaviour, such as greeting people, making and responding to introductions, thanking someone, making a complaint politely, making an enquiry, and so on. The teacher's example is important here, but there is also a need for some teaching and discussion and plenty of opportunities to practise. Drama lessons may well offer this kind of opportunity.

In adult life the majority of people have reason to work with others to an agreed end from time to time. We want children to be able to get on with others and live and work with them to achieve group goals, sometimes leading and sometimes following. There are skills involved in doing this which are discussed later.

We also want children to be sensitive to others. Sensitivity is closely linked with the ability to see through the eyes of another. A teacher needs to find ways of extending children's understanding of how things look from other points of view. Stories are often a help and it is worth trying to make a collection of stories which help to develop such understanding. Drama or role-play games in which each child has to study the part he or she is playing and see things from the point of view of a particular character may contribute.

Discussion about this is also important and it is often possible to use the occasion when a particular child's behaviour has hurt someone else to get that child and others to think through how it looked from other view points. Very young children find this very difficult to do but development is likely to come through encouragement to think about other views. As children grow older they need continued help and constant encouragement to view things this way.

Social education as well as religious education must include moral education. Moral behaviour is sometimes confused with obedience to a particular set of rules. While we need some rules to regulate the way we do things because life would be very difficult without them, mere obedience to them is not really enough, because they can never cover all eventualities.

A person who is acting morally needs to be able to weigh up the facts in a moral situation, look at it from different points of view as well as his or her own, generate or refer to principles and see if they fit in the situation and then make a choice and act with intention.

At the primary stage of education teachers can do a great deal to help this development. At the beginning of the primary stage, children need to be bound by the rules of the adults in their world, whether parents or teachers, because they are not yet ready to generate their own rules for living. By the time they leave the primary stage, some are already examining the principles offered by adults and thinking deeply about how to deal with moral situations in their own lives.

3 Developing a framework of meaning for life and a value system
Children start to develop a framework of meaning and a value system during their years at school. As they grow, they gradually develop their own frame of reference by which they make judgements about people, events and things. Everything that happens to them contributes to this, rather as it does to their self-images.

Initially children take on the values and ideas of their parents and these are gradually modified and developed as teachers and other adults and children put forward different ideas. Eventually children reach the point where they have an internal set of references. They can then use these to make judgements about new people and new situations.

Each person's frame of reference constitutes a view of the world and life and where people have widely differing views of what constitutes *good*, their views may be very difficult to reconcile. You may find, for example, that the parents of some of your children have views about bringing up and educating children which are very different from your own, particularly if they come from a different culture.

Those with a religious faith accept with it a set of values, many of which they make their own, so that the values enshrined in their faith become part of their frame of reference. There is an important sense in which Christian values are part of the frame of reference of most British people because they are part of British history and culture and much of our thinking is rooted in the values of Christianity. This is likely to change as the other cultures in our midst influence the way we think. It is the fear of this change which has caused some of the argument about the nature of religious education in our schools.

Information technology

Information technology should be part of every subject area from the beginning of school. Children will need to become familiar with the keyboard from an early stage and use word-processing as a means of drafting work as often as equipment makes it possible. The advent of small lap-top computers may make it possible before long to supply these on a much wider scale so that it becomes a normal part of drafting to use a word-processing program. They will also need to learn how to use a database and opportunities should be sought to make this part of work on different projects. Work with other electronic equipment may also be valuable and they may use turtles, electronic keyboards and perhaps concept keyboards.

The *Technology programme of study* (1990b) also envisages that children should learn that many pieces of equipment are now controlled by computers.

THEMES

Economic and industrial understanding

There has recently been much work linking schools with industry and a number of primary schools have learned a great deal from their industrial links, from visits to farms and factories and other work places and from broadcasts which enlarge their ideas about how things are done. This is particularly important in a society like ours where children do not see their parents at work outside the home and therefore have only the haziest ideas about the world of work.

The task at the primary stage is to see that children acquire some knowledge of the way in which wealth is created and industrial society functions. This is most likely to take place in the context of links between industry and schools.

Careers education and guidance

It could be argued that careers education is very much the province of the secondary school. However there are elements in the work of the primary school which may have relevance for future careers. The work done on linking with industry and anything which gives children an insight into the world of work may sow seeds which will grow later. Work on citizenship will also give children some idea of the work done in public services and this may be of later importance.

The Curriculum Guidance publication *The whole curriculum* (NCC 1990a) suggests that the first requirement in careers education is self-knowledge, a topic which is equally relevant at the primary stage when the self-image is being formed.

Health education

There is a great deal which is relevant in the *Science in the National Curriculum* (DES 1989a) under Attainment Target 3. This states that:

'Pupils should develop their knowledge and understanding of the organisation of living things and of the processes which characterise their survival and reproduction.' The Statements of Attainment then cover nearly all the topics needed in a health education programme.

Schools are expected to have a clear policy about sex education and in most cases this will be part of the curriculum. It will be important to set the information in context, stressing the need for loving relationships and providing a caring environment for children.

Education for citizenship

Social learning also involves learning about the society in which we live. Children need to learn something about how democracy works nationally and locally and this is reinforced if the teacher uses opportunities which arise in the classroom for making democratic decisions and then relates this to democratic decisions made elsewhere.

Some aspects of this are likely to be covered by the history programme, which should introduce children to some of our history and cultural background and that of other groups and nations. It is important also that children know something of how people behave in groups and something about the way our society functions, including its institutions and practices, the way we are governed, the need to generate wealth and the way present-day life differs from the past. Some of these aspects are among the themes suggested in *The whole curriculum.*

Children also need to learn about the part played by industry and about the rule of law. Some of this may come from relevant visits or visitors such as the police.

Children also need to be introduced to those values in our society which are commonly held. There will be many opportunities to introduce the values of the school which are part of wider values. These values will be evident in the way teachers deal with children and encourage children to deal with each other and with other people and in the way the school tackles children's misdemeanours. Assembly is traditionally a way of reinforcing values.

In today's multicultural schools there are considerable problems about putting over values because different groups within our society have different values. However, there is a certain amount in common on which early work can be based. As children grow older it may be possible to discuss some of the differences.

Environmental education

One of the most important issues for children to learn about at the present time is that of the environment. They need to know what is happening to the world in terms of the greenhouse effect and the human behaviour which is creating it. They also need to be concerned about maintaining an environment in which we can live in comfort with areas for leisure and recreation as well as places for work. It could be that as industry develops further the ability to work with computers and whatever comes after, much land now covered with factories will become available for public use. We need to give thought to the way we might want our towns and cities to develop.

The National Curriculum Council booklet *Environmental education* (1990c) list ways in which the Statements of Attainment in science, technology, geography and history contribute to this particular theme.

In thinking about the environment it may also be sensible to think about human behaviour and ways in which we might change it. Discussion about such issues as graffiti and vandalism, football hooliganism and drugs at the primary stage might have an effect in the primary school which would be difficult to achieve at a later age.

DIMENSIONS

Equal opportunities

Most young children come to school with fairly firm ideas about male and female roles. In most households it is still the mother who stays at home while the children are very young and she is therefore the person with the time to undertake the household chores and feed the family. Small children naturally take this as the norm, as is evident from the way they play in the Wendy house and elsewhere.

A view of women as subservient to men is reinforced in many schools where the head is a man.

The school has a substantial task to do in helping children to appreciate that women need not take the background role but can offer many of the contributions made by men except where these require considerable physical strength. Boys need to appreciate that men are no less masculine if they are sensitive to others and take their share of domestic chores.

This task is made more difficult by the fact that children are themselves trying to sort out their roles as future men and women. Boys are under pressure to seek macho behaviour and avoid anything which has overtones of the feminine. Girls experience less pressure in some senses but are growing up in a society which is very uncertain about the role of women and this makes life difficult for them.

There is also a need to consider issues of equality where children with disabilities are concerned. Are they being treated in the same way as other children so far as this is possible? Are they getting all the opportunities that other children have where they are able to gain from them? Handicapped people are continually surprising us with the things they are able to do.

A further area in which there is the need for equal opportunities is in social class. It is very easy to favour middle-class children by giving them more opportunities for taking responsibility, more praise, more opportunities in the classroom, and so on.

The teacher can seek out many ways of reinforcing equality, avoiding treating either sex in a special way and ensuring that each has similar opportunities and is encouraged to use them. There should be frequent opportunities for discussing male and female roles and stressing the need to treat both equally. It is also necessary to consider from time to time how you are treating children with special needs and working-class children.

Education for a multicultural society

Schools in areas where the population is ethnically mixed have usually done a great deal to enable the various groups to appreciate each other. There is much work on celebrating each others' festivals, understanding each others' point of view and generally respecting and tolerating differences. This may not always be successful but there is no lack of appreciation of the need for the work to be done. There will continue to be a need to combat racism in all its forms and every school needs to consider how occurrences of racism should be dealt with and how children can be led to realise its dangers.

There is also a difficult task in the areas where there are few children from ethnic communities and a lack of realisation that in these circumstances there is also much to be done. Children, and their parents also, often have a very limited idea of people of other nationalities, especially those who are black, and the school has an important job to do in broadening this view. Contacts with schools where there are substantial black populations would be valuable, but there should at least be discussions about people who are different in various ways, including stories and films about other nationalities, work in religious education on other religions, including some work on festivals.

Provision for pupils with special needs

Provision for children with special needs is discussed in greater detail in Chapter 11. The important thing to remember is that the National Curriculum provides that pupils with special needs should be given as much access to it as possible, unless, for some reason, the clause about disapplication is applied. In this case the school will have to offer an alternative curriculum.

Preparation for adult life

It might be argued that all education is about preparing children for adult life. It might also be said that certain aspects of this preparation such as preparation for employment, marriage and parenthood are really the province of the secondary school, since it is then that children begin to look forward to adult life and experience work related to possible careers.

Yet preparation for adult life is really a continuum which starts before school and continues into the nursery school and reception class, with children playing out the adult activities they see taking place, such as shopping, cooking, caring for the home and children, visiting the doctor or hospital, and so on. Some of these activities become more directed as children grow older and they may experience cookery or sewing or perhaps gardening or caring for animals and learning about how babies are born and grow. None of this is a very conscious preparation for marriage and parenthood but it is a starting point and a valuable contribution, likely to affect later attitudes.

Schooling at any stage may be regarded as induction into the adult world. Part of the induction process is introducing children to their cultural legacy, teaching them about their past and that of other groups, reading and telling stories, hearing of great men and women and events, and so on. This is one of the reasons why the study of history is important and likely to play a larger part in the primary curriculum than formerly.

Children learn a great deal about living with others at all stages in their schooling and the ability to share, to work together, to take responsibility, to lead and to follow are all useful parts of learning to be members of a community.

A further aspect of adult life which has its roots in the primary school is the development of leisure interests, skills and hobbies. This involves opportunities for learning to enjoy music, dance, drama, art, practical opportunities for developing craft skills and playing games, the development of interests such as reading, stamp collecting, electronics, photography, astronomy and many other likely and unlikely studies, depending on the enthusiasm and skills of teachers and anyone outside the school willing to be drawn in.

The whole curriculum (NCC 1990a) makes the point that the preparation for adult life now means 'life in a multicultural, multilingual Europe which, in its turn, is interdependent with the rest of the world'.

Teaching and learning are not tidy pursuits. A good deal of important learning goes on outside the curriculum and much that is important is apparently learned incidentally. No teacher can do everything and none of us can do everything at once. The value of considering a set of aims is that it gives you a frame of reference for teaching and enables you to look at

ANALYSIS 7.1:
THEMES, SKILLS AND DIMENSIONS

Complete this analysis by marking where the subjects of the national curriculum meet the aims listed

		English	Mathematics	Science	Technology	History	Geography	Music	Art	Phys. educ.	Rel . educ.
SKILLS	Communication										
	Numeracy										
	Study										
	Problem solving										
	Personal and social										
	Information technology										
THEMES	Economic and industrial understanding										
	Careers education and guidance										
	Health education										
	Education for citizenship										
	Environmental education										
DIMENSIONS	Equal opportunities										
	Multicultural education										
	Special needs										
	Preparation for adult life										

what you are doing with a wider perspective from time to time. A great deal of what has been suggested overlaps so that several things can be tackled at the same time.

The list in Analysis 7.1 is intended to enable you to consider where the skills, themes and dimensions fit with the subject areas of the National Curriculum

8 The learning programme

A good teacher is always searching for the best way of using the time, space and other resources available for the children's learning. The advent of the National Curriculum has made this even more important since there is now a pressure on primary teachers to complete certain parts of the curriculum within a given time. You need to seek the most efficient way of using time and resources.

The HMI report on *The implementation of the National Curriculum in primary schools* (1989) found that planning was one of the weakest areas of teachers' work. They say that teachers 'seldom attended adequately to sequencing work to achieve progression or took sufficient account of the different levels of attainment in topic work'. They were also concerned about the planning of time. Many schools seem to be finding that so much time is being spent on the core subjects that it would appear to be difficult to find time for the rest of the curriculum. This may be simply because teachers are finding their feet with the core subjects but the planning of time and planning for progression are certainly important.

Whatever your style of work and chosen pattern of organisation, there must be planning and system behind what you do, particularly so far as the National Curriculum is concerned. The Programmes of Study and the non-statutory guidance papers give general guidance about the way it is intended that work should take place. *Teacher assessment in the classroom* (SEAC 1990a) suggests that the National Curriculum helps you to:

- make an appropriate teaching plan. A teaching plan is your way of introducing the statutory Programmes of Study
- identify what is noteworthy. The noteworthy points in pupils' knowledge, understanding and skill have been described in the Statements of Attainment
- identify what each child should do next. The Attainment Targets map out progression in children's competence and help you to pace your children's progress through the Programmes of Study

Planning is needed both for the long term and for day-to-day work. Some of the planning may be for topics and some for specific lessons but the teacher has to find the best path between making the decisions him or herself and leaving too much to the children. If you decide exactly what is to be done and how it is to be carried out, the children may learn some things extremely well, but they will not become independent learners. You will also miss the inspiration which children very often bring to work when they have a measure of freedom about how to do it. If, on the other hand, you leave too much to them, they will lose the inspiration and the ideas which you bring to them as their teacher and may not learn what you intend. You need to plan in outline so that your plan may be adapted if this seems to be the right thing to do.

Different pieces of work provide differing opportunities for children to contribute ideas about learning. In some situations you may need to dictate fairly fully what is to be done and what is to be learned and how the learning is to be carried out. In other situations there can be much more freedom and the opportunity for children to choose and develop ideas of their own. Some of both approaches are needed.

When you first start work in which there is a good deal of freedom to choose with a group of children for whom it is new, they will need a lot of help if they are going to do any of the planning themselves. At this stage you could discuss with the children possible ways of working. A question such as 'we need to learn how living things differ from each other – how do you think we might set about it?' may bring useful suggestions. Not all the work you may want to do can or should be dealt with in this way, but a good deal of the planning could be shared with the children, with the teacher adding in ideas where the children find it difficult to make suggestions. This approach helps children to become learners by making them think about how the learning process takes place.

You need to plan at three levels:

Long-term planning for the year and term

Your teaching plan for a particular piece of work which may spread over several weeks

Planning for day-to-day work

LONG-TERM PLANNING

Every teacher needs to plan on a long-term basis as well as from day-to-day. It will be important to plan work for the whole year, using various approaches to the National Curriculum. While you may not wish to select topics too far in advance, you will need to select what it is that any given topic is designed to teach so that you spread over the year the demands of the National Curriculum

An important planning task is to consider the time scale of what you are intending to do. Note the points at which you hope to introduce new material. These need not be too definite. It is useful to set in earliest and latest dates so that you can allow for the stage the children have reached and their readiness to move on to another piece of work. A suggested planning chart is given in Figure 8.1.

There is a great deal of research evidence to suggest that the teacher who has clear objectives is more likely to be a successful teacher than someone who has not defined work in this way. The National Curriculum both makes the setting of objectives more important and at the same time gives a clear lead in defining the learning tasks in the Statements of Attainment.

It may also be helpful to consider what use might be made of the computer both for planning and for recording. Work which one tries to repeat with another group is never quite the same and it may be helpful to store outline plans on the computer so that you can come back to them and update them when similar work is in hand. It may also be helpful to have a database of where individuals are with progress through the Statements of Attainment. This will enable you to list out all the children at a particular stage as part of your planning.

Finally it is important in long-term planning to consider your objectives in training children to work in the organisation you have in mind. What do you need to do to train them to become independent learners? How are they going to acquire learning skills? These can all be acquired as part of the learning which is in hand, but you need to be conscious of what is involved and how you can develop the necessary skills. These were discussed in Chapter 7.

YOUR TEACHING PLAN FOR A PIECE OF WORK

It may be helpful to consider planning for a piece of work in various different ways. There would seem to be a number of alternatives.

- Attainment Targets and their related Statements of Attainment can be tackled directly.
- Particular statements can form the core of topic work.
- Statements from different programmes can be linked together to form a basis for topic work.
- A topic can be selected which meets the Programmes of Study and this can be used to provide opportunities for children to develop the knowledge and skill required for some of the Statements of Attainment.

Subject area.. Term.................................				
Earliest date	Latest date	Subject matter	Attainment target	Level

Figure 8.1 Planning chart

It may also be possible to use opportunities which occur fortuitously to help children to achieve particular Statements of Attainment. For example, mould growing on something within the classroom may create an interest which could be followed up in a study of moulds and might lead to Attainment Target 1 in the science programme which is concerned with the exploration of science – 'Pupils should develop the intellectual and practical skills that allow them to explore the world of science and to develop a fuller understanding of scientific phenomena and the procedures of scientific exploration and investigation.'

In the past there have also been many occasions when primary teachers have taken advantage of something topical or something which interests the children and used the stimulus to help them to learn. Local events like the fiftieth birthday of the school, the opening of a new motorway or bridge, national and international events such as royal events or the Olympics, annual events such as Easter and Guy Fawkes day have all been used, as can topics which interest particular children, such as riding or football. Teachers have picked up these events and interests and used them in a variety of ways. The task now will be to look for opportunities to use them as a means of helping children to achieve the Attainment Targets. This is not to suggest that other ideas should be set aside, but as with all the work involving topic-type activity, it will be important to keep an eye on time so that the statements are not forgotten in enthusiasm for other learning. This will become easier to do as you become more familiar with the National Curriculum and begin to carry in your head many of the Statements of Attainment.

This should not be the normal way of working, however, partly because of the time element, but also because of the need to be concerned with progression in many of the Attainment Targets. It is very difficult to ensure progression if work is too opportunist. The development of scientific understanding, for example, requires progression in the ability to identify questions which could be investigated and to apply scientific thinking to the investigation, and much the same is true of other subjects. If progression is to be achieved it must be planned.

Most primary school teachers do some work which is subject specific. Nearly every subject has at its core, knowledge, concepts and skills which are particular to that subject and need exploring in their own right, and even where a great deal of the work is integrated teachers will spend time with children on work in individual subjects. This is necessary if full understanding and skill is to be achieved. It is also usual to find that more work is subject based as children grow older.

Topic work

Primary schools also do a good deal of work which is topic based or thematic. It is perhaps worth considering at this stage the reasons why primary schools use topic work as a learning medium. In the first instance, a topic helps to place learning in a context. Children learn about a number of related things at the same time and this makes it more likely that learning will be retained. A good topic will involve a strong element of first-hand experience as well as a variety of different approaches to learning. Children will observe, question, use first-hand experience and books to find out; write, draw, paint and make models. The teacher will also give them information and lead them to form appropriate concepts. They will develop and practise skills of various kinds. They will also learn to work together if group work is part of the activity. All these approaches help to reinforce learning.

There are also some problems about topic work. Different children undertake different tasks and it is difficult for the teacher to be sure who has learned what. This has particular problems for work with the National Curriculum. A child may also get a biased view of a particular topic because he or she has chosen certain aspects of it to work on. Topic work tends to make continuity difficult because of the different tasks which children have undertaken and, as HMI have noted, it is difficult to ensure progression in the context of a topic. You have to allow for these difficulties, mainly by the care with which you record what each child has done. With older children it will be possible to ask them to do some of the recording of the ground they have each covered in a particular topic.

Some elements of all the patterns given above are needed. The use of Statements of Attainment in topic work helps to ensure that children understand the use of what they are learning and the linking of different programmes makes it possible to use the same experiences to provide background for several different pieces of learning. There may be other situations where you feel that the most effective way of working is to base work directly on a particular statement.

Whether you are using a topic as the basis of your teaching in a particular area or are dealing with a specific subject directly, the following need consideration in planning:

1 Children's existing experience
   What have children already experienced on which I can build?
2 First-hand experience needed
   What experiences must I provide for children so that they understand the work we shall be doing?
3 Language
   What words and phrases will children need to understand the work we shall be doing?

What new language will they learn as a result of this work?

What varieties of language can be practised?

4 Knowledge

What do I hope children will know at the end of this piece of work?

5 Concepts

What do I want children to understand at the end of this piece of work?

6 Skills

What should children be able to do as a result of this piece of work?

7 Creative work

What creative work might grow out of this work?

8 Outcomes

How will this learning be demonstrated?

This pattern of planning can be used for planning whole topics or a series of lessons based on a particular Attainment Target or for individual pieces of work. The plans given below set it out as a form which could be adapted for use.

This type of plan gives you a clear picture of what the outcomes of your work might be but does not necessarily limit the possibilities which may emerge. With a new group you might plan the broad areas in which they will be working. For example, you might plan the field work involved in the *living things* project described below and discuss with the children what they might see and what they might collect. You then feed in ideas like the quadrat as a means of helping observation. Gradually you build up a list with the children, rather like the lists on pages 146 and 148, and you can then add to this ideas from the lists you have prepared yourself. Although the outline is given here in detail, in practice quite a lot of the items might be those suggested by children.

From there you go on to plan which children shall undertake which tasks. A great deal of the organisation here will be a matter of children choosing tasks which interest them, but as they become more familiar with the National Curriculum, they are likely to be receptive to being asked to undertake a particular task because it is one they need to meet the Statements of Attainment.

The conclusion of any piece of work is important for learning. We have already seen that there is some evidence (Bennett and Kell 1989) that teachers do not always judge what has been achieved in terms of their original intentions. The same study also suggests that teachers often do not make it clear to children what is the object of a given piece of work. If children are to be partners in their own learning, it is essential that they know the purpose of any work they do. The National Curriculum now makes it important to judge work in terms of intended learning. The conclusion of any piece of work should therefore demonstrate what has been learned in a way that enables you to assess whether your intentions have been achieved. In planning you need to decide how the work will be concluded. Will there be an exhibition or talks or presentations by groups of children? How will you draw things to a close and what important points do you need to bring out in doing this? This will be even more important now because of the National Curriculum learning which should be taking place.

Approaches to teaching and learning

1 Statements of Attainment can be tackled directly
   There will be some statements, particularly in mathematics and to some extent in science and English, which you will want to tackle directly, organising lessons involving a variety of strategies and methods with the specific objective that the children achieve what is involved in a particular statement. It may be useful to go through the programmes picking out statements which you want to tackle in this way. Very often you may wish to deal with a statement directly in the first instance and then to use it in the context of a particular topic. For example, the statement: 'know the most commonly used units in length, capacity weight and time and what they are used for' may need work on the units in the first place and they can then be used in the context of a topic.

2 Particular statement (s) can be the core of topic work
   The science programme includes Statements of Attainment on materials which include the following statements at level 3 (it has rather similar statements at level 2): 'know that some materials occur naturally while many are made from raw materials' 'be able to list similarities and differences in a variety of everyday materials'.
   The programme in Figure 8.2 may meet the requirement to learn what is involved in the statements given above.

3 Statements from different programmes can be linked together to form a basis for topic work.

A different approach to planning might be to take one or two statements from the National Curriculum and look at how these link up with others so that a topic can be undertaken which covers a considerable number of statements. We can, for example, take Attainment Target 2 from the science curriculum and select two items from level 3: 'be able to recognise similarities and differences among living things, and 'be able to sort living things into broad groups according to observable features'. This will involve providing children with experience of a considerable variety of

Existing experience		Experience of a variety of materials in everyday life – fabric, food, furniture materials, building materials, use of yarn in clothing, knitting, woodwork, experience with clay, etc.
First-hand experience		Visit local street and small manufacturing unit, e.g. a pottery; bring in fabrics; dig clay; collect sheep's wool; collect similar sized twigs of different woods; survey buildings; visit building site
Language		Names of different fabrics, dye plants, stones, woods, etc. Transparent, opaque, porous, inflammable, saturated, flexible, rigid, man-made material, natural material Discussion of how to test materials; presentation to others of findings; use of books to find out; writing of reports of findings
Knowledge		Sources of different materials; their characteristics; uses of different materials
Concepts		Some materials are natural and some are man-made; different materials have different characteristics which determine their use
Skills		Testing materials for different characteristics, e.g. hardness/softness, flexibility, etc.; making bricks and pots; making dyes; spinning; weaving
Creative work		Making a picture with stones; making bricks and pottery; making dyes and using them; making a fabric collage; spinning and weaving; writing about how different materials make you feel
Outcomes		Exhibition of work; discussion of experiments and findings; planning for presentation to parents

Figure 8.2 Analysis of thematic material

Figure 8.3 Topic based on science Statements of Attainment

Existing experience	Observation of plants, birds and animals in environment; plants grown in classroom; keeping of pets; observation in gardens and parks; television wildlife programmes
First-hand experience	Visits to field, woodland, pond; growing plants in the classroom; keeping small animals in the classroom; observation in school environment and home areas
Language	Names of plants and animals; names of their parts; words describing plants, e.g. deciduous, evergreen. Words describing what animals do, e.g. hibernation; descriptions of animal movement; words describing animal homes and their young; explain work being done; relate events in the life of a plant or animal to other children
Knowledge	Plant and animal life cycles; some of the habitats of different plants and animals; some of the food chains of different animals; the effects of season and weather
Concepts	Basic life processes are common to all living things; living things grow and change over time; different living things require different habitats; a habitat must have appropriate conditions for the plants and creatures that live there; plants and animals can be classified in various ways.
Skills	Making classes and sorting; devising questions for research; making and using a database; speaking to the class; using lenses; making tables/bar charts; recording over a period; making and using a quadrat; drawing and naming parts of animals and plants
Creative work	Making pictures of the areas studied and of plants and animals using different media; writing poems about the areas studied and setting these to music; drawing plants and animals as they grow; writing stories about animals which include knowledge of their life style; making leaf prints; making lino blocks from drawings of plants and animals; printing materials.
Outcomes	Exhibition of what has been discovered; talks by individuals and groups about their findings; making of books; sharing of creative work; class discussion about what has been learned

Figure 8.4 Analysis of thematic material

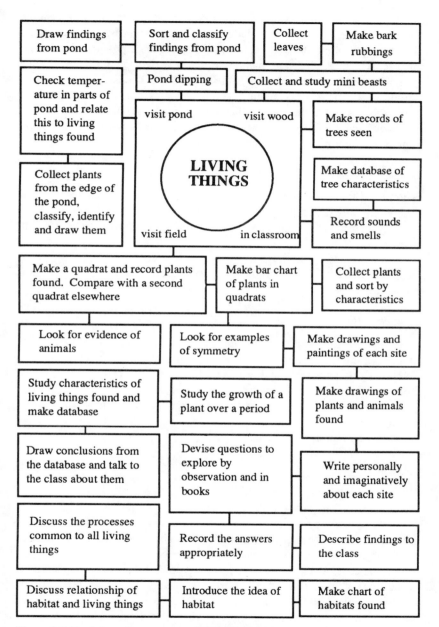

Figure 8.5 Topic based on statements about living things

living things, both bringing them into the classroom and also visiting them in their habitats. The starting point is to list the living things you wish the children to see. This should include plants, animals, birds, fish and insects with the opportunity to study several kinds of each. If possible you should plan to visit more than one habitat so that a variety of life forms can be seen. The outline given on page 148 suggests that if possible the children should visit a field, a pond and a wood. This may not be a possibility for some schools and more urban habitats may need to be studied.

If you then look at what other statements might be studied at the same time, you might make a list such as the following:

Science

Know that the basic life processes – feeding, breathing, movement and behaviour – are common to human beings and other living things.
Identify and describe simple variables which change over time, e.g. the growth of a plant.
Record experimental findings in tables and bar charts.
Select and use simple instruments to enhance observations, e.g. a stop clock or hand lens.

Mathematics

Choose and use appropriate units and instruments in a variety of situations, interpreting numbers on a range of measuring instruments.
Explain work being done and record findings systematically.
Enter and access information in a simple database.
Recognise the reflective symmetry in a variety of shapes in two and three dimensions.
Construct and interpret bar charts.

English

Produce a range of non-chronological writing.
Relate real or imaginary events in a connected narrative which conveys meaning to a group of pupils, the teacher or another known adult.
Devise a clear set of questions that will enable them to select and use appropriate information sources and reference books.
It will, of course, require careful planning, if you are to provide learning opportunities for each of these statements in the process of dealing with the two original statements from the science curriculum. You will also need to check to see which children have covered which statements because it will depend to some extent on the work they choose or are

given to do which statements get covered. It will be particularly important to draw together the learning from the topic as you come to the end of it. You may do this through class discussion in which you draw out the particular points which are important. Or you may have an exhibition with children talking about their particular contribution. You can then stress anything which seems to you to be particularly important in what they say.

4 A topic can be selected and used to provide opportunities for children to develop the knowledge and skill required for some of the statements of attainment.

The *National Curriculum – making it work for the primary school* (ASE 1989) describes how to take a topic which is a common one in the primary school, such as food, and then to look at which parts of the curriculum could be served by it. A topic such as communication might, among other material, provide a way of introducing the following statements. These are all at level 2.

Science

Record findings in charts, drawings and other appropriate forms.
Know that there is a variety of means for communicating information over long distances.
Know that sounds are heard when the sound reaches the ear.
Be able to explain how musical sounds are produced in simple musical instruments.

Mathematics

Help to design a data collection and use it to record a set of data leading to a frequency table.
Read, construct and interpret block graphs and frequency tables.

English

Participate as speakers and listeners in a group engaged in a given task.
Read accurately and understand straightforward signs, labels and notices.
Produce, independently, pieces of writing using complete sentences, some of them demarcated with capital letters and full stops or question marks.
Produce simple, coherent, non-chronological writing.

SHORT-TERM PLANNING

In addition to planning long term and planning major pieces of work you will need to make plans for day-to-day teaching. The more experienced you are, the less detailed these plans need to be, but the need for planning remains, however long you have been teaching. The following need to be prepared in advance:

1 The range of activities you intend to pursue during the day
   It is essential to think clearly about these since some will need careful preparation of the classroom.
2 The provision you intend to make for the range of pupils
   Some activities will concern the whole class; others will be for different groups and individuals.
3 Questions you plan to ask in relation to the activities planned
   We have already noted the importance of questioning. Higher order questions, in particular, need to be considered in advance because it is often difficult to think of suitable questions on the spur of the moment.
4 The materials and equipment you will need
5 How you plan to undertake changes of activity and clearing up
   If you are experienced and your class is well trained this issue needs no preparation. Inexperienced teachers would be well advised to plan changes and clearing up very carefully, since this is the time when things can go wrong.
6 The children to whom you need to give some individual help
   You will have identified some children from the previous day's work who need some help in the work they are doing.
7 The children whose work you plan to check

   If you are to succeed in making all the assessments required by the National Curriculum, you will need to make a small number of checks each day. You may have a list you are working through, or you may select children each day who seem to be at a stage when it would be worth checking. If you check a number of things by inspecting children's work, you will need to see only two or three children for checking each day.

Existing experience	TV and radio; observation of forms of communication; use of telephone; signs and symbols in environment; possible experience of other written language symbols; sounds of musical instruments
First-hand experience	Opportunity to handle musical instruments; experimental work in making sounds; visit to printer; observation of signs and signals
Language	Names of forms of communication, e.g. books; graphs, newspapers, maps, etc.; words connected with sounds and the way they are made, e.g. vibration; names of types of communication, e.g. signs, braille, language of deaf, etc.; know something about musical notation; know something about how to match speaking or writing to an audience or readership
Knowledge	Know how musical sounds are produced and the types of instrument making them; know how advertisers capture our interest; know the ways in which we communicate over long distances
Concepts	Sound is produced by vibration; vibration is caused in a variety of ways; we use many forms of communication which are not dependent on language, e.g. road signs; we speak and write in a different way according to the audience or readership
Skills	Work with a group on a communication task; collect information about types of communication and organise it as a block graph; write about findings using full stops and capital letters correctly; prepare and give a talk to a specific audience (e.g. children from another class), matching the talk to the audience
Creative work	Invent a language; invent signs; create a newspaper; devise musical instruments; devise advertisements
Outcomes	Exhibition and presentation to another class; class newspaper

Figure 8.6 Analysis of thematic material

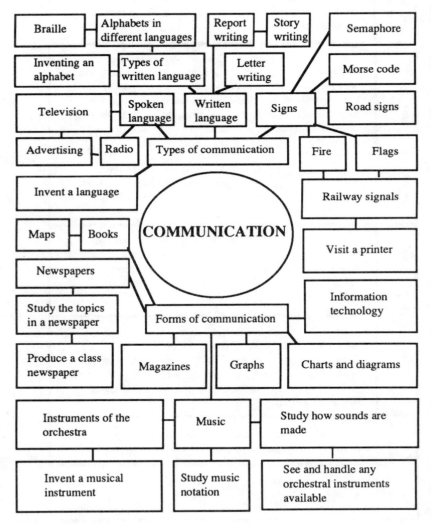

Figure 8.7 Topic based on theme of communication

9 Organising children for learning

The range of children in a school is decided by the LEA, which determines the age groups it caters for. The way children are organised within the school is the decision of the head and staff. Classes and groups can be formed on the basis of age, ability or stage of development or achievement in a particular activity. Children can also be grouped randomly or by friendship or family. Teachers can work solely within a particular class or they can take some subjects with another group or they can work with other teachers taking joint responsibility for a group of children.

The way a teacher organises work has a hidden or partly hidden curriculum which should be considered from time to time so that it is no longer hidden.

The extent to which you work with the class or with individuals or groups affects the kind of contact you have with each child. Your organisation also has implications for the development of study skills and independence in learning. The extent to which you encourage competition or cooperation will affect attitudes to learning and to other people. Encouraging children to work together or to compete with one another will have implications for social behaviour and the extent to which children eventually come to regard others as fellow workers or rivals.

The way a teacher organises work is a very personal matter and there are many good ways of working, each with its own collection of strengths and disadvantages and pitfalls. No one way of working suits everyone.

Classroom routines

If teaching is to take place, it is essential that the classroom is well organised. Neville Bennett and Joy Kell in *A good start?* (1989) described poor classroom organisation which showed itself in lack of pupil involvement, wandering about, interruption, lack of interest or motivation and poor use of resources. Children played about without the teacher apparently being aware of it. The same study was also critical of some of the use of play activities in the youngest classes. It is described as

> characterised by such child behaviour as fighting, throwing, knocking, wandering, messing and ill-considered and half completed projects. The activities themselves lacked purpose, structure, any kind of clear demand for process or product or challenge. There was poor monitoring, no discussion and no extension or assessment.

Cleave *et al.* (1982) noted that in their study there was three times as much queuing to see the teacher in infant classes as there was in the nursery.

This description identifies a number of the things which can go wrong. Children will not work well if the work they are given lacks purpose in their eyes or if they are unclear about what is being demanded. Clarity in giving instructions about work is essential for a well-organised classroom. There also needs to be structure in what is required so that children know what to do when they have finished a piece of work. A classroom in which there are long queues to see that teacher is a badly organised room where children are wasting time.

Another important point is that of monitoring. The teacher needs to be aware of what is happening in the classroom at all times, even when he or she is engaged with a group or individuals. The habit of scanning the room quickly and catching the eye of children who are not on task or who need help is an essential teacher skill. Monitoring also involves being aware of the work children are doing and how it is going.

A well-organised classroom has routines, so that children feel secure in knowing what to do. You need to have rules about the following:

1 Movement about the room
   Children should know when they are allowed to move freely about the room and when you expect them to sit at their tables. They also need to know how many people are allowed to undertake any one activity at the same time.
2 The things for which they need your permission
   This needs to be made very clear to children from the beginning. Most teachers would expect to have to give permission for children to leave the classroom, although where there is working space outside, further definition may be needed.
3 What to do when they come into the classroom first thing in the morning and after the breaks in the day
   You may want them to continue with work in hand or have some other task for them to do, but they need to be clear about what is required.

4 When they are expected to be quiet

There will be times in the day when you want quiet. There will also be situations when you want attention from everyone. You need an understood signal for quiet, such as clapping your hands or raising one hand and should insist that everyone stops and listens when you give this signal.

5 What to do when they have finished the work they are doing

Try to avoid the situation where children come to you every time they finish a piece of work. If you give them more than one piece of work at once, the occasions when they need to come back to you will be fewer. Some materials can have a structure that makes it clear what comes next. On the other hand, you need to keep track of some individual children who may avoid coming to you at all.

Forms of organisation

There are a number of different ways in which a class can be organised for learning.

Whole class teaching

The whole class can be taught the same thing at the same time. This is appropriate for teaching things like safety measures and rules for classroom behaviour but it is rare for a whole class to be at the same stage at the same time. It is a good way of introducing something, however, when you can rouse enthusiasm for a new piece of work which children will explore at different levels. It is also useful for summing up a piece of work at the end.

A major problem of this approach is that you need enough material and equipment for the whole class.

Class works on one subject at different levels

You can organise so that everyone is doing mathematics, but there is grouping after an initial introduction and each group or individual is doing work at a different level. You move round the groups or spend time teaching one group if the others are sufficiently well occupied. This method of working has the advantage that matching work to pupils is easier because it is accepted that work will be at different levels. It requires very good organisation to keep everyone going. It can work best if your materials are set out in an order which children recognise and it is agreed that if the class is not pursuing a topic which concerns everyone at his or her own level there is a pattern of materials through which children are working.

This sort of organisation is particularly useful in science where there is a need for a lot of discussion at both class and group level. Children may therefore be working in groups at different tasks but come together at the end as a class to talk about what they have learned.

This approach also requires you to have enough material for the whole class. It is also very demanding to have everyone doing practical work at the same time.

A rather different approach to this is the situation where the whole class works at the same subject but the approach is sufficiently open-ended for children to be able to respond at different levels. This is a very usual way of working in English but is also appropriate in the other core subjects and technology.

Class works at different subjects in groups

Each group in the class has a programme of work in two or three subjects and groups will change the subject they are doing at a certain point in time. This makes it possible to give some groups work which is less likely to make demands on the teacher, leaving you free to spend time with one of the other groups.

This approach has the advantage that not all the equipment and material is needed at once. You can also arrange things so that only one or two groups are doing practical work and the others are working at their tables. The disadvantage is that it is less easy to have class discussion about what each group has done.

Children work on individual programmes

This is appropriate for some aspects of work, but it is important not to have too much of the time spent in this way. Written work, in particular, lends itself to individual programmes, especially where children have some choice. There will also be individual work in topics, with children choosing different aspects of the topic. As you gradually become more skilled at assessing where children are with the Statements of Attainment, there will be a need for quite a number of individual programmes matched to the needs of particular children. These are likely to be most effective if the children are aware in some form of the statement they are attempting to achieve. Individual work is also useful as a kind of fall-back position. For example, everyone can have a personal mathematics programme which he or she pursues when there is no other mathematical work taking place. It is also useful for children to have interesting work to do if they finish early or if they are waiting for the teacher to take the register.

The evidence from the Mortimore study (1988) is that less progress is made in this organisation. This is probably because if it is taken too far children lack the stimulus of other children and the teacher. HMI (1985) also noted that 'individual work, when overdone, allows the teacher little time to discuss difficulties with the children in more than a superficial way and provides too few opportunities for the children to learn from each other'. This is probably less of a danger if there is plenty of opportunity for class and group discussion.

Children work together in groups, each making a specific contribution to the group task

The decisions about the work each child does may be made by the teacher or by the group. If the decision is made by the teacher, children will get to work more quickly, but there will be little need for discussion and negotiation. Decision-making in groups needs to be introduced carefully with a limited range of areas of decision in the first instance. This can gradually be increased.

Children work together in groups which plan the task and organise the work

This is the stage to aim for. This kind of group planning provides good opportunities for collaborative work, which is part of the National Curriculum. Further suggestions about work in groups are given below.

All of these forms of organisation have a place in planning. The organisation should match the tasks being undertaken. This means that all the patterns are likely to be found at some point in time.

The purpose and value of group work

Schools as we know them plan children's development and learning on the basis of groups of children working with a teacher. Even schools committed to a team approach and those where there is a strong emphasis on individual learning, must still group children for some purposes and it is important to recognise that children learn a great deal from the group that they are in. There are also activities such as drama, some kinds of music and games which must be carried out in a group

A number of recent studies suggest points to note in considering organisation. *The Oracle study* (Galton *et al.* 1980) quoted in detail earlier, gives a great deal of information about the way teaching and learning styles affect each other, and while labelling of any kind tends to over-simplify, the value of this study is that a teacher can look at his or her own style and see some of the effects of it.

School matters (Mortimer *et al.* 1988), the ILEA study quoted earlier, also makes a number of points about style. The most effective teachers in this study spent quite a lot of time communicating with the whole class, which, the study is at pains to point out, is not the same thing as class teaching.

An older study, *Extending beginning reading* by Vera Southgate *et al.* (1981), found, rather disturbingly, that the *more* time a teacher spent in hearing individual children read, the *less* good was the overall reading attainment of the class. This suggests that the time being spent with individuals was perhaps not being used to the best advantage and that a different approach, possibly with groups or with the whole class, might be more effective. The study does not suggest that the teacher should stop hearing reading, nor is it an argument for ceasing to work with individuals, but rather that the teacher should look at the overall efficiency of the organisation.

Tizard *et al.* (1988) found that 65 per cent of all teacher contacts in the infant schools in their study were with the whole class; 17 per cent were on a one-to-one basis and 19 per cent was group teaching. Individual work was common, but individual teaching was not. Group teaching was also not common.

Wynne Harlen (1985) suggests a useful way of using diagrams in planning to show whether work is with the whole class or with groups (see Figure 9.1).

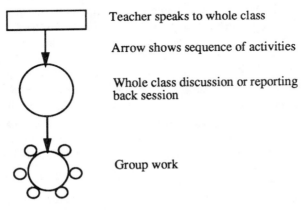

Teacher speaks to whole class

Arrow shows sequence of activities

Whole class discussion or reporting back session

Group work

Figure 9.1 Organisation diagram
Source: Harlen (1985)

The National Curriculum Council in *A framework for the primary curriculum* (1989a) lists the purposes of working in groups as follows:

- for some purposes it may be important for pupils at the same level of attainment to work together
- the National Curriculum requires the development of collaborative skills and working in groups will help to develop social skills, mutual support and leadership skills; for young children working in a group may be a new experience and one which they take time to get used to
- the economic deployment of resources may allow only small groups of children to be engaged on a practical activity
- grouping can allow teachers to concentrate their time on a group which requires support while other groups work on practice or consolidation which needs less constant attention.

The Plowden Report (1967) made a good deal of the value of group work. Its authors saw groups as the natural social unit for primary school children, contributing to the process of socialisation. Group work also has value for children in the language opportunities they are offered and the chance to work together on topics and to help other people. The development in language also helps the ability to solve problems in mathematics and science and technology, since verbalising will help thinking and children will help each other.

The Oracle study (Galton *et al.* 1980), taking up this point some years after Plowden, found that children were seated in groups in many classes. Groups were formed according to different criteria and were sometimes stable and sometimes changing; but as we have already seen, the most striking of their findings was that children seated in groups normally worked individually and to find a group working together at something was the exception rather than the rule, with some 90 per cent of teachers in their sample never using group work in this sense.

Neville Bennett and Elisabeth Dunne (1990), in a paper on classroom groups, analysed the conversation which took place in groups studying different aspects of curriculum. They found that when children were genuinely working together, task related talk was very high, averaging 88 per cent, being highest in technology and computer tasks and lowest in language work. Children working in groups where they were expected to cooperate to achieve the task demonstrated much greater involvement in their work and the amount of task related talk was 22 per cent higher than in groups where children were working individually. Language tasks, in particular, appeared to generate a good deal of abstract talk, although this might be the effect of the nature of the tasks set. Talk about action predominated in all the groups. The majority of the teachers involved in this study were 'amazed or delighted at the perseverance of even the youngest or lowest achiever'. They also felt that the children produced better results than usual in the action tasks. In addition, more able children tended to take on the role of teacher, leaving the teacher free to stimulate by asking questions and encourage higher order thinking.

This study is of particular interest in view of other studies, such as that of Tizard *et al.* (1988), which found that cooperative group work occurred rarely.

Maurice Galton in his book *Teaching in the primary school* (1989) gives some information about his findings in children's preferences for types of organisation. Children preferred working individually with the teacher or by themselves. They next preferred whole-class teaching. They liked group work least!

If we look at the way people in many occupations in adult life are expected to work together, it is perhaps surprising how little attention has been paid in schools to the necessary skills of working in a group. This is changing fast in the secondary sector, where TVEI and GCSE in particular have encouraged work in groups. The demands of the National Curriculum will also encourage group work particularly in language development, where spoken language is now given a much more important place, and also in science and technology.

We also tend to pay too little attention to the effects of different kinds of grouping and the relationship of the organisation chosen to the overall aims of the school and the teacher, and the nature of any particular activity.

Types of group

Children can be organised for learning in groups of many kinds, varying in size, composition and permanency. Each type of grouping has its advantages and disadvantages for particular activities and particular children and a strong case can be made for doing some work on an individual basis, some in a variety of different groups and some on a class basis.

We can consider each type of grouping in turn.

Individual work

This term can be used to describe any of the following situations:

1 Children work at individual tasks which may be chosen by the child or be given by the teacher
   These tasks could arise from topic work or a class activity or be a development of the child's own ideas.

2 Children work at their own pace through a structured scheme
This may mean that everyone is doing English or mathematics at the same time, but the actual work each child is doing is different.
3 In creative work children may work either at their own ideas or their interpretation of a group theme
They also develop a personal style.

All children need some experience of each of these types of individual work. Individual work would seem to be most appropriate for:

- a situation in which there is a range of ability within the group, but a common theme. For example, an environmental study might involve a variety of different questions and working plans so that the work could be matched to the ability range of the class.
- learning which needs to be step-by-step such as those aspects of work in mathematics which are concerned with individual understanding and practice.
- learning which is matched to individual need and differentiates children according to their ability, stage of development and the stage they have reached in the work in hand and in the National Curriculum.
- providing individual opportunities for creative and practical work, though this may contribute to a common goal.

Pairs and trios

This form of grouping has a good deal to offer and is probably insufficiently used. A pair of children tackling a mathematical or scientific problem may benefit considerably from talking it through. This not only helps the mathematical or scientific learning by making different aspects of the problem explicit, but it makes demands on each child's language ability. This also applies to the situation in which one child teaches another.

Small groups (ten or fewer)

Groups of this size are valuable for a variety of activities, but children need training in working together if the intention is to do group work. A group of this size working with a teacher is particularly valuable, but in a single class, the programme for other children needs careful thought if the teacher is to be able to concentrate on the group. This is much easier to do in a team-teaching organisation where teachers can take it in turns to work with small groups while someone else supervises the others.

In a well-prepared programme it may be possible for students from a college of education to work with small groups, or children from a local secondary school studying child development or undertaking work experience or community service. A teacher may also involve parents in supervising the body of the class while working with a small group, providing the work for the other children has been clearly defined and there is a supervision task which can be done by a non-professional. Conversely a parent might supervise the work of a small group which has a task clearly defined by the teacher.

Groups of this size are valuable for the following:

1 Discussion
   A group of this size is small enough to give everyone a chance to contribute and large enough to get a variety of ideas.
2 Group tasks
   A teacher may form a group to undertake a particular activity, such as a group project or some drama or work in science.
3 Work which is matched to the learning needs of a group
   At any particular time there may be a group of children who are ready for a particular piece of teaching. A group of not more than ten enables the teacher to question and check that everyone in the group has understood.

There should be opportunities for work of this kind with and without the teacher.

Large groups

A large group can be anything from a class group to the whole school. A large group does not lend itself to discussion as well as a smaller group and it is much easier for a child to opt out in a large group. On the other hand, there are activities, such as some aspects of music and dance, where the large group provides an experience of involvement and participation which is very valuable.

Large groups require much more detailed preparation than small groups. Some questions for teachers may be:

1 Is this the most efficient and effective way of teaching this particular thing?
2 Are all or almost all the children going to get something from it or would some do better working on their own or in smaller groups?
3 Can we, by showing a film or a television programme to more than one class at once with one teacher in charge, provide opportunities for other teachers to work with individuals or small groups?

Teachers in the past have had very little opportunity to consider the size of group likely to be more or less suitable for different activities, unless they happen to have been in a team-teaching situation. It may be more possible to group children according to the needs of the activity in the future if we are able to staff primary schools rather more generously or have the benefit of teaching aides, but even in present circumstances group size for given activities should still be considered.

ANALYSIS 9.1: GROUPING FOR LEARNING	Indiv-idual	Pair/trio	4–9	10–19	20–29	30–39	40–49	50+
Direct teaching								
Studying text								
Working on mathematical problems								
Mental arithmetic								
Science experiments								
Practical work in technology								
Discussion								
Listening to radio/ watching TV								
Listening to the teacher reading								
Drama								
Topic work								
Practical music making								

Analysis 9.1 is intended to help you to consider group size in relation to different kinds of activity. The items across the top give you possible group sizes and some suggested items for types of activity are given down the side of the page. You will need to select from these those which are appropriate to your situation and then add any others which seem to be relevant. Then tick the appropriate cell for the type of group which seems most suitable for each particular activity.

As with many of the analysis suggestions in this book, it may be valuable to discuss this with other teachers.

In considering what may be appropriate grouping for different activities it is useful to consider grouping from the child's point of view. We actually know very little about how children view the groups they are in. Does a five year old, for example, know all the children in the class? At what stage does an assembly of the whole school have meaning for a child and to what extent are some children frightened by being part of such a large group?

In a small group it is difficult for an individual to opt out or day-dream. While too much day-dreaming or day-dreaming at the wrong time may be a nuisance or worrying, there may be a case for providing some opportunities for children to be inactive and to think. This is probably more difficult in today's active classrooms than it was in traditional settings, where class teaching sometimes became a background for a child's own thoughts. Times when everyone is quiet are needed not only for the teacher's peace of mind but in order to allow children to reflect.

The formation of groups

Another important question about grouping for learning concerns the criteria by which the groups are formed for the purposes they are intended to achieve.

Different kinds of grouping are needed for different activities and it is better not to have groups which are too fixed. A child who is always in the same reading group, for example, comes to see his or her reading ability as being at the level of that group and this may limit progress. This is particularly true of the lowest ability groups. Such a child may also lack the example of more able children.

The *Non-statutory guidance in English* (1989b) makes the point that children should have the opportunity to be part of different groups and that grouping should be flexible and varied. Group composition should be a conscious decision on the part of the teacher.

HMI in their survey *The implementation of the National Curriculum* (1989) found that about half the classes they saw grouped children by attainment for English and mathematics. Group work was more common in science than in the other two core subjects and individual work was common in mathematics with children working through a published scheme supplemented by work cards.

Neville Bennett and Joy Kell in *A good start?* (1989) found that in the reception classes they studied, grouping by ability was used by about half the teachers. A third used age or intake as a criterion for grouping and a third used flexible grouping. Twenty-five per cent used mixed ability groups and about one in six used friendship groups.

Groups may be formed as follows:

Grouping for class management

There are many situations where the teacher needs to divide a class in order to undertake particular activities. This kind of grouping is very common in physical education and in art/craft activities because there is a limited amount of space and equipment which has to be shared. It is also necessary to group children from time to time for the teacher's benefit to make work easier. For example, you may wish to demonstrate or show children something which cannot be seen properly if the group is too large.

Grouping by age

The majority of primary schools group children into classes by age when they can, although an age group may represent a wide ability group. There is evidence from the HMI *Primary Survey* (1978) that so far as junior age children are concerned, children in classes with a single age group tend to achieve more than those in classes of mixed age. The HMI *First School Survey* (1982) also shows this as far as the older children in the first school are concerned.

This information comes at a time when falling rolls are inevitably leading to a considerable increase in the number of classes with mixed age groups. There may come a time in any primary school when to maintain classes of a single age group is grossly unfair because the numbers in different year groups are very uneven.

The maintenance of single age group classes may mean cutting out any chance of withdrawal of children for particular activities because there are no teachers free to do this. In some of these situations classes of mixed age may be the better solution, especially if the teachers involved consider the children as individuals and are concerned to extend the thinking and achievement of the older and more able children as well as that of the younger children.

We noted in Chapter 2 that the study *School matters* (Mortimore *et al.* 1988) found that teachers were not sufficiently aware of age differences among children within the same class and made little allowance for this. Younger children were generally regarded as less able even though they made normal progress but from an earlier starting point.

A child's date of birth may have all sorts of consequences for his or her education. A child who is among the oldest in the class may appear to do well and this in turn may be motivating. A child who looks mature may be treated as older and is thus encouraged to behave in more mature ways.

A child who is one of the youngest may be stimulated to emulate the older children and may thus make good progress. On the other hand such a child may become depressed about doing less well than older children and develop a self-image which suggests a person who is not very competent and consequently may cease to try very hard. A child who is young within the class may also be under-estimated, especially a child who is small and immature. Teachers and others will speak to him or her as to a younger child and their expectations may be lower than the child's ability justifies. We need to be aware of our tendency to treat children as being the age they appear to be and the effect of this.

Ability grouping

Studies of the effect of ability grouping suggest that other factors may be more important in their effect on children's learning and that less able children are often under-estimated in a streamed situation.

Joan Barker-Lunn's study *Streaming in the primary school* (1970) and others show that streaming has an effect on teacher expectations and attitudes, with teachers in streamed schools tending to make more hard and fast judgements about children. Even in the sixties when this research was carried out there were difficulties in finding enough primary schools that were streamed and it is now a rarity to find a primary school using this form of organisation throughout although schools often set for mathematics in the later years. However, many classes group by ability within the class.

Two other findings feature in studies of streaming, including studies in secondary schools. Teachers in streamed schools tend to under-estimate the less able, who tend to do better in mixed ability classes. Teachers in streamed schools also believe that they move children from stream to stream more often than they in fact do. These problems are also present in year groups where there is setting and in grouping within a class.

The attitudes and expectations of the teacher and the school make all the difference to the way children view ability grouping and to its value as a form of organisation. A good teacher can make each group feel that they are special and deserving of the best attention or that the children in some groups are failures, although few teachers deliberately reinforce failure. It is also important that the school encourages more able groups to be sympathetic to less able peers. Children withdrawn in a less able group and others may also draw conclusions about themselves from the accommodation, books and materials provided for them which demonstrate the value placed on them by the school and the teacher. A group which meets in poor accommodation with ancient books and materials, possibly designed for younger children, draw their own conclusions. Withdrawal grouping becomes more acceptable if the very able are sometimes withdrawn and if other groups, formed with different criteria are also withdrawn from time to time.

What is true of ability grouping within the school will also be true within the classroom, especially of grouping which tends to be permanent.

The classroom teacher has the opportunity to re-group for different activities, however, and this will help to prevent some children assuming that they are in the bottom group for everything and poor at all school work. If you use ability grouping for a large amount of work, you perhaps need to ask yourself some questions about whether the more negative findings of studies of ability grouping apply in your classroom.

It is equally important not to take the opposite view that ability grouping is something to be avoided under all circumstances. Ability grouping may be the most efficient and effective way of teaching some things, offering the right level of group stimulus to the children and using the teacher's time most effectively. For example, some aspects of work in mathematics may be best done in ability groups, although there is much mathematical work which can be done effectively with a mixed group.

Other work may gain from a mixed ability organisation. This is particularly true of the creative aspects of work such as art and drama and the content, though not necessarily the presentation, of personal writing.

Developmental groups

Here the teacher is concerned to achieve a measure of homogeneity not by grouping for age or ability but by grouping according to the stage of development. This is most likely to be relevant in practical work like physical education, but might be used in other areas.

Conversely a teacher might consider the developmental stages of a group of children and deliberately mix the stages, so that the immature might learn from the more mature. This might be a useful thing to do in drama, for example.

Grouping by learning needs

There will be occasions when a teacher selects a group who are at about the same stage to work with, perhaps introducing new work, checking or consolidating past work or drawing together the work of a previous session.

This would seem to be a useful practical compromise for some work. It is particularly valuable with an integrated day or team-teaching approach where groups of any size can be withdrawn for work with the teacher. Grouping by learning needs allows groups to vary from day-to-day and week-to-week as children progress and their needs change. It also makes evident the value of analysing the needs of individuals. We are likely to see more of this kind of grouping with children grouped according to the stage they have reached in the National Curriculum.

Interest groups

Most teachers provide some opportunity for choice of interests in the course of the day or week and this may involve allowing children to choose a group working at a particular topic.

Social learning groups

Children need to acquire the skills of working with others and this is discussed in more detail below. A particular individual may also benefit from working with children who provide good models by virtue of being older or good workers or good group members or just a good influence.

Friendship groups

Most of us like to work with our friends and there will be occasions when friendship groups work well. There are two caveats, however. At the primary stage friendship groups will nearly always be single sex and there may be occasions when a mixed group would be preferable. There is also the problem of the child whom no one wants and the group where one dominant child does all the work. You may need to do some engineering in such cases.

A teacher needs to use a mixture of groupings, sometimes forming ability groups or groups at the same stage of learning, sometimes deliberately structuring groups, so that children learn from one another, and sometimes using friendship groups. This enables children to gain from the differing contributions of other children.

The questions you need to ask in planning grouping might be as follows:

ANALYSIS 9.2: GROUP COMPOSITION								
	Friendship	Interests	Social learning	Learning needs	Stage of development	Ability	Age	Class management
Mathematics								
English								
Science								
Drama								
Physical education								
Environmental studies								
Topic work								
Technology								

Which activities need homogeneous groups?

Mathematics is one area which is commonly expected to need homogeneous groups but a good deal of mathematical work needs to be individual, with group activities providing a stimulus. Some of the more open-ended mathematical activities can be undertaken with the whole class and children can follow them up according to their ability. It depends to some extent on the teacher's personal preferences and ways of working, but nearly all work benefits from discussion and you need to consider what can be discussed in a group where the ability differs widely and what requires a more homogeneous group.

Practical activities in mathematics can involve the whole ability range initially, although as work continues, it is important to structure it carefully so that the most and the least able have enough challenging work to do.

It could be argued that some physical education would be better in groups of comparable ability, but it is very unusual to find this. The same could be said of music. One hears few primary teachers complain of the problem of the mixture of ability within the group in these subjects. Nevertheless, it might be worth considering whether there is not a case for arranging some work where children have the opportunity to work with others of a similar physical or musical ability.

Which areas of curriculum gain from being undertaken in a mixed ability group?

Most creative work provides a situation in which a mixture of abilities is possible and often useful. While the view that the less able are compensated by being good with their hands is not really tenable, inventiveness and creativity are not the province of only the intellectually able. This is likely to become particularly evident as the technology curriculum develops. Almost any area of curriculum can be undertaken with mixed ability if the work is open-ended.

Does the organisation I provide offer children the opportunity to work in different kinds of group in the course of a week?

If different types of group offer different learning opportunities, this suggests that it would be beneficial for children to have experience in different types of group.

Am I training children to work together rather than alongside each other?

Children will work together without a great deal of encouragement as they grow older, but their ability to do this is likely to develop more quickly if they are given both encouragement and training in the skills of corporate working.

We have already seen that there is a difference in working with a group towards a common end and working alongside others with similar tasks. The first requires certain social skills and is important for adulthood. It is also the intention of the National Curriculum that children shall learn these skills as part of their work. While children may acquire the necessary skills incidentally in the process of attempting group work, they are likely to acquire them more quickly if you work consciously to develop them.

Teaching of group skills is a normal part of life in infant classrooms, although teachers may not be very conscious of doing this. It is largely a sub-conscious process and teachers do not usually see it as part of the curriculum which needs to be checked for each child, although records may well include comment about how well a child is getting along with others. The more this is discussed and considered, however, the better the learning is likely to be.

Training in group work skills starts with such elementary tasks as learning to share, to take turns and listen to other people and try to see their point of view. Children advance from this stage to develop readiness to contribute to common goals and to sink personal differences in order to achieve something.

These continue to be necessary skills for members of a group of older children or adults and there is a case for working consciously at developing these skills, perhaps checking how well each child is doing in developing them. They are very important for a happy and productive adult life.

The teacher needs to make a point of praising children for being good group members from time to time, so that group work is seen to be valued.

Assessing the National Curriculum (SEAC 1990c) suggests that children may need help:

- to know how to look at their own work and develop and continue discussion
- to learn how to look constructively at the work of others
- to know when they should ask teachers for help, resources or other assistance

The primary school in a changing world (Button 1989) stresses the importance of children experiencing cooperation at school as part of their preparation as world citizens.

Teachers are sometimes tempted to create a group spirit by setting up teams or other similar groups and getting them to compete against each other. This is useful but has to be kept within bounds, especially with younger children. Too strong an emphasis on competition can result in children giving their best only when the situation is competitive and being unprepared to cooperate with others. Sherif *et al.* (1954) found that competitive activities tended to provoke feelings of hostility and collaborative activities more positive feelings. Lynch (1987) listed the benefits of cooperative work. They were 'superior academic learning, achievement and productivity, improved self-esteem, better relationships between pupils of different racial and ethnic backgrounds and between handicapped and non-handicapped and greater trust and concern'.

Group project work, art/craft and technology tend to contribute well to group work skills since these place emphasis on working together to create something.

With older children the skills of group leadership can also be discussed and fostered. Some tasks can also be carried out by groups without leaders.

When you start encouraging children to develop skills as leaders, it may be a good idea to choose leaders in the first instance. At a later stage other children will know what to look for in a leader and will be able to make wise choices themselves. Explain to all the children that you expect the leaders to do certain tasks and want their groups to support them in carrying them out. Some useful tasks to practise in the context of a piece of group work might be the following:

1 Getting ideas from the group
   A group leader gives shape and direction to discussion about a task and the action following it, e.g. a group leader asked to prepare the group for a visit to a local farm might start by getting them to list what might be available for study.

2 Sharing out the tasks
   When the lists of possibilities have been made, the group leader has to see that the tasks are reasonably distributed. This is more a matter of saying 'Who would like to do this?' than of telling others what to do. It will include seeing that all the tasks are covered and that they are fairly distributed, taking into account the particular people in the group.

3 Pacing the work
   The group leader needs to keep track of what is happening and see that anyone getting left behind is helped to catch up. He or she may also need to discover whether anyone finishing early has a further contribution to make.

4 Encouraging and supporting
   Encouraging others is an essential part of leading a group and often makes all the difference between a person who leads well and is accepted as a leader and the person who cannot get others to follow him or her. Very few people do this by themselves and you need to encourage children leading groups to tell others that they are doing well or to thank them for contributions, and so on. The teacher's example will, of course, be important here.

5 Considering the way the pieces fit together

If the group is to present its findings to others, the form of the presentation needs to be agreed. The leader will need to keep a running check on how the various contributions fit together and how each contributes to the whole, bringing the whole group together to discuss this.

The existence of a leader in a group implies the existence of followers. If a group is to work well together, its members must accept the leader's role and work with him or her. This can be difficult for children who are natural leaders, but it is an important piece of learning for them. Group members also need to learn to listen to one another and consider the contributions made by others.

It could be argued that these are very difficult skills which adults do not always achieve or practise. On the other hand, much that teachers already do in the classroom helps towards ends of this kind and a more explicit attempt to develop group work may achieve even more.

Analysis 9.2 provides an opportunity to consider types of group in relation to activity. As with the previous analysis, the types of group are given across the top of the page and some activities have been listed down the left hand side with space to add others

There are a number of further questions you may like to ask yourself about your organisation (see Analysis 9.3 overleaf).

ANALYSIS 9.3:
CLASSROOM ORGANISATION

1 Have I an established classroom routine which children follow?

2 Have I the right balance between class teaching, group and individual work?

3 Are my children really learning to work in groups?

4 Is the grouping I am using satisfactory for its purposes?

5 Do children have the chance to work in a variety of groups?

6 How well do I match work to individual children?

7 What opportunities do I offer children to contribute to the planning of their work?

8 Are they becoming independent learners?

9 Have I the right balance between teacher directed work and choice by children?

10 Am I providing enough opportunities for discussion in pairs, small groups and as a class?

---

10 The use of time and space

Organising work in the classroom involves not only managing the children and planning the curriculum, but also managing time, space and resources. As we have already noted, HMI (1989) in their study of the implementation of the National Curriculum were generally rather critical of planning, particularly of the use of time where they felt that there was a lack of analysis of curriculum in relation to the time available. They say

> Adjustments may well have to be made to the balance of individual, group and whole class teaching to make effective use of time, improve the pace and progress of work to match the range of ability in the class and to offer the full curricular range.

THE USE OF TIME

The National Curriculum has created a pressure on time for teachers. There is now a great deal to do in the time available and since a primary teacher usually has considerable freedom to plan the programme of work in the way that seems best for the children, the use of time requires a good deal of planning. The primary teacher, unlike the secondary teacher, has few fixed points in the day, although the demands of the National Curriculum are probably leading to a more formal programme in some schools. There may be the use of a shared facility like the hall or playing field or a television programme to be watched live, but generally speaking, teachers are able to plan the use of time as seems best to them.

Since time is finite and you cannot get any more of it, it is important to use what you have as well as you can. This means that you need to be very conscious of how you and the children are using time. While it is almost certainly impossible to organise so that you and your children are always using time to the best advantage, this is, nevertheless, the goal you should be trying to achieve.

The problem about organising time in the classroom is that individual learning times and the need for practice are so varied. The mixture of class, group and individual work which takes place needs to allow for this. Your aim is for every child to be working profitably with no one simply occupied because you haven't time to deal with him or her. This means that for much work you will need to provide at a variety of different levels.

Teachers do this in various ways, by working with groups of children, using materials which differ, providing individual work for some children, and so on. The advent of audio-visual materials and the gradual development of computer-assisted learning will gradually make it easier to provide programmes which match individual need, but there is still an important place for group teaching and learning, since children need the stimulus of both the teacher and other children. We have already seen that research has suggested that a mixture of class, group and individual teaching is associated with good achievement.

The National Curriculum is requiring teachers to think differently about the use of time. The National Curriculum Council in *A Framework for the primary curriculum* (1989a) suggests that there may be a need for re-thinking, that teachers should consider how time is used at present, what restrictions there are currently on the use of time (assembly, registration, movement around the school, etc.) and how much time is left for the curriculum.

Studies of the use of time

There have been a number of studies of the way teachers and pupils use time. HMI (1989) found that the most common practice in primary schools was to blend separate subject teaching with integrated teaching to practise basic skills across a broad curriculum and to benefit from single subject teaching as necessary. They found the following breakdown of time was the average in year 1 where about 70 per cent of time was given to the core subjects:

English	7 hours	33%
Mathematics	5 hours	23%
Science	3 hours	14%

The range of time used was very wide.

	Minimum		Maximum	
English	2 hours	9.5%	12 hours	57%
Mathematics	1 hour	4.7%	10 hours	47%
Science	1 hour	4.7%	8 hours	38%

The ILEA study *School matters* (Mortimore *et al.* 1988) noted that between

66 and 75 per cent of teachers used a timetable and that this practice increased as the children grew older. This study also gives the amount of time which teachers were using for preparation, which were as follows:

Hours per week	% teachers
less than 1	2
1 – 5	25
6 – 10	59
11 – 15	10
15+	4

This study found that managerial aspects of the teacher's job took approximately one tenth of the time available. It seems likely that these figures would be considerably higher if the study were done today.

Tizard *et al.* in *Young children at school in the inner city* (1988) found that in top infant classes, less than half the day was devoted to work activity. Forty-three per cent of the day went on routine activities such as registration, toilet visits, lining up, tidying up, meals and playtimes. During the part of the day when children were actually learning they were on task for 66 per cent of the time.

This kind of dilemma for teachers was also evident in *The Oracle study* (Galton and Simon 1980), which suggests that individualised learning is more apparent than real because teachers do not have the time for the kind of probing discussion with individuals implied in *The Plowden Report* (1967). This study found that a typical pupil is fully involved and working directly on task for 58 per cent of the time. For 40 per cent of the time, the pupil is working alone, not interacting with anyone. For 12 per cent of this time the pupil is interacting with or listening to the teacher and for 5 per cent interacting with another pupil. The typical pupil interacts with the teacher for only 2.3 per cent of lesson time.

An American study *Time to learn* (Denham and Leiberman 1980) makes some related and relevant comments about the use of time in classrooms. Findings on the relationship between *engaged student time* and achievement showed, not very surprisingly, a high correlation, though we need to note that *engaged student time* is not the same as the time that children are *supposed* to be engaged with a particular piece of work. It is the time which *The Oracle study* describes as *on task,* when children are actually engaged in the work they are supposed to be doing.

The *Time to learn* study also showed that high achievement went with high success and that the child who frequently needed and obtained extra help still achieved less. The study implied that the teacher might get the slower children to achieve more and use time more effectively by doing more to anticipate the needs of such children and giving them work in which they could succeed by taking a series of small steps which were demanding for them but which they could take without help. This might be more effective than responding to requests for help which implied that the child had already realised that he or she was failing.

What can be learned from this study is that the best teaching occurs when the teacher is able to match individual learning needs in such a way that children have work which challenges, but at which they can succeed.

The teacher's use of time

As a teacher, you are responsible for the way you use your time and the children's. Your task is to fit in all the aspects of curriculum covered by the National Curriculum and this is not easy. It is important to consider the areas in which learning in one subject complements and overlaps work in another – how, for example, the Statements of Attainment in English can be met through work in science and history and geography and other subjects, where mathematics is a relevant part of work in science, and so on. It will also be necessary to consider more thoroughly than has been common in the past, how the time available in the week and the term can be broken down to ensure that every aspect of curriculum is getting a fair share of attention. It may be that time is allocated to core skills and physical education each week, but that some other aspects have concentrated time for a period or perhaps a project centred on them.

How you use your time depends also on your teaching style and on your view of the teaching/learning process, but it is very easy under the pressures of day-to-day classroom life to believe that you should be using time in a particular way and end up using it completely differently, sometimes without realising it.

A good starting point, therefore, may be to work out what you think you ought to be doing, perhaps using the log sheet in Analysis 10.1. Then try to find a way of recording what you are actually doing. Most studies show some difference between what teachers think they are doing and what they actually do, so don't be too surprised if this is true for you.

It isn't easy to find a way of recording how you are using time because of your involvement in what is actually happening. The ideal would be if you and a colleague were able to observe each other and note the use of time against a check list. Most teachers are likely to have to do this for themselves, however, and you will need to find a way of recording which you can manage to use in the classroom. There are several ways of recording time spent and you may like to design your own check list, but you need some kind of classification against which you can check.

ANALYSIS 10.1: TEACHER'S TIME LOG

Complete this analysis by writing in the amount of time spent in each activity

Name... Date.............................

	Class or group activities						Contacts with individuals			
	Talking/listening to class or group	Organising activity	Radio, TV, films	Leading practical work	Questioning/discussion	Other activities	Explaining to individuals	Talking/listening to individuals	Checking work Hearing reading	Other activities
1										
2										
3										
4										
5										
6										
7										
8										

One possible starting point is to have a tape recorder running for a time, recording what is going on. You can then listen to it and decide on categories of activity which could be checked with a list as you work. It may also be a good idea to note different uses of time on different days, recording, for example, on one occasion, the time you spent talking to the whole class, or the time spent dealing with the kind of task which doesn't require your skill as a teacher (I can't find my book, my pencil's broken etc.) or the number of times you praised or scolded a child and who it was.

Another way of recording is to go through a list at each break in the day, estimating the time you spent on different activities. Almost any aspect of work can be incorporated into this approach and if you use a chart you make it easy to abstract information as well as making it easy to record.

The log sheet in Analysis 10.1 is a suggested record for this purpose which can be adapted to suit whatever you want to find out. You may wish to extend it to provide more cells. You can record either by noting how long each item takes, or by noting starting and finishing times. If this requires too much attention, you can simply tick in a cell each time you undertake something. A number of activities are suggested on the log sheet but you can adapt it to fit your own situation. This will be useful also if you involve children in analysing their use of time, since you can compare their records with yours.

Children's use of time

Studying your own use of time will inevitably involve studying aspects of the way children are using time. How you set about studying this must depend partly on the age group you teach and whether they are able to make some observations of their use of time for themselves, perhaps as part of mathematical work on the use of time.

You may be able to coopt some outside help in making detailed observations of what a sample group of children is doing at agreed intervals. College of Education or Education Department staff and students are often interested in undertaking this kind of study and it can be helpful to you to have someone with whom to discuss findings.

The involvement of children in studying their own use of time might be part of work on graphical representation. The log sheet for children which follows in Analysis 10.2 can be adapted for your particular class.

If possible give every child a copy of the log sheet and discuss what each item means. Bring in a pinger egg timer and set it to ping at regular intervals – about every ten minutes might be a good starting point – with a child given the job of re-setting it each time it goes. When the pinger goes, everyone, including you, puts a tick in the column which shows what he or she is doing. The children's log sheet below can be used for this and you can adapt the teacher's log sheet for this purpose.

ANALYSIS 10.2: CHILDREN'S TIME LOG

Name..................................... Date...................................

When you hear the pinger, tick the column which says what you are doing

	Listening to the teacher	Answering questions/discussion	Practical work like PE, music	Watching TV, film, listening to radio	Using the computer	Doing work I should be doing	Talking about work to a friend	Talking about other things	Doing nothing in particular	Talking to the teacher	Getting help from the teacher	Getting work checked	Reading to the teacher
1													
2													
3													
4													
5													
6													
7													
8													
9													
10													

Although this appears to be a bit disrupting, what you may find is that the number of children who are doing what they should be doing when the pinger goes, actually increases, because they want to be able to write down that they are doing the right thing. Ideally you want to do this on several occasions over a number of weeks, perhaps doing it for a quarter of the day or half a day, so that you eventually get a fairly typical pattern.

The records themselves have a number of uses. They tell you at given points in time how many children are doing what you want them to do. You can also relate your own activity to that of the majority of the children. For example, which activities on your part are associated with which activities on the children's part? When you were explaining something to an individual child, what were the rest of the class doing? How much time do you and the children spend on each of the activities listed and how do you feel about these proportions? Can you get nearer to what you would like the division to be?

You may find it helpful to discuss your results with a colleague who is also undertaking these studies. It will be helpful to compare notes about the way each class is using time.

You can also use the results to discuss with children how far they feel they are using their time properly. It may be an opportunity to discuss with older children possible ways of studying and to provide an opportunity for each child to choose the order of some of his or her work and discover his or her best way of working We all have our own ways of using time and we need to know whether we work best in long or short spells.

Children may also like to set personal goals to improve their patterns of working and it may help them to identify and state something they plan to improve and keep a log of whether they are achieving this. This is all part of the process of becoming an independent learner.

Further investigations and action

These exercises will almost certainly throw up things you will want to do something about. Your areas of concern will to some extent be personal to you, but the following suggestions for considering your findings may be useful. If you made a statement earlier about the way you thought you should be using time, this will give you a useful yardstick against which you can assess how well you and the children are doing.

1 Consider the balance of class, group and individual work
   The grouping of children for learning was discussed in the last chapter. Here we are looking at whether the balance of grouping you are using is the best fit for your class in terms of the time spent in each kind of

organisation. This means studying the differences in children. These include not only differences in ability, skill, knowledge and understanding, but also differences in learning style.

The following may help you to take your analysis a step further:

Select a time when you are teaching the whole class using exposition and questioning

As soon as possible afterwards go through the class list classifying children as follows:

– those for whom what you did was probably exactly right
– those who had either learned what you were doing already or could have learned it much more quickly
– those who needed more work and explanation before they grasped what you were talking about.

Most of your children will come into the first category and you will probably have made use of those who knew it all to stimulate the others and make them think, perhaps also asking open-ended questions which challenged the thinking of the most able and took their thinking further. Those in the third category will have made a start which you will be planning to follow up later.

If you can honestly say that this is what happened then your class probably spent time profitably. But if you find that you have quite a number of children in the middle and third categories, then you should perhaps consider whether they might not have used time better working individually or in small groups. You might have used your own time better in teaching them in groups.

Consider whether the group and individual work taking place is making the best use of your time and that of the children

There are a number of ways you could look at this:

– Take a point in the day when everyone should be working individually and look around the class noting how many children are really engaged and involved in what they are doing, so far as you can tell. Do this several times over a period. Note the children whose names occur most frequently among those not involved and consider whether a different form of organisation might do more to engage them.
– Note over a period of time which children respond best to teacher stimulated and directed activities and which do better given more freedom to work on their own.
– Listen to what happens when you ask a group of children to work together at something, thinking about the skills involved in group work and considering how you foster them (see pp. 174, 175).
– Set up an experiment by selecting two very similar topics and then deal with one as a piece of class teaching and the other on an indi-

vidual or group work basis. Check at each stage how many children are fully involved in learning in each case and try to make some comparison of the success of each piece of work.

— Ask each child to do a week's work in one notebook, differentiating in your own mind which pieces of work arose from class work and which from individual work. While written work is by no means the only, or even the best, way of assessing what children are learning, it nevertheless gives you valuable information. Studying the children's notebooks also gives you clues about the learning styles of different children and the approaches which best suit them. The notebooks also give you interesting information about the amount of work different children actually do in the course of a week. The notebooks can be kept and used in this way occasionally, perhaps once a term, which gives you an interesting record of progress.

The outcomes of these investigations into the use of time may not change your practice all that much and, of course, you can never cater equally well for all children. Nevertheless they should provide some food for thought and perhaps a greater awareness of the children who benefit most from the different approaches. This may give you some criteria for deciding how to set about a particular piece of work.

Study the occasions when you are speaking or reading to the whole class

The value of these activities lies mainly in the extent to which you can stimulate interest and thought. The review suggested above, where you check through the register thinking about what children have gained, is probably your best check on the value of such activity. On the other hand, you must remember that some inputs by the teacher may not have immediate outcomes and yet have important long-term benefits. Much reading and story telling might come into this category.

If you are near the beginning of your career, you may have doubts about your ability to stimulate children in a large group. The skills involved can undoubtedly be learned. It is easiest to stimulate others if you are enthusiastic yourself.

Examine your work in questioning and leading discussion

This is a most valuable way of supporting children's learning. You need to consider whether you do enough of this kind of activity or too much and whether you are happy with the quality of what you do. Stimulating questioning at the right moment which demands thought and goes beyond questions which are a matter of recall may do a great deal to help children to assimilate their learning and to explore ideas. The ability to draw thinking together through discussion is also valuable.

Further investigation here must be concerned with quality as well as quantity and you may find it helpful to tape two or three sessions of this kind for analysis. You may like to turn back to pp. 181 and 183 where there is an analysis of different kinds of questions which you can use to help you analyse the questions you actually asked. You can also speculate about what was achieved perhaps looking at the following:

– Which questions got the most response and which the least? Why do you think this was? It you changed some questions would you get a better reaction?
– How many children actually gave or wanted to give answers?
  It may be useful to make a seating plan and tick each child who answers a question. This will give you several pieces of information. It will tell you which children actually answered questions and which were either silent or not called on. You will discover something about the differences in quality of answer, especially if you listen to the children again on tape. You will also be able to check whether there is any pattern about who answered and speculate about whether this was the result of your selection of children to answer or lack of contribution from some children.

  Do the children who contribute most, for example, come from any particular part of the classroom? Are you unwittingly missing some children because of where they are sitting? There is some discussion of this on page 201. Are the girls answering fewer questions than the boys and is this your selection of children to answer or the natural behaviour of the two sexes?
– If you go through the register, for which children can you say that this was a valuable use of time; for whom was it of some value and for whom was it of very little value? How many would have learned more from personal reading? How many didn't need the session anyway?
– Could you, by better planning, better questioning and better follow up, have increased the number for whom this session was valuable?

2 Study the time spent on organising children, space and materials
  Many of the studies of the use of time in school show that teachers spend quite a lot of time on this kind of activity. *School Matters* (Mortimore *et al.* 1988), the account of the ILEA junior school project, found that on average teachers spent about a tenth of their time on classroom management. This is time which it is in everyone's interest to reduce to the minimum.

  It isn't easy to check the detail of this type of use of time, but if you keep a copy of the list in Analysis 10.3 below beside you during a morning or afternoon and tick it when you deal with any of the matters listed, you will begin to see where some of your time goes and you can then consider whether you can reduce the time you are using for this kind of activity.

ANALYSIS 10.3: WHERE THE TIME GOES	
Tick in the appropriate box each time you do one of these activities	
Tell children what to do	
Explain work to individual who hasn't understood	
Answer child asking what to do next	
Answer child asking where to find something	
Answer child raising query about work, e.g. spelling, maths problem, etc.	
Answer child checking that (s)he is doing what you want	
Answer child asking permission to do something	
Make disciplinary comment	
Check/mark child's work	
Other	
Other	
Other	

Using this list should help you to identify priorities and see which activities are using too much time. Each of the items can be considered in turn:

Tell children what to do

The following points may be considered:

1 Could you more often give children their work in writing?
   Even with young children you can build a vocabulary which allows this
   to some extent and the instructions can give reading practice. With
   older children more can be done and this, too, will provide practice in
   reading comprehension.

2 Could you organise materials so that their sequence is more evident to
   children?
   In a number of areas of work, there is a sequence and if children know,
   for example, that the blue mathematics group is this week working
   through the next four work cards or exercises in the book, with
   intervention by the teacher for group or class discussion, they can get
   on without coming back to you at frequent intervals to check on how
   they are doing. This is partly a matter of getting materials organised
   and getting a number of ways of learning and practising certain things
   very clearly structured so that you can say to a child 'Start work here
   and when you have finished you may take anything from shelf A or box
   B', knowing that these materials will offer the practice the child needs.

   Or to another child you may say 'The work cards over there are in
   order. Start with the first box and if you can do it easily go on to the
   next box. Come and see me when you get to box 3.'

   This kind of approach gives you time to deal with more complex
   issues, although it is not suggested that having given a child work, you
   ignore him or her. The point is that you may become more able to
   decide when to intervene if you are not all the time responding to the
   demands of individual children, but are able to select where to direct
   your attention.

3 Children who have genuinely developed skill in working in groups will
   often turn to each other to ask questions which in other circumstances
   they would ask the teacher.
   Children can be encouraged to ask each other and to come to you only
   as a last resort.

Explain work to an individual who hasn't understood

The best way to cut this down is to look at the kinds of questions children
are asking you and then to use the information about problems that this
gives you to modify the way you give out work. It may be, for example,
that the language you are using is too difficult, not perhaps in vocabulary,
but in complexity of sentence structure. You may also be unwittingly

referring to things outside the children's experience. You may be giving too much information at once and it will help to have some of it in writing so that a child can check it over after you have finished speaking.

A different way of tackling this is to get a child who has understood to explain it to one who hasn't but in such a way that it is clearly seen as the responsibility of the explainer to see that the child to whom he or she is explaining really does understand.

This offers useful practice in using language for the more able children and will help to reinforce their own learning.

Answer child asking what to do next

This links with your arrangements for giving work to children. However, there will be children who are working individually who need your guidance. There will also be attention seekers, who ask questions to make contact with you. However, if you start getting a lot of questions on a particular aspect of the work then you should take a look at the following:

1 Your organisation and the way you give children their work
   The suggestions made earlier should help with this.
2 The need to train children to work independently
   We noted in the chapter on curriculum that there was a need to train study skills. You then need to identify the ways in which you want children to work and make sure that they gradually become independent of you.

Answer child asking where to find something

It is a good idea to treat queries of this sort as a signal that the way your environment is set out is not perfect and that you may need to improve the way you organise. Of course, this is not always the case, but many such queries are the result of insufficient labelling of equipment and materials and a lack of consistency, usually on the part of the children, in returning things to the right place. You should aim at a situation where such questions are rare.

Answer child raising query about work

Some such queries are inevitable, but you need to minimise them. The following are very common queries:

1 How do you spell ... ?
   There are various ways of dealing with this. You can encourage the use of dictionaries and word indexes. For some children it may be useful to ask another child before asking the teacher, although one has to watch

the problem of children not being able to get on because of queries from other children.

You can also ask children to have a go before they come to you or suggest that they write the word in rough, without worrying about spelling, and then discuss it with you when the work is finished. This helps to avoid the loss of concentration involved in getting words from the teacher.

You can encourage children to do the best they can over spelling in some pieces of work and then work on the spelling problems afterwards.

There are also now spellcheckers on the market which allow the writer to check the spelling of a word. These are getting cheaper all the time and could be a boon to the teacher, as could spelling programmes on the computer which provide a similar service.

If you press children too much about always spelling correctly, they will tend to use only those words that they know they can spell. This makes it more difficult for you to help them to enlarge their spelling vocabulary, because you can't tell what is in their spoken vocabulary. An approach which encourages children to have a go allows you to pick out words on which the child should concentrate attention. This also gives you clues about the cause of some problems.

2 How do you do this sum?

This is more difficult than spelling, because you really need to explore a child's thinking and level of understanding in order to help. If you are getting many queries about a particular piece of work, however, you are obviously pitching it at the wrong level for a number of children.

It is also helpful to try to note the types of query over how to do something. It could be a matter of not understanding the language involved, inadequate number concepts or understanding of number operations or one of several problems.

As with spelling, it is useful to note the kinds of queries and errors, both those made by an individual and those made by a number of children. By generalising from these, you can often improve the ability of the children to cope without recourse to you.

3 What does this mean?

Try to get children to re-phrase this question as 'Does this mean x?' This encourages them to try to understand before coming to you. Again too frequent queries mean that you have pitched the work wrongly, perhaps for an individual or for the group.

Answer child checking that he or she is doing the right work

The children who constantly turn to you to ask this kind of question tend to be children who are a bit insecure. You need gradually to build up their confidence in themselves and in you, so that they know that you won't be cross with them for doing the wrong things. It may be a good idea to check at the beginning that such children have understood and at an early stage, if possible, make encouraging sounds about what they are doing so that they know they are doing the right thing.

Answer child asking permission to do something

A teacher normally expects children to ask permission to go out of the classroom unless there are work areas adjacent, but as you work with a group of children you should be able to reduce the number of occasions for asking permission to a bare minimum. Note the occasions when children ask permission and see if you can organise so that some of these requests are not needed.

Make disciplinary comments

These include both telling a child not to do something and praising a child for doing the right thing. There is a lot of evidence to show that the latter is more effective than the former. There is also evidence to suggest that teachers do not very often praise children for behaving correctly. As your class gets to know you, there should be a declining need for negative comment, although there will always be children who need to be restrained from time to time.

It is also useful to look at the children to whom you offer each kind of comment. It is not unusual to find that some children get negative comments all the time. If you find this to be so, you need to think of possible positive comments which could be made, remembering that what you comment on positively is likely to be repeated whereas negative behaviour which is the subject of comment does not necessarily disappear.

Just looking for what could attract positive comment for a child who seems always to be doing the wrong thing can sometimes be productive.

A major problem for teachers is finding enough time to make assessments. A number of the suggestions above may be relevant in providing more time when you are not dealing with the many queries which come up in the classroom. You also need to have some types of work which you know children can be left to do without interrupting you when you want to check a child's learning. Reading is an obvious one with older children and various forms of play with younger children, although, as we have seen, play is less useful if no adult is involved. It may be possible to give children a number of tasks to do so that they can go on to another if they find difficulties with one. It will also be helpful if you have parents or ancillaries working with you who can help to deal with problems while you are dealing with an individual child. Team-teaching also helps in this context because if there is more than one teacher in the room one can deal with the queries of a large group which has been given work which all of them should be able to manage easily, while the other deals with individuals.

THE USE OF SPACE AND RESOURCES

Children learn from everything that happens to them and the classroom environment is a tool for the teacher to use which can affect children in the following ways:

It can set aesthetic standards for children

Children should be able to get pleasure from what is around them. This has several benefits. What we know about learning suggests that attitudes towards school and towards learning are formed early. A pleasant environment is likely to contribute to the formation of good attitudes.

We set standards by the environment we offer to children. We need to provide things of quality and give children a chance to handle and enjoy them. This becomes increasingly difficult with ever smaller budgets, but it is still possible to provide plants and reproductions of paintings and to provide some things which are comparatively inexpensive to look at, handle and discuss. This is how standards are formed and maintained and the less likely children are to get such experience at home, the more important it is for the school to offer it.

The classroom can set standards of presentation

The teacher sets a standard of displaying work and teaching material which will be reflected in the children's own work. This should lead gradually to children putting up displays themselves and learning about how to display material effectively.

The working environment should be functional

The classroom should provide for the work you want to do. This means careful thought about storage and the way in which the grouping of children and the pattern of work relate to the environment and the resources available. We have already noted that if you organise so that different activities take place at the same time, you can manage with less, but have more varied equipment. You also need to think about circulation in grouping children, noting the path which children will take from different parts of the room to get what they need.

In being functional the classroom contributes to the formation of good working habits. Any practical area needs to have tools and materials laid out, each in its marked place, with clear rules about how things are to be used and returned.

The classroom should be easy to maintain

You need good arrangements for getting things out and putting them away and with a new class you need to spend time training children to do this properly. There should be a definite place for everything and every place should be labelled appropriately so that it is easy to see where to put things.

The classroom should stimulate children

This means that you should display some material designed to start children thinking and asking questions and sometimes to start them working. It also means that you should change the display fairly frequently and check that what is on show is really used. It is not unusual to find that a classroom with a considerable amount of attractive material displayed is having no impact because the teacher has not stimulated the children to look at what has been displayed for them.

You need to train children to look at displays and to see what is there. It may sometimes be better to display less, use it more and change it more frequently.

Organising the use of space and resources

The way you decide to use your classroom and the resources available, will affect the way children learn. In industry a firm tries to keep its equipment in use for as much of the time as possible, so that it earns its keep. While there are all sorts of obvious differences between schools and industry, there is, nevertheless, a case for seeing whether you are getting as much use as possible out of the equipment you have.

If you have a computer, for example, how much of the time is it in use? Could you use it more if you organised differently?

Most schools and teachers feel that they could do with more resources than they have, but are you sure that you are using everything available? It is surprising how often a teacher who is clear what is needed finds ways round the difficulties imposed by limited funding. There is very often equipment and material lying unused in someone else's classroom. There would seem to be a case for much more sharing of materials and equipment and for a school organisation which lists where things are, so that teachers can borrow them when they need them.

It is rare for a teacher to get exactly the furniture he or she would like and rarer still to get a sufficient amount of storage. Most teachers have to make the best of what they have and do a good deal of improvising and arranging things to meet the needs of their children's work.

In most primary classrooms the vast majority of the week's work has to take place in the same space, with only a small amount of specialist accommodation available, if any, even in middle schools. The classroom has to be used for many different activities, some of which don't go too well together. It is never very satisfactory to have to use materials such as paint and clay in the same space as clean work, however carefully you clean up.

The task in making what is available match your needs is therefore to arrange space, time and resources so that your environment is both functional and attractive.

You may find it helpful in thinking out how best to use your room and equipment to work through the following questions:

1 What space is actually available?
    − Is there space outside the classroom which could be used for some or even all of the time? This might be corridor or cloak space or shared space.
    − Draw a plan of the space available roughly to scale to use for planning purposes.
2 What activities will need to take place in the space in the course of the day or week?
    Most teachers will have a list which includes reading, writing, mathematics, science, using apparatus, discussion, painting, working with materials (both clean materials like fabric and messy materials like clay). The list may also include things like drama and music making. With very young children you will need opportunities for different kinds of play. You also need to think about the storage you need.
3 What kind of programme do you want to work?
    If you feel that it is really important that your whole class should be able to sit at tables and write at the same time, this will affect the other activities. Similarly if you feel that it is important for every child to have a table and chair of his or her own, this affects how you use your

furniture. It may help to list, over a week, the activities which actually took place in your classroom, giving the furniture needed. The chart below sets out a few entries for one day in one classroom.

Table 10.1 Use of furniture

Activity	Furniture	No. of children	Time taken
Basic skills	Tables and Chairs	15	2 hours
	Work-tops	10	
	Floor of book corner and easy chairs	5	
Topic	Work-top	10	1.5 hours
	Easels	4	
	Tables	16	
Story	Chairs	10	0.5 hours
	Floor	20	

If we make the assumption that this is typical of the rest of the week, there are various conclusions which can be drawn. The first is that sixteen tables would be sufficient for all the table work needed. If you are prepared to use work-tops for work rather than display or laying out materials, it may be possible to manage without a chair and table place per child. This can make movement easier. Or alternatively you can have different places in the room for doing different things such as painting or working with mathematical apparatus which can be set up for several days at a time or even permanently.

There is also a case for having some work-tops for use standing up. Many primary children spend a lot of time on their feet and it is not unusual in a primary classroom to see almost everyone standing and the chairs very much in the way.

Some form of integrated day undoubtedly makes better use of space and facilities than a more formal programme because each facility can be used by a small group at a time and all the facilities can be used for much of each day. A cooperative teaching situation does this even better.

On the other hand, you may not like the situation this creates and your children may not respond to it. We have already noted that there is research evidence to show that children appear to work more effectively in a situation in which they have only limited choice. Particularly if your control is shaky, you may be wise to see that each child has a place to sit and keep his or her things. The children themselves usually prefer this, although we have created the situation in which they regard this as the norm.

If you decide not to have a chair and table place for each child, it will be important to allocate storage space to each one. Human children, like many other animals, need territory of their own and if you take away the table/chair territory, you need to think about the territory each child really needs.

4 What does each of the activities you plan need in terms of space, equipment and storage?

Lists will be needed for each of the following activities and possibly for others:
 − Language work including group discussions and listening and the use of audio-visual media
 − Mathematics
 − Science
 − Technology, including art and craft, work with materials of all kinds, work with computers, etc.
 − Environmental studies including geography, history and social studies
 − Expressive work such as music, dance, drama
 − Physical education (this will take place out of the classroom but you still need to think about its requirements)
 − Religious education
 − Play activities
 − Children's storage of materials and equipment
 − Teacher's storage of equipment and materials

5 How can the space available be best used to provide for all these activities?

Inevitably you must compromise to some extent, but it is useful to make some basic plan. If you have drawn a plan of the space available which is roughly to scale, you can go on to make scale cut-outs of the base of each of the pieces of furniture you have. This allows you to try different ways of arranging it.

There are advantages in having particular areas for particular activities. Even if you teach fairly formally, it may be a good idea to have storage and display bases for some work. When there is a variety of activity going on for most of the time, there can be places to which children go to paint or do mathematics or science, and so on.

The fundamental divisions are into clean and messy activities and quiet and noisy ones. These pairs need to be separated either in time or space. Noisy activities can be confined to a certain time of day or you can perhaps place them in an adjoining area if they don't disturb other people and you have this kind of space.

The messier activities are best placed as near to water as possible and this often fixes the space used for work with materials and sometimes, by contrast, the areas used for quiet work. If classroom and corridor or cloakroom are being used, you can either confine the noise and mess to the classroom and put the quiet activities outside or conversely, depending on the particular circumstances and the geography of your working environment.

Space for particular activities can be marked off using cupboards at right angles to the wall or screens or open shelves or tables. The backs of cupboards can be shelved to use for storage or covered with paper or fabric as a background for display. Tall or unstable cupboards should be fixed to the wall or floor or you need to put very heavy things at the bottom of them so that there is no danger of their falling over. Open-shelf units can be made from timber or specially designed materials. They have the advantage of providing a good deal of storage in a small space and they can be used as room dividers with access from both sides.

When you have arrived at an arrangement of furniture which suits you and have put it into action, try to find time to observe how it is being used and then move things accordingly if you find that your plan isn't really working as you intended.

6 How can you furnish the spaces to provide what you need?

You have to start with what you have, arranging it to provide as far as possible for the activities you want. There are a number of ways in which furniture can be modified or used differently, however.

All work areas need surfaces at which children can work. These may be built-in work tops, locker desks, tables or hinged flaps on the wall to give an extra surface when you need it.

Another way of providing suitable surfaces for messy work is to make table covers with hardboard with battens round the edge to keep mess from falling on the floor. These can be made to fit over one or more tables. Floor vinyl makes a good surface for such covers or for old tables with bad surfaces. You can also use a roll of floor vinyl to cover the floor or tables.

It has already been suggested that there are advantages in using work-tops for working and open shelves for storage. In providing shelving, it is useful to remember that space between shelves which is not used is wasted space. The shelves therefore need to be fairly close together, though not so close that you can't get to the back.

We have also noted that chairs take up a lot of space and are not always used. With younger children the floor is often a good place to work if it is carpeted and if you decide not to have a table and chair place for every child, some chairs can be packed away.

Stools are generally more versatile and less space-consuming than chairs and can be pushed away under tables when they are not needed. If your school has some really old chairs and the head is willing, you may like to saw the backs off some of them and cushion the seats to make some stools.

Storage is a problem in most classrooms. You need to store things in such a way that they are easy to find, placed so that a child does not have to wander round the room to collect things to do one job, easy to return and keep tidy as well as using space as economically as possible. Start thinking about storage by considering what you need to store for each aspect of your work and then see how this matches up with the space available. You are likely to need to find ways of improvising storage which matches the work you want to do. Look for spaces which could take additional shelves, including some high shelving for storing things not often needed. Look also for existing shelving which uses space uneconomically, which might be adapted for better use.

Cupboards are often more useful without their doors, or you can plan that when the doors are open your storage is carefully set out and the doors used for pinning up information or suspending material in pockets.

Flat materials can be suspended in bags, clear plastic if possible. These can be hung on wire coat hangers which in turn can be hung on a rail.

Trolleys are always useful, particularly for materials like paint, where you need to clean the surface where they are stored. A deep box trolley is very useful for various kinds of scrap material and for clay, provided there is a lid.

It has already been suggested that cupboards might be used as room dividers. Room dividers might also be made from corrugated card, wound round large tins filled with concrete or some other heavy material. You can also use wooden lattice, or, if you can afford it, you can make or buy room dividers of various kinds.

Earlier in this chapter we noted the importance of display as a teaching tool. Although one can put too much on display so that none of it is properly looked at, most primary teachers feel they could use more display space than they actually have. Pinboard is a very desirable wall covering, but if you have only a small amount, you can add to it in various ways.

Hessian wallpaper which takes pins is a very attractive surface which can be stuck straight onto plaster or over pinboard which has become unsightly. Corrugated card can be used in many ways and in particular will make bays. It can also be pinned to a small piece of pinboard to make a much larger display space. Carpet tiles of the cheapest kind also make a good pin-up surface and have the added advantage that they absorb noise. They are more expensive than pinboard but provide a more attractive background to display and can be bought a few at a time.

When you have arrived at the best arrangement of your furniture that you can devise, you then have the problem of how to keep it in order. It is important to train children to return things to their proper places after working with them, giving them the idea that it is their environment and that they need to care for it.

However good your children and however well you train them, the environment will stay attractive and well ordered only if you organise it well. A first rule is that everything must have its own labelled place. Where possible draw the outline of the item you are storing on the shelf or on the board where you plan to hang it and label the space. This enables you to make an immediate check as to whether things are in the right places. It also offers reading practice for younger children.

Similarly you can attach lists of pieces to all collections of apparatus and train children to check the items against the list each time they use the particular material. Small items such as rubbers and Sellotape which can often get lost need a large piece of wood attached to them, rather as hotels often attach large labels to their keys. They can then be hung from labelled space on peg board.

One fairly simple way of making sure that everything remains in its proper place is to allocate to each child a small area of classroom storage for which he or she is responsible – perhaps one shelf or section of a cupboard. That child's name can be stuck to the section together with a list of what should be there or things which must be checked or cleaned. You can then provide a short time at the end of each working session for each child to check that everything has been returned to its place and that the space is clean and tidy. This enables you to clear up very quickly and make sure that everyone takes a fair share of the work of clearing up.

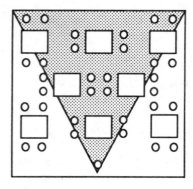

Figure 10.1 Teacher's sight lines

A quite different problem in the use of space concerns the suitability of your seating arrangements for the work you want to do. The way a group is seated makes a difference to their readiness to respond and interact with one another and with you. You may like to consider the following points:

Sight lines.

When a class is seated facing the teacher, the teacher's sight lines are as shown in Figure 10.1.

This means that the children in the non-shaded portion of the room are less easily seen than the others and it is surprising how often the very children who concentrate least well manage to be in this position. It is made doubly difficult, as can be seen from the diagram, by the fact that children normally have to turn their chairs round to face the teacher for work on a whole class basis.

Seating for discussion

If you want to encourage discussion with children interacting with one another as well as with you, you need to seat them so that they can see each other. A rough circle or U-shaped arrangement allows this. If you seat children round a square of tables and wish to use this for discussion, it is as well to remember that people tend not to talk with those on each side of them when they are sitting in a row, mainly because they cannot see each other's faces easily. The arrangement in the right-hand diagram in Figure 10.2 is less likely to encourage discussion than the arrangement in the left-hand diagram.

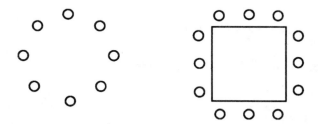

Figure 10.2 Arranging seating for discussion

7 Consider defining territory

We have already noted that children as well as adults like to have defined territory. It can be a bit disconcerting when sitting at a round table to find that one's territory is less defined than it is when sitting at a rectangular table (see Figure 10.3).

Figure 10.3 Defining territory

ANALYSIS 10.4:
THE USE OF TIME, SPACE AND RESOURCES

1 Could I improve the way I am using time?

2 Could I improve the way the children are using time?
   How much of the time are they on task?

3 Do children spend time waiting to see me?

4 Am I using space to the best advantage?

5 Does what I have displayed at the moment include
   both children's work and material to stimulate?

6 Are the children learning how to display things well?

7 Has everything in the classroom its proper place?
   Are all the places labelled?

8 Is there an established routine for the use of space and
   resources? Are all the children aware of it?

9 Are resources easily accessible and close to the places
   where they are to be used?

10 Have I a good scheme for getting everything returned
    to its proper place?

11 Is circulation about the classroom as good as I can
    make it?

One further point worth noting is that when you are asking children to work in pairs, it may be helpful to know that there is some evidence that young children prefer to work sitting beside a partner rather than sitting opposite and facing him or her as an adult would probably do. This may be something to consider in sitting down to help a child.

11 Individual children

Catering for individuals within a class is never easy, but the National Curriculum has made it more than ever necessary to think in terms of individual progress, since the teacher is now required to assess the way each child develops in relation to the Attainment Targets. This is a matter of not only establishing the point a child has reached but of using this to plan his or her future progress. It is clearly not possible to make an individual plan in every case and managing a class depends upon being able to deal with the needs of most children, if not in a class group, then in a smaller group of children at around the same stage in their work. You can then use the knowledge gained from assessment to match individuals whose needs are different from those of the majority and to select individuals within the groups who need some particular help.

In every class there will be children who need not only individual help with some of the work of the class or group but also, for some of the time at least, an individual programme. This is particularly noticeable since the *Education Act* (1981) which encouraged the integration of children with disabilities of all kinds. You may have one or two children in your class who would formerly have been in a special school. Since it is the responsibility of every teacher to try to teach every child in the class, you must do your utmost to provide for such children without neglecting others.

Children who have learning difficulties are at risk, whatever their age. They cannot afford to waste time. A lack of progress in the core subjects will make all their school learning difficult and this difficulty may increase as they grow older. It is therefore essential that they receive appropriate help as soon as possible.

Brennan's study of the curriculum offered to slow learners *Curricular needs of slow learners* (1979) showed that such children frequently achieve at a much lower level than their ability suggests. Low expectations on the part of teachers lead to a lack of confidence on the child's part and this is reinforced by each subsequent failure.

If you look at this problem from a different angle, you might say that every class is made up of individuals. Some of these individuals will be at about the same level for some work and will be able to learn together for part of the time. Others, for various reasons, may need a good deal of individual provision. This group is likely to include children with:

Low ability
Specific learning problems
Emotional/behavioural problems
Problems of sight or hearing
Physical disabilities
Gaps in schooling
Language problems including non-English speaking home background
Outstanding ability of some kind

It is often tempting for a busy teacher to provide time-filling activities for children who don't fit with the majority or to try one thing after another, without ever getting down to the particular needs of the individual. This is understandable, given the pressures on teachers, but you need to find ways of overcoming this problem if you are to enable all your children to make progress. In any case, the *Education Reform Act* (1988) commits you to giving access to the National Curriculum for all children.

Your first task is one of diagnosis. You will have discovered from records and observation which children have problems. Some of these, such as the child with a physical disability or a lack of English, are easy to identify and see the reasons for the problems; other problems, such as that of the child who is nine, but whose reading age is six, are comparatively easy to identify but it may be difficult to discover the reasons for the problem and still more difficult to know what to do about it. Yet other problems may pass unnoticed for a time, such as the child with an undiagnosed hearing problem. This is especially true where the child is quiet and well-behaved.

It is tempting to group together all these children but this isn't really the right answer. It may be helpful at this stage to look briefly at each of the groups listed and decide which of the categories above fit each of the children you have identified, remembering that a child may come into more than one category.

CHILDREN WITH LOW ABILITY

Children with low ability are likely to need a certain amount of special attention at every stage of schooling and this needs to be accepted and planned for. They are likely to be at an earlier stage of the National Curriculum than other children in the class and you will need to do a great deal to encourage them and reward their progress with praise and encouragement so that they are not depressed by this. You may also need to break down the Statements of Attainment into smaller steps that these children can actually take.

The extent of the special attention they will need will depend upon the class they are with. If they are in a class where the average IQ is well below 100, the work is likely to be nearer their needs than if they are in a class with an above average ability range. A child with a much higher IQ may need individual help if he or she is with a group of high flyers. This makes it difficult to talk about children with low or high ability in the abstract. Although the terms are defined by national norms of ability, the extent to which the level of ability of a particular individual child affects the work of the school or class is a matter of the norms within it as well as the particular ways in which the child's ability differs from the norm.

We have already looked at motivation for learning. It is particularly important to look at what motivates these children and to use this to help them to learn in appropriate areas. You also need to look at what they do and do not know within the core subjects and plan work to fill the gaps you discover. Teachers sometimes take the view that since children who are slow learners are poor at reasoning, they should learn by heart. This is unlikely to be a successful ploy, since they are likely to have a poorer memory than the majority anyway. What is needed is work designed to help them to learn to reason and develop appropriate strategies for learning, so that they gradually become more capable learners. All children need this teaching but in some ways the need to provide this for slow learners is greater than it is for others because of the limited amount of time you have to work with them.

Children with low ability tend to need short-term goals. You are more likely to be successful in teaching such a child if you identify clear objectives which you share with the child, which can be achieved with one lesson, or within an even shorter period. You then give praise when the objectives are achieved and perhaps record achievement somewhere for the child to see.

It is likely that there will always be children of low ability in your class. It is therefore worth while making or buying specific material for them, firstly for developing work in the core subjects and secondly to provide for them to develop their work in other aspects of the curriculum. This material can be used many times. If you add to this collection a little at a time and start with material you know you will need time after time, you gradually build a collection and this makes it easy to provide for children at the right level. The same approach is needed for very able children.

CHILDREN WITH SPECIFIC LEARNING DIFFICULTIES

These children form a very varied group. There will be some who are apparently of average or above average intelligence but who are not achieving at their proper level. There will be others who appear to have difficulties in one particular aspect of their work while managing the rest quite well. There may be children with minimal brain damage which creates problems for them and there may also be children with problems which have not yet been diagnosed except insofar as some of their school work seems to be well below average.

Children in this group may need special attention for a period and may then be able to cope normally. It is particularly important for the teacher to spend time analysing what they know and do not know and what they can do and not do, if time is not to be wasted. You may find the tests and suggestions in *Framework for reading* (Joan Dean and Ruth Nichols 1986) helpful so far as reading and writing are concerned. These tests cover all aspects of reading and the book then goes on to suggest what you can do about the problems you find.

CHILDREN WITH EMOTIONAL/BEHAVIOURAL PROBLEMS

Most teachers find the children in this group among the most difficult to deal with and the most demanding professionally. Mary Evans and Mary Wilson write in *Education of disturbed pupils* (1980) of teachers' views of the kind of school situation most likely to cope well with these children and found the most important characteristics to be as follows:

- warm, caring attitudes in adult /child relationships
- improvement of child's self-image through success
- individual counselling and discussion
- a varied and stimulating educational programme
- continuity in adult/child relationships
- firm, consistent discipline

Successful specialist teachers of these children tend to use one or both of two main ways of working with them. They make considerable effort to know the children well and this leads into counselling and discussion about work and behaviour. It sometimes involves teaching a child how to behave in a given social situation because sometimes children behave badly through ignorance of the acceptable thing to do.

The second approach is that of behaviour modification. This involves setting very specific goals which appear to be within the child's capacity to attain. For example, you might agree with a child that he or she will work quietly for ten minutes by the clock without getting up or speaking to anyone. If the child achieves this goal, you reward him or her with praise and perhaps a mark on a personal chart. You then go on to set further goals. If the child was unable to achieve the goal set then you make it easier – working for five minutes, for example. A detailed account of this way of working can be found in *Positive teaching: the behavioural approach* by Kevin Wheldall and Frank Merritt (1984).

In some cases you may find that a child who is easily distracted is helped if you can arrange for him or her to work in a carrel or booth. You can create corners for individual learning by placing hardboard between two tables or placing a cupboard at right angles to the wall. The child then sits facing the wall. Working there should be treated as a privilege rather than a punishment, since a distractable child may wish as fervently as you do that he or she could behave like other children. You may find that other children also like working in this situation.

From time to time you may experience a child who creates a situation which challenges your authority as a teacher and perhaps demonstrates to the group that he or she is managing you. The child swears at you, defies you, deliberately does something you have forbidden and creates a dramatic situation where all the children are waiting, breathless, to see what will happen. When this kind of situation occurs you usually have little time to think. The first thing is to retain a professional calm, acting the part of someone calm even if you are boiling inside. You can then take one of several courses of action.

1 You can separate the child from the others
   You may do this in various ways. You may perhaps take him or her out of the room or at least out of earshot, if not out of sight of other children, in order to talk without an audience. This is probably the best solution and has the advantage of ending the drama. How you deal with the child then will depend upon the particular child and the situation, but you have a better chance of making an impression when the child is not playing to the gallery.
2 You can assert your authority
   You can do this in any way you think may be effective. Some teachers demonstrate blank astonishment that anyone could do such a thing; others produce a show of anger, looking directly at the child and maintaining eye contact while moving towards him or her. Both of these can work, but you have to feel reasonably confident that this kind of action won't lead to further defiance. It is also easier to stay in control of the situation if you are acting as if you are astonished or angry and not really feeling it. This is often difficult to do.

3 You can pass it off lightly

You can imply that it is not important or treat it as a joke or by saying something like 'I'm sure you didn't really mean that. How about starting again?' Then you take a later opportunity to talk to the child in question and try to find out what caused the outburst.

4 You can behave as if nothing has happened

You can more or less ignore the behaviour at the time and discuss it later. If you are dealing with a child whose behaviour is known to be abnormal and recognised by the other children to be so, this is not an unreasonable thing to do, especially if you can couple it with an opportunity to retract or re-phrase what was said. A comment like 'I didn't quite hear that. Would you mind repeating it?' very frequently produces something more moderate.

It may also be useful to keep a note of the situations where a child has been particularly difficult, noting also what led up to the situation. If you do this over a period, you may be able to see a pattern in what triggers unacceptable behaviour and this may enable you to avoid situations which create problems or discuss them with the child in question to see if he or she can overcome the problem.

PROBLEMS OF SIGHT AND HEARING

One result of the 1981 *Education Act* is that you may now have within your class children with serious problems of sight or hearing. They may be with you for only part of the time and in a school-based unit for the rest of the time, but you need, nevertheless, to be aware of the problems they have and the implications of those problems for you as teacher.

Children with poor vision need very good light for their work. They certainly need to sit near a window and may need an individual reading lamp. They also need to sit near the board and may need someone to read what is on it to them. Whiteboards are easier for them to read than blackboards and they may manage better with work written in felt pen on a large sheet of paper, providing the writing is large enough. Worksheets also need to be in black on white.

You may need to familiarise such a child with the classroom layout and where things are when he or she first joins you. Such children may also need familiarising with the school layout, but it is likely that this will be done by a unit teacher. It is useful to use clockface directions in describing where something is if the child is old enough to understand them.

If a child has had poor sight from birth, he or she will have developed a rather different picture of the world from a sighted child and this may affect the way concepts have been formed.

One very common sight defect which is not sufficiently noticed in schools is colour blindness. You are quite likely to have at least one child in your class who has a degree of colour blindness. This creates problems for the child when things are colour coded as well as problems in art and craft and in daily life. This is a defect which cannot be remedied, but if you know about it, you can help the child in question by giving other references as well as colour.

It is easy to check whether you have any colour blind children by asking everyone to draw a flag with diagonals on it which make four triangles. You then ask them to colour the section as you do and you show them a flag coloured with some sections red and some green. Colour blind children will have difficulty in doing this because red/green colour blindness is the most common. They will, however, have learned to make up for their deficiency and will identify red and green crayons, perhaps by reading their labels or by some marking on them. It is important not to give any clues by saying the colour names. They will also look to see what other children are doing. It may therefore be best to divide the class in half. One lot of children might then be asked to colour their flags in blue and orange, which are the other colours often confused, and the others red and green and then they could change over. Look out for children who are looking around to see what other people are doing. They are quite likely to be colour blind.

Children with hearing problems also need to sit near the board and they will need to see your face as you speak if they are to understand what you say. Try to avoid talking while you are writing on the board or asking children to look at something on their tables while you talk about it. A child with hearing problems will find this very difficult.

A child who has had poor hearing from birth will almost certainly have more limited speech than his or her contemporaries and will therefore have more difficulty in understanding. Speech problems will include not only pronunciation but also limitations in vocabulary and language structure and this may need explaining to other children who may find such a child odd, because of the peculiar speech. It is best to do this some time when the child in question is not there.

In both the case of visually impaired and hearing impaired children, it is important to see that they have with them and are using the aids they need. Glasses and hearing aids are essential to them but they do not always want to use them. The teacher can do much to help the child to find these aids more acceptable.

CHILDREN WITH PHYSICAL DISABILITIES

You may also have in your class a child or children with physical problems of one kind or another. It is very easy to assume that such children will make slower progress than children without such problems, but this is not necessarily the case. Children with physical disabilities probably represent the same range of ability as that in the normal population and their needs need to be assessed in much the same way.

The major problem you have to tackle with such children is what they can do physically. There will normally be advice available to you about what the problems are and how best to tackle them. They may have considerable difficulty in subjects like science and technology if their hands are affected by their disability and you may need to find ways in which they can be enabled to do the work that others do, perhaps by working with a partner or by supporting them in some way. They may be able to do some things in physical education and generally should be encouraged to join in as much as possible, provided that medical advice allows this.

You may also have children with a variety of medical conditions including such problems as epilepsy and possibly AIDS. Each needs to be dealt with according to the advice offered by doctors and parents, but you would be wise to find out all you can about any disability suffered by a child in your class. Your task is to help him or her to learn and if your knowledge, is good you can make provision with more confidence.

CHILDREN WITH GAPS IN SCHOOLING

A child may have missed a period at school through illness or for other reasons. He or she may also have been taught badly or missed something by changing schools. This will be much more evident now that all children are working through the National Curriculum. It should also be rather easier to discover where the gaps are. Careful analysis will be especially important for initial reading and number operations. It is a good idea to have some appropriate test material on tape or on paper so that you can find out, for example, whether a child has all the phonic knowledge needed at the stage the rest of the class have reached, or whether the child has sufficient knowledge of spelling rules, what his or her knowledge of the four rules of number actually is, and so on. Suitable tests for reading and writing skills are given in *Framework for reading* (Dean and Nichols 1986), and in many other places, but it is not difficult for a teacher or a school to make tests for such a purpose.

It is not sufficient to discover what is missing, however. You also need teaching material you can use with such a child on an individual basis. Once again the best way to build an appropriate stock of this is to make or buy a little at a time, each piece having a specific purpose.

CHILDREN WITH LANGUAGE PROBLEMS

Language problems range from the child who comes into the school with virtually no English because this is not the language used at home, to the child whose language is so far from standard English that he or she has difficulty in understanding and being understood. They also include children who have some impediment in their speech or difficulty in using and understanding normal language. Where there is a group of children with similar problems who can perhaps be helped together, perhaps by a specialist teacher, this is less of a problem than where the situation is one of a single individual who has problems which create demands on the single classroom teacher with everything else to do. On the other hand, if the problem is that of not speaking English, the lone individual may make more progress than the child in a group where there are other children speaking his or her own language.

Almost all language problems involve some work on a one-to-one basis and it is clearly impossible for a teacher with a normal class to provide for this on any scale. You therefore need to consider what other help you can muster and, if you find it, how you can organise the work so that the time is well used. Parents may be willing to come in to talk to children who need practice in English. The *Non-statutory guidance in English* (NCC 1989b), suggests that it might be helpful to invite in speakers of the child's mother tongue who would read stories in that language and then go through the same stories in English.

Other parents might come in to help these children, perhaps introducing words and phrases in everyday use in the classroom. In dealing with children with a limited knowledge of English it is important to use the same phrases many times in the same context. In managing the day-to-day work of the classroom there are many occasions for this. Phrases like 'put your things away'; 'put your coats on'; 'wash your hands for lunch' and so on, will soon be picked up by children learning English who will be able to see what the phrases mean by the actions of other children. You can then get different children to say the phrases so that those learning English get practice in speaking.

Individual work for such children might involve work with tapes and pictures or tapes and slides, designed to teach the names of everyday objects and actions.

Work with children with language disabilities should involve advice from the speech therapist. This is likely to vary from one child to another, according to individual need.

THE CHILD WITH OUTSTANDING ABILITY

In any class there will be children who are more able than the majority in some or all of the work of the class, who will need individual programmes for some work. From time to time you may encounter a child who is so far ahead of the group that he or she needs an individual programme for almost everything or at least a variation of the class or group programme. It is tempting to believe that such children are easy to identify and don't need any extra help because they can get on by themselves. The evidence from a number of studies suggests that this is not the case; that some gifted children use their ability to hide their gifts and that not all of them are known to their teachers, particularly if they are disinclined to conform and do as they are told.

If you want to be sure that you are catering for children of outstanding ability you need to do the following:

1 Develop your skill in identifying children of outstanding ability
   Look particularly for the child who is unusual in some way, who asks unusual questions or has original ways of looking at things. Where you have queries about such a child, ask if he or she can be seen by an Educational Psychologist.
2 Make sure that your overall programme is rich and varied enough for latent gifts to emerge
   Some people reveal their gifts only if the circumstances are right and when something strikes a chord for them.
3 Consider possible teaching approaches for a child of outstanding ability
   Try to ensure that you ask questions and present material at a variety of levels and that you include open-ended questions in any questioning session.
4 Assess carefully levels of ability and stages of development within the class
   Examine the ways in which you check on the abilities and stages of development of your children. Is it possible that you have a child who could do much more demanding work than you are giving him or her? It may be a good idea to go through the register asking this question and then check up on any children whom you think may have more ability than is apparent, by talking further with them and looking at their work.
5 Organise work at different levels
   With any topic work you plan to do with the whole class, see that there are, within the plan, opportunities for doing more or doing work which is more demanding. Very able children don't necessarily want the next stage of the work which is in hand, although it may sometimes be appropriate to go on to the next level in the National Curriculum. They are often able to do more than their peers and can enjoy a richer programme involving their own investigations or ideas which you or

they suggest. It is a waste of any child's time to do more of work that is already mastered, although it can sometimes be difficult to avoid this.

6 Consider the basic curriculum in relation to such a child

Since able children are likely to learn fast, their basic learning can be more concentrated than that for other children. It may be a good idea to look through the books and materials you are using to see if there are short cuts or ways in which a child who grasps things easily can get through the essential work more quickly than the majority. Try building a collection of material for the faster workers. It multiplies the material available if a group of teachers collaborate in making and collecting such material and share it.

A child who works quickly has time for other work. Try to find some genuine problems which are within the capacity of such a child and if possible enlist help from parents, students and others who may be interested. For example, the production of a school or local guide book for new children and their parents or for people in the area is a project which requires a good deal of research and needs to be written and presented with a particular readership in mind. Such project material must actually be used, however, and the child must be aware of this from the outset; otherwise the discipline of working in a real situation will be lost. A further project might be to evaluate the success of this work.

We noted that children with learning problems need to be encouraged to become independent learners, as much, if not more, than other children. Children of high ability have a particular need to acquire learning skills so that they are able to work independently and are not too dependent on a busy teacher.

SPECIAL NEEDS AND THE NATIONAL CURRICULUM

Work with children with special needs takes on a new challenge with the advent of the National Curriculum. The National Curriculum Council's guidance paper *A curriculum for all* (1989e) starts with the statement 'All pupils share the right to a broad and balanced curriculum, including the National Curriculum'. This document makes it clear that it sees all pupils working towards the Attainment Targets, even if some spend a very long time getting to the starting point. It also makes it clear that all pupils are intended to follow a curriculum which is wider than the National Curriculum.

Many teachers find it difficult to provide for children with learning difficulties because their training did little to prepare them for this kind of problem. There is nothing mysterious about the skills needed, however. They are an extension of the skills needed by every teacher and can be learned by anyone ready to make the necessary effort.

Successful work with children with learning problems

It may be helpful to look at the factors associated with successful work with children with learning problems. You are most likely to be successful in teaching such children if you:

1 Study them as individuals with interests and a preferred style of working and make a careful diagnosis of the nature of their problems.
2 Devise a programme for each child to meet the needs revealed by the diagnosis and involve the child in setting and achieving realistic short-term goals.
3 Break down the necessary learning into steps which are small enough for the child to take successfully, but which also have purpose in his or her eyes and involve decision-making and thinking and are not over-dependent on memory.
4 Enable each child to see his or her own progress and reinforce learning, including the behaviour you want, by specific praise and encouragement and perhaps by charting progress in some way so that the child can see how he or she is doing.
5 Provide opportunities for each child to learn to take responsibility and become independent.
6 Provide genuine opportunities for these children to contribute to the life and work of the class.
7 Gain the cooperation of each child's family and work with the parents to help them to find specific ways of helping their child.
8 Keep careful records and review progress regularly, often involving the children themselves.
9 Maintain a positive attitude in all circumstances and provide many opportunities that are more likely to lead to success than failure.

It is possible to take a positive approach even in the areas in which a child is weak. Most children are anxious to do well and if you can get a child to join you in setting targets and achieving them in a given time, you enable that child to work positively to improve and add to achievement.

For example, suppose you want a child to improve his or her knowledge of multiplication facts. One way forward would be to agree a target day by which some of this learning would have been achieved and then discuss all the possible ways of working to achieve this. A child might, for example, dictate tests onto tape and then play them back, writing the answers. Another possibility would be to work with another child playing games designed to teach the particular learning needed, and so on.

Legislation following *The Warnock Report* (1978) means that all schools may eventually contain children with disabilities. This has many advantages for the children, both those with special needs and others, but it also poses problems, because children with serious disabilities will be expected to cope with as much of the normal school programme as possible and to follow the National Curriculum. It will take time for teachers to discover how much a child can do and what may be expected of him or her. This is knowledge which will be built up over time as schools get experience of integration.

It would probably be fair to say that many people with disabilities can, if motivated, do more than other people think they can and this should be encouraged. Older children, in particular, need to be encouraged to be helpful but not to make pets of small children with physical disabilities but to treat them as they would other children except where their disability requires particular attention. In the main, the way children with special needs are treated by other children will come from the example set by the school staff.

The children we have been considering, both those with serious disabilities and those with various kinds of learning and other problems, may or may not be a problem to the teacher. They may give you a permanently guilty conscience because you feel you should be doing more, but they will not necessarily disrupt the work of the class. Some of them and some other children also will be disruptive and you need to consider these children as individuals too.

Children with and without disabilities may pose problems in school. Difficulties such as poor sight or hearing or motor control problems, hyperactivity and others may make the normal programme of work inappropriate or lead to problems of understanding which result in disruptive behaviour. Maladjusted children may create a range of disturbances and may have difficulty in relating to others. Personal problems may occupy a child's mind to the exclusion of everything else.

Although there is provision in the *Education Reform Act* (1988) for disapplication of the National Curriculum to certain children under particular circumstances, it is clear from the National Curriculum Council's booklet *A curriculum for all* (1989e) that this is not intended to be used to any great extent. The booklet says:

> Only a few pupils should require 'exceptional arrangements' for modifications or exemptions and only when the National Curriculum requirements are impossible to achieve or are inappropriate to the pupil's very specialised needs.

It is unlikely that a child with special needs in a primary school will be allowed exceptional arrangements, although it must be accepted that there will be children who spend most of their time in the primary school achieving level one in some subject areas. The task of the teacher is therefore to seek ways of helping all children to achieve.

From your point of view, while it is valuable to know what causes a particular difficulty, the more important question is how to deal with it. Part of knowing how to deal with it is knowing enough about it to know

---

ANALYSIS 11.1:
INDIVIDUAL CHILDREN

1   Which children in my class need to be treated individually for much of the time because of their special needs?

2   Have I diagnosed the problems of each of them?

3   Have I provided suitable programmes for each of them which are designed to meet their particular needs?

4   Have I any children with outstanding ability? Can I recognise the signs of outstanding ability when the child in question tries to disguise it?

5   Am I aware of all the children who have problems of sight or hearing? Could there be some children with these problems which have not been diagnosed?

6   Have I any children who are colour blind? If so, what am I doing to help them?

7   How well am I coping with children who have behaviour problems? Have I strategies for dealing with the difficulties they create?

8   Am I creating situations in which children with special needs experience success?

9   Does my organisation enable me to spend time with these children? Have I organised their work so that they do not waste time?

what is possible and what is impossible. It is easy to be so concerned by what you discover about a child's background and so sympathetic towards him or her that you give too little attention to learning needs. The fact that Jackie lives daily with violence and family rows, may make you sympathetic when she finds it difficult to concentrate, but it may be that the most helpful thing you can do is to help her to succeed in learning to read. Every teacher needs to be a sympathetic human being, but no teacher has enough time to be a psychologist as well. It is generally better to concentrate on the professional task of being a teacher, showing human understanding as part of your everyday relationship with children.

12 Working with parents

One important effect of the National Curriculum is that parents will be given a much clearer picture of how their children are doing in school. This has implications for the teacher who may now need to work more closely with parents than ever before.

Many schools have developed excellent work with parents but research suggests that there is still quite a way to go if schools are to create the kind of cooperation with parents which will truly support their children's learning. Janet Atkin *et al.* in *Listening to parents* (1988) suggest that when parents understand what the school is trying to do, identify with its goals and support its efforts, understand something of their role as educators and take an interest in and provide support for their children's school work, then the effects can be both dramatic and long lasting. They state that 'parents are an essential resource and also have unique opportunities as educators'. The school needs to harness this resource for the learning of children.

Both parents and teachers have stereotypes of each other and the parents' view of teachers will be largely formed by their own experience of school. This has left some people very hesitant about entering a school and talking with their children's teachers. The stereotypes held by parents will depend upon their own level of education and past experience. They may see teachers as the fount of all knowledge and wisdom, as intimidating figures or as rather underpaid employees. Teachers, for their part, often blame parents for the problems their children create in school and frequently comment that it is the parents who do not come to school whom they would most like to see. Teachers may also hold the view that working-class parents are not particularly interested in their children's progress at school and this is particularly so where black parents are concerned. Tizard *et al.* (1988) note that 70 per cent of teachers in their study made negative comments about black parents – mainly that they were 'over-concerned with their children's education', 'had too high expectations', 'lacked understanding of British education' and so on. The same study found that virtually all parents said they gave their children help with school work and more black than white parents started to teach their children to read before they started school. It would seem that there are really very few parents who are not interested in their children's progress but some are hesitant about coming to the school to meet teachers

Janet Atkin *et al.* (1988) suggest that schools do not give parents sufficient of the right sort of information. Parents get their ideas of what the school is doing mainly from their children and from looking at the work their children are doing. They will probably not be aware of the educational philosophy of the school, its policies and teaching strategies. Teachers too rarely explain what the term's work will consist of and suggest ways in which parents might help. Nor do they explain the processes by which they are helping children to learn. In general parents tend to get the message that teachers would rather they left the business of educating children to them. In practice most parents try to help and this help is a resource which is too rarely harnessed.

Tizard *et al.* (1988) found that teachers did not give a great deal of feedback on children's progress. In the reception class, 41 per cent of white parents and 16 per cent of black had been told how their child's reading compared with that of other children. In the middle infants these figures were 44 per cent and 23 per cent. They were concerned to find that only 20 per cent of parents had been told that their child was having difficulties when testing suggested that the overall figure was considerably higher. Only 12 per cent of reception parents had been told that their child posed behaviour problems although the teachers said that 26 per cent of children posed such problems. There was also the feeling on the part of some parents that teachers tended to be defensive about problems rather than being prepared to discuss them openly.

Bruce Carrington and Geoffrey Short (1989) suggest a number of ways in which the school may contribute to the non-involvement of parents. This may happen when:

- teachers are unwilling to work with parents who are regarded as non-professional and therefore not qualified to offer anything
- teachers foster the view that the parent's duties cease at the school gate
- the school structures visiting arrangements for parents in such a way that some parents are prevented from coming by work commitments

PARENTS AS PARTNERS

Listening to parents (Atkin *et al.* 1988) gives a list of concerns and suggestions:

1 The development of practical arrangements for effective communication between parents, teachers and pupils lies at the heart of good home/school relationships. Parents need to see, discuss, experience and develop understanding.
2 Effective basic communication needs to be backed up by a range of appropriate opportunities for parents to participate in their children's schooling
3 Schools need to recognise, support and strengthen the crucial role of parents as educators.
4 Parents represent a valuable but often unacknowledged resource which can be tapped to great effect in the education of children and young people.

The studies all suggest that there is much to be gained from treating parents as partners in the education of their children. If the large majority of parents are keen to help their children to do well in school, this is a resource which teachers would do well to use. Parents who are keen to help their children will do this anyway, however much teachers discourage them. The studies quoted above suggested that in mathematics, teachers generally discouraged parents from helping, but nevertheless many parents worked with their children. When we consider how many opportunities parents have for teaching their children mathematics in practical situations, it seems a pity not to encourage them to make use of these.

Nursery and reception class teachers are well aware that children's home background makes all the difference to the way that children settle into school. Wells (1985) found the strongest association with attainment at age seven was the child's knowledge of written language at entry to school. Tizard *et al.* (1988) found that letter identification at nursery stage was a stronger predictor of reading ability at top infant level than concepts about print or word-matching. They also found that the children of parents who tried to teach them to read and used books scored higher at later stages. The number of books a child had access to was also a predictor of good performance.

Tizard *et al.* also found that families with high incomes did no more than other families to help their children, but gave them more experience with books. They were also likely to have a greater knowledge of schools and believe that success was due to family influence. Mothers with higher educational qualifications were more likely to have positive attitudes towards helping their children but did not give their children significantly more help. Progress in reading and writing through the infant school was significantly related to parental contact with the school.

Hughes (1986) investigated the mathematical knowledge possessed by pre-school children and found that when children were asked to work in practical situations, it was considerably greater than might be expected. However, he found that even at this stage, there was about a year's difference in performance between children from working-class and middle-class homes. This suggests that schools need to do everything possible to help parents of pre-school children to prepare them for school. A number of schools have developed packs of material which parents of pre-school children can use at home with their children in preparation for school. These encourage parents to use opportunities for children's learning and help them to understand what the school may want later.

There are a number of ways in which a school can facilitate home – school links, including the obvious ones like establishing a parents', teachers' and friends' association. Schools can also :

– provide social functions where parents, teachers and other interested parties can mix on an informal basis
– organise parents' meetings in a flexible way so that everyone has the chance to come
– provide opportunities for parents to meet in small groups to discuss common problems with teachers. This requires skill on the teacher's part but could be both helpful to parents and also to the teacher in understanding how parents view things.
– establish a parents' room where parents can meet, make coffee, look at books and undertake work for the school's benefit
– develop a plan in which a parent is responsible for involving parents in each particular road in the catchment area, welcoming new parents and visiting parents who don't come to meetings
– develop shared reading plans where the parents agree to hear the child read at home each day and note what has been done
– involve parents in other work, such as mathematics, asking them to use opportunities for children's mathematical learning and work with children to practise necessary skills
– involve parents in topic work, perhaps asking for stories about their youth or inviting them to help with an outing or in collecting material and information
– ask parents to help with recording stories on tape for children to follow with text
– ask parents who can type to type stories by children at their dictation. These stories then become reading material for the child who has written them and for others.

COMMUNICATION WITH PARENTS

Parents have a unique view of their children which is much more comprehensive than a teacher's can possibly be. Teachers have therefore a good deal to learn from parents about the children they teach, but little opportunity is usually provided for this. What is needed is a regular meeting where both teachers and parents inform each other. The parents inform the teacher about the child and how they view what seems to be happening in school and the teacher informs the parents about the work which the child's class will be doing and how they can help. Both teacher and parents also discuss frankly the problems they are encountering and discuss how they can work together to overcome them.

The studies suggest that there are two further ways in which teachers are not always effective in communicating with parents. In talking about how parents can help they tend to dwell on what not to do, rather than on what to do. They are also inclined to use what parents see as educational jargon. The problem about jargon is that one person's jargon is another person's technical language. Teachers quite properly have ways of talking about what they do which are particular to the education profession but are confusing to other people. It is a good idea for a group of teachers to try to think of all the words and phrases they use which will be seen by others as jargon. For example, topic work, environmental studies, sets, mapping, number, RE, CDT, not to mention all the language which has come in with the *Educational Reform Act* – key stages, levels, Statements of Attainment, Attainment Targets, SATs and many other words and phrases are unfamiliar to parents because they have all come into being since parents were at school themselves. They need either explaining or avoiding.

The appearance of communications to parents is also important and with word-processing and desk-top publishing it is becoming possible for anyone to produce good looking-material. General communications to parents should be short, arranged so that they are easy and quick to read, perhaps with large headlines which stand out. The language needs to be friendly and lacking in jargon and complicated sentences should be avoided. Parents have usually a good deal to distract their attention and anything complicated or long probably will not be read. Where appropriate, communications will need to be in more than one language so that they are intelligible to all the parents. Parents themselves may be able to help with the problem of translating and re-writing documents in other languages.

If parents are really going to be partners in their children's education they need to be taken into the confidence of the school a great deal more than is often the case. Many of the plans for learning need to be discussed with parents. At the level of the individual class, each teacher needs to consider how to inform parents about the work being planned. There is much to be said for meetings of parents of one class at a time when you can talk about the work the class will be doing and the way in which parents can help with it. Methods need to be explained as well as outcomes so that parents can learn how to work with their children in ways which complement the work the teacher is doing. There is also a need for plenty of time for questions and discussion.

You may also like to consider a class newsletter which informs parents about the work in hand and how parents can help. This might also include information about school journeys and visits and what is needed for them as well as what may be needed for different aspects of other work. A newsletter may also be a good place to ask for specific help with particular activities, such as helping with a trip or making costumes for a play. It will, of course, be important not to cover the same ground as any school newsletter and it may be necessary again to enlist the help of certain parents to translate the letter into other languages.

The major piece of communication with parents is now the discussion of each child's progress. Teachers must inform parents of where their child has reached in the National Curriculum, and although this can be done on paper, there should also be a meeting at which the details of what is being said can be explained.

Assessing the National Curriculum (SEAC 1990c) suggests that the intentions behind reporting are as follows:

— to widen access to information about the school's curriculum plans and objectives for individual pupils and classes in the case of parents and more generally for the school as a whole
— to provide parents with the information necessary to support an informed dialogue with the school and with the children themselves about their achievements, progress and future work throughout their school career
— to encourage partnership between schools and parents by sharing information and explaining its implications
— to enable a school to report on the overall accomplishments of its pupils in ways that not only parents but also the wider community can appreciate

Most teachers will regard it as important that children see their progress as improving on their own performance and tend to discourage too much comparison with other children. However, parents will certainly want to know, not only where their child stands currently, but how he or she stands in relation to other children of the same age. In most cases this will be a fairly complex picture with children being well up with the age group or beyond it for some work and doing less well in other areas. The chart below has been suggested by the School Examinations and Assessment Council for recording a seven year old pupil's achievement in mathematics. It shows the areas in which the pupil is doing well (Attainment Target 2 and 3) and the areas in which he or she is doing less well (Attainment Target 6). Attainment Target 7 does not apply to this age group. It gives the teacher a picture of the areas on which the child needs to concentrate and would be valuable in discussion with the child's parents although it would take some time to prepare this kind of graph for all the children for each of the three core subjects. However, the basic graph could be duplicated so that all that is needed is to fill in the line of the graph. This record would also be valuable to the next teacher.

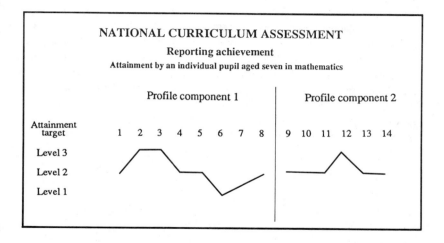

Figure 12.1 National Curriculum assessment chart

This kind of visual presentation will still require quite a lot of explanation if parents are to understand about levels and Attainment Targets but it helps to answer questions about how the child stands in relation to other children because it can readily be seen that the answer is a complex one. Every child will have a different profile.

Discussion of this profile needs to be followed up by discussion of what teacher and parents can do to help the child in the areas where he or she is at the lower levels. Try to have some really positive suggestions about ways in which the parents could help and give them a clear idea of what you are planning to do.

It is important in these discussions to keep a positive view in all that is said. Try to emphasize the areas in which the child is doing well and be positive about action to be taken where he or she is doing less well. Try also to avoid over-stressing what not to do and concentrate instead on what they can do.

Discussions with each child's parents need to go further than discussion about the core subjects. Progress in other areas needs to be discussed and any problems of behaviour. Teachers, not unnaturally, feel that this is a very delicate area which could imply that they are not doing their job or that the parent is not doing his or her job. Tizard *et al.* (1988) report that in the one in four cases where teachers actually discussed behaviour with parents 35 per cent of parents responded positively; 36 per cent agreed with the teacher; 25 per cent responded negatively and 15 per cent couldn't see the problem. There was also a good deal of difference between the views of parents and teachers. Thirty per cent of children regarded as a problem by teachers were also thought a problem by parents and 34 per cent of those seen as problems by parents were seen as problems by teachers. This suggests that children often differ in their behaviour between home and school and that there is everything to be gained from parents and teachers each knowing about the problems the other finds and working together to overcome them. Parents are also often grateful for the opportunity to discuss the problems they encounter with someone else.

It has been customary for most discussions about children to take place on the school premises. However, there is a great deal to be said for visiting the children's homes to discuss them with their parents. Parents feel more confident on their own ground and usually appreciate the fact that a teacher has taken the trouble to come to see them. This kind of meeting can be more relaxed than a meeting in school where there may be others waiting to see the teacher and it gives the opportunity for you to learn about the parents' view of the child. You can also learn a great deal about a child by seeing his or her home setting and the discussion tends to go better than it sometimes does at school. This takes time but is very rewarding. It is important in doing this to acquire techniques for finishing a meeting so that you do not spend too long in any one home. Usually putting one's papers together and making summarising statements give an indication that the meeting is ending.

Schools also now have to send parents a written report on children's progress. This needs to state where each child has reached in the National Curriculum and also report on other areas of work and such areas as work skills, behaviour, attitudes and any problems. It will also need to give information about the average class performance. Decisions about the nature of such reports will be made at school level, but again it will be important to be positive as well as honest and there is much to be said for a report which allows parents to comment and, possibly with older children, for them to comment also.

PARENTS IN THE CLASSROOM

It has become common practice in primary schools to invite parents to help in the classroom or about the school. This has a lot of advantages in that parents begin to see how teaching takes place and this not only helps them to support their own children, but may well make them good advocates for the school. The teacher is also helped in many of the tasks which take time from the more professional aspects of teaching.

There are also problems. The first and most difficult problem is that of whether you select the parents who come in to help or take all comers. Where parents are selected this can lead to a good deal of bitterness and upset, but avoids the problem of the parent who wants to take over or the parent who is not very literate. On the other hand, it may be that the kinds of parents who are not selected are just those who would benefit most from being in the school and working with teachers. The problem of the parent who appears to want to take over may disappear if the teacher is clear what he or she wants and the problem of literacy is partly a matter of the tasks parents are asked to do. However, this too is something of a problem since there are inferences to be made from the tasks which are allocated to parents. It is also important to stress to parents helping in the school the need for confidentiality about the work of other children than their own.

In inviting parents to work in school, you will need to discover what any individual parent can offer. A parent may have special knowledge and skills which could be used very widely in the school. It is also important to plan the work of parents and any other ancillary help in considerable detail. Neville Bennett and Joy Kell in *A good start?* (1989) make the point that in many of the classes they observed, ancillary helpers and parents were left to their own devices and in some cases were not supporting the teacher in a very satisfactory way because the teacher had not thought out how to use their services.

They list the tasks done by parents and auxiliaries in the infant schools in their study as shown in Table 11.1 overleaf.

The *Non-statutory guidance in English* (NCC 1989b) suggests that bilingual parents might help by reading and tape-recording stories in the home language of children in the class and then working with them to assist in translating the story into English.

If you have parents helping you in the classroom, think out in detail what you want them to do and how you want them to react to children. If you have parents hearing reading, for example, you should make it clear what you want the parent to do if a child is stuck for a word. If parents are supervising children playing with sand or water, or working at cooking, they need to know how they can introduce appropriate language and encourage children to experiment and discover. Play is more effective for learning when an adult takes part, but the adult needs to know what he or she is doing. Some parents will do these things instinctively. Others will need help, but in helping them to see what is needed in the classroom, you will also be helping them to see what it is important to do in the home.

Table 12.1 Percentage division of tasks by parents and auxiliaries

	Auxiliaries	Parents
Pre-language and mathematics	70%	40%
Work with materials	66%	32%
Art and craft	56%	51%
Domestic care	54%	15%
Reading	38%	34%
Home economics	32%	51%
Imaginative play/talk	25%	17%

This all suggests that teachers need tactfully to give parents some training in some aspects of helping in the classroom. It may be best to ask them to undertake tasks like preparing materials in the first instance and gradually to involve them with children.

ANALYSIS 12.1:
WORKING WITH PARENTS

1 Do I know all the parents of children in my class by sight?

2 Do I discuss each child with his or her parents at some time during the year?

3 Do we discuss behaviour as well as academic and other progress?

4 Do I listen to what parents can tell me about their children as well as telling them what I have discovered?

5 Do I try to avoid jargon and explain the terms we are using in school?

6 Am I ever too defensive about what I am doing?

7 Do I keep parents informed about the work we are doing in class?

8 Do I explain to parents the way I am trying to teach their children?

9 Do I make positive suggestions about ways in which parents can help their children in different aspects of the curriculum?

10 Am I making use of any particular skills and knowledge among my parents?

11 Am I making use of parents in the classroom?

12 Do I plan what they do each day, so that they reinforce my work?

13 Evaluation and assessment

We have heard a great deal about evaluation and assessment in recent years and the *Education Reform Act* (1988) has built into it a requirement for testing children at 7, 11, 14 and 16. It would be easy to forget that we all evaluate all kinds of things throughout our lives and teachers have always evaluated the work of their children. The change we are experiencing is towards more systematic and regular evaluation with outcomes available to parents and others.

Normal living involves us all in the process of making judgements about people and events in order to predict what may happen and decide what to do next. We do this from a very early age and it becomes our normal response to new situations. This is evident when you go to a course or if you are on holiday and meet new people. You listen to them, look at them and ask questions to discover the ways in which they are like you and the ways in which they differ and what their interests are, and so on. The judgements you make may not always be accurate, but this may not matter in such circumstances, particularly if you are aware that you are making judgements on inadequate evidence.

As a professional teacher, however, you need to be much more sure of your evidence because much depends upon the outcome of your judgements. You therefore need to extend the everyday practice of making judgements in order to make sure that the judgements you make are as valid as possible. This is one of the purposes of the Standard Assessment Tasks (SATs).

As a teacher, irrespective of external tests, you need to check and test and observe children, question them and explore their thinking about what they are doing, so that you can lead them on from the point they have reached.

There is now a legal requirement for teachers to keep records which must include for each pupil material on the pupil's academic achievement, other skills and abilities and progress in the school and this material must be updated at least once a year. This record will chart each child's progress through the National Curriculum and it will be a record of current performance, rather than future potential.

The report of the *task group on assessment and testing* (DES 1988) makes the following point:

> The assessment process itself should not determine what is to be taught and learned. It should be the servant, not the master of the curriculum. Yet it should not simply be a bolt-on addition at the end. Rather, it should be an integral part of the education process, continually providing 'feedback' and 'feed forward'. It therefore needs to be incorporated systematically into teaching strategies and practices at all levels. Since the results of assessment can serve a number of purposes, these purposes have to be kept in mind when the arrangements for assessments are designed.

The *Non-statutory guidance in English* (NCC 1989b) suggests two key principles:

1 Assessment is an integral part of learning; teachers must provide children with the opportunity to reflect on what they have done, that which is kept, collected and selected by the child and the teacher will help the child to review the success and progress of his or her learning

2 It should lead to a response; gathering and recording evidence is not an end in itself but a means of informing the next stage of learning for the child and teacher

Assessing the National Curriculum (SEAC 1990c) also offers some principles:

1 The assessment should arise from current classroom practice
2 A task should build on a pupil's previous experience
3 A task should be clear to the pupils who need to know what is expected

The report of the *Task group on assessment and testing* (DES 1988) which looked at how the assessment of individual children might be undertaken starts by stating that a school can function effectively only if it has adopted:

– clear aims and objectives;
– ways of gauging the achievement of these;
– comprehensible language for communicating the extent of those achievements to pupils, their parents and teachers, and the wider community, so that everyone can take informed decisions about action.

The report goes on to give four criteria which it feels any system of assessment should satisfy:

1 the assessment results should give direct information about pupils' achievement in relation to objectives: they should be criterion-referenced;

2 the results should provide a basis for decisions about pupils' learning needs;

3 the scales or grades should be capable of comparison across classes and schools, if teachers, pupils and parents are to share a common language and common standards; so the results should be calibrated or moderated;

4 the ways in which the criteria or scales are set up and used should relate to expected routes of educational development, giving some continuity to a pupil's assessment at different ages: the assessment should relate to progression.

There is a fair amount of evidence to suggest that teachers have not been very good at recording in the past. HMI state in their survey of the implementation of the National Curriculum (1989): 'In nearly all the schools...the existing arrangements for assessing children's progress were at best barely satisfactory.' They go on to stress the need for a better link between planning and assessment.

In *Education 8–12* HMI (1985) comment on the fact that while assessments of reading are generally satisfactory, the situation is less good in other subjects. In particular the assessment of science does not pay sufficient attention to scientific understanding and competence in many schools. They also thought that the range of criteria needed to be widened to relate more clearly to the aims and objectives of the curriculum. They felt there was a need for more diagnostic work and that more attention should be paid to talking with individual children about their work in order to gauge their understanding.

Neville Bennett and Joy Kell (1989) found that even when assessment was carried out, little use of it was made to adjust planned work to match the needs of the children.

The process of assessment and evaluation is continuous. It isn't just something you do at the end of the term or the year or when the time for the SATS comes round. It starts before the children come to you and must be there at every stage in between, sometimes as part of a formal process, but more often as part of your day-to-day observation of children at work. You also need to evaluate your own performance, skills and abilities as well as those of the children and many of the previous chapters of this book provide tools for assessing yourself and your children in order to decide what to do next.

In the past the fact that a teacher was making formative assessments all the time often meant that there was only a very limited attempt to stand back and assess consciously in order to evaluate what was happening in more general terms. There has also been more limited summative assessment than the National Curriculum demands, as is evident from the comments by HMI quoted above. This takes time and since time is always in short supply during the school day one could easily feel guilty at taking time to assess when one might have been preparing teaching materials or going through children's work. The temptation now is to put a great deal of effort into assessment of individual children's progress and performance and not enough effort into overall evaluation of the teaching approaches and their effectiveness.

Colin Corner (1990) quotes the reactions of a deputy head, who had attended a long course on the assessment needed for the National Curriculum as having learned the following:

1 To value my own experience and judgement about my children based on evidence which I collected through close observation
2 The value of knowing what a child *can* do at any given moment in time measured against his own abilities and *not* those of others
3 The value of organising myself to document incidental occurrences of importance in the classroom, as well as actually organising specific assessment tasks, which were embedded in on-going learning
4 The absolute necessity of being able to think positively about the whole business of assessment and making it a meaningful part of curriculum planning

THE PURPOSES OF ASSESSMENT

A framework for the primary curriculum (NCC 1989a) lists the purposes that teachers' records should serve:

1 They will identify which attainment targets a pupil has studied;
2 They will record a pupil's level of attainment and speed of progress as measured against nationally prescribed statements of attainment;
3 They will provide a teacher with information which will enable schemes of work, allocation of resources, teaching methods, staff deployment and classroom organisation to be evaluated or modified where appropriate;
4 They will provide important information when pupils change schools (e.g. to a different phase of schooling or to a school in a different part of the country);

5 They will provide feedback to pupils and a basis for discussion about their achievements and areas for future effort;

6 They will provide evidence which will be used as a basis for negotiation and discussion with parents about the achievement of their children;

7 They will provide material to be used in discussion with governors, LEAs and the DES, about the performance of the school and groups of children within it.

THE LANGUAGE OF ASSESSMENT

The words *assessment* and *evaluation* are frequently used as if they were interchangeable. They are not really quite the same. There have been many definitions of these two words and they tend to mean slightly different things in different contexts. For the purposes of this book *assessment* refers to the process of gathering and collating evidence; *evaluation* occurs when you make judgements based on that evidence.

If you are to decide what evidence to look for in making an assessment, it is important that you have in mind certain criteria against which you weigh the evidence you find. This means that if, for example, you are checking to see if a child can add numbers to ten, you are clear what the evidence is on which you will base your judgement. Are you looking for this ability as mental arithmetic? Are you prepared for the child to use apparatus of some sort to help in the calculation? What about counting on the fingers? It will depend on the age of the child which of these is acceptable, but you need to know what you are looking for before you set out to check in each situation.

There are a number of words used in the process of evaluation which is may be helpful to define:

Formative evaluation

Assessment of work while it is in the process of being carried out so that the assessment affects the development of the work.

Summative evaluation

Assessment carried out at the end of a piece of work.

Process/product.

In any evaluation you can look at what children are getting out of doing something (process) or at what they finally achieve (product).

Validity

A test or assessment is said to be valid if it can be shown to test what it sets out to test. Thus a written intelligence test given to a child who is unable to read might be said to be an invalid test of his or her reasoning ability.

Reliability
To be reliable a test or check needs to give similar results when given to the same person on different occasions.

Criterion-referencing
A criterion-referenced test is one in which the results are compared with previously defined criteria or objectives.

Norm-referencing
A norm-referenced test is one in which the results are compared with norms for children of a particular age. Norms are usually established by extensive testing on large samples of population.

Sampling
We can never know everything that is in a child's mind. Any test is a sample of what he or she knows, understands and can do and may not be a true representation of that child's ability or achievement. It is no more than the best information we can obtain.

METHODS OF ASSESSMENT

The National Curriculum is demanding a great deal more assessment and, more particularly, recording, than most teachers have been in the habit of undertaking. If you are to make a judgement about whether each child has achieved each Statement of Attainment you will need to be observing and recording all the time.

This sounds more difficult than it may be in practice, because what it involves is teaching diagnostically. A great deal of the work that you do will be geared to the Statements of Attainment and the fact that you have done work towards a particular end with a group of children in itself tells you something about their progress towards achieving the statements. You will still have to check whether each child has achieved the appropriate learning, but you know that at least everyone has had some practice. If there is written work following then this will also help you to know what each particular child has achieved.

The National Curriculum Council paper *A framework for the primary curriculum* (1989a) speaks of the importance of formative assessment in indicating what children should do next and how schemes of work may need to be modified. It notes the need for summative assessment to indicate what children know, understand and can do and also speaks of *informative* assessment as the provision of accurate information for parents, governors, the LEA and DES about curriculum achievement, both individual, in the case of parents, and more generally in the case of the other recipients. It also suggests that schools should be monitoring the performance of constituent groups, such as boys and girls and members of ethnic groups, looking at how successful resource allocation, schemes of work and teaching approaches and INSET involvement have been.

The basic method of assessing children is that of observation. This may be observation of the child's performance or of his or her work. Observation may be extended by testing. These can each be looked at in more detail:

Observation

The evaluation needed for assessing children's progress in the National Curriculum depends, as the evaluation by teachers has always done, on the skill of the teacher in making observations. Teachers have always assessed their pupils by observing what they do, talking with them and questioning them. The validity of judgements made in this way depends upon the skill with which the observation and questioning are carried out and the experience the teacher can bring to the interpretation of the situation.

There is a sense in which all forms of assessment are a kind of observation. Tests and examinations, records and check lists are devices to make observation more systematic and therefore more likely to be accurate. But you can assess only what is evident. A child may know and be able to do more than he or she can demonstrate in a test situation. You need to be continually asking yourself whether a child's performance is representative of what he or she knows and whether the sample piece of work or behaviour you are considering is typical and whether the result would be the same on another occasion.

The same is true if you want to make assessments of the class as a whole. One reason why a teacher's observation may sometimes be more accurate than a test is because the teacher helps the child to demonstrate what he or she knows and can do in all sorts of situations. The sample of the child's performance is thus likely to be a valid one and to reflect his or her potential.

Observation in the normal sense has the advantage that you can take into account many features acknowledged to be important but not easy to test at the same time. For example, in hearing a child read, you may note the words he or she is able to recognise, the ability to put them together in sentences, the child's understanding of what he or she is reading and the mistakes made and their possible significance. It would be difficult to find a test which could do all those things at once with any validity, and while you may be mistaken in your judgements, you are in a position to follow up your findings and check them further.

One disadvantage of this kind of assessment is that you will see only what your experience, background and frame of reference will allow. You may miss things which a more experienced observer would see because you have not encountered them before. For example, if in hearing a child read, you have no experience of considering the significance of the types of errors made by children, you will probably miss some of the particular clues being offered.

Perhaps the really significant point to note here is that the skill of observation is one of the most important skills a teacher can have and it is one that teachers need to work to improve all the time. One way of improving your own skill in observation is to look at children and their work with other teachers, who, because they are different people, will see differently from you and may thus enlarge your seeing. This is particularly important at the beginning of your teaching career, although experience can sometimes make a teacher look less sensitively, if teaching becomes a matter of habit. This kind of assessment can be used in all aspects of work in school.

It should be noted also that observation is not confined to what one can see. It involves checking by questioning and discussion and exploring how children see things. Observation is also the main way in which we assess children's progress in more nebulous areas like personal development. Such areas need as much thought and care in assessing them as in making assessments of children's academic work. Teachers are sometimes reluctant to make formal judgements about more personal aspects of a child's development, but actually do it informally all the time. While it is natural to be hesitant about putting statements about such matters as the ability to relate to others on a child's record, it should be remembered that personal development happens and teachers affect it whether it is recorded or not and it may be better to give it careful consideration, thinking about the needs and problems of each child, than to leave it to chance. You don't avoid making assessments by not discussing or considering them.

You can assess by observation informally or formally. In the process of your day-to-day work there will be points which arise which you need to note. A child will give an answer which makes it clear to you that he or she has understood something important or made a major step forward. There will be other situations where the opposite happens and a child whom you thought had grasped something, demonstrates a lack of understanding. There may be evidence from children's mistakes and errors about the way they are thinking. There will be situations where you discover that you have over- or under-estimated a child's ability in the work you have allocated and it will be important to remember this and make a change for the next piece of work. There may also be critical incidents in the classroom when you learn something about the way particular children react to particular situations or discover that your organisation or planning is less good than you had thought.

It is not easy to find time to note such occurrences, yet they offer you valuable information. It may be that you reserve time at lunch time and at the end of the day to note down anything of this kind which you have noticed in the course of the day. There may also be some opportunities during class time when you can make a note. It is important that these notes are made in places where you will link them with the notes you make when you are checking on particular children's learning. Having a page per child for odd notes is valuable and this can be placed alongside notes for each child about other progress.

Observation is also carried out more formally to check specific aspects of learning. This may be observation of a group or an individual. Here you need to decide in advance exactly what you are looking for, the way you are going to check it, whether you are simply going to observe or enter into conversation with the child or children to see what their thinking may be. You may also need to decide in advance whether you are going to use the opportunity to extend thinking or whether you are simply observing. You need to be clear how you are going to record what you observe. Then you need to decide after observation whether the children in question have grasped the work or whether you need to observe further.

You may be assessing not only the actual learning that has taken place in terms of the Statements of Attainment but also children's learning ability. Where you are observing a group, you may be looking at how children share group tasks, the kind of discussion which takes place, the involvement of the group members, the emergence of leaders within the group, time spent off the task, and so on.

Testing

A test might be regarded as one way of making observation rather more objective. Teachers need to give tests for a variety of reasons and there is certainly a place for both teacher-made and standardised tests, and although the need for standardised tests will diminish with the use of SATs, there is still a case for testing potential.

Teachers often feel that there is something special about standardised tests which makes the results of a child's performance in such a test much more reliable than a teacher's judgement. While it is certainly true that occasionally a test result will make a teacher think again about a child, the judgement of an experienced teacher is also a very good guide. Standardised tests should never be more than one factor among a number used to evaluate the performance and potential of an individual. The same goes for the SATs.

One of the reasons for feeling that standardised test results give special information is because they are the nearest thing we can find to an objective assessment, and subjective judgement is often doubted. There is a sense, however, in which all assessment must be subjective. In the first instance there are subjective views involved somewhere in the choice of test, whether chosen by the DES, an LEA, the head or the teacher. There is also subjective judgement involved in interpreting the results.

If you accept that most of your evaluation is subjective, even when you use tests, you can try to be aware of ways in which you might be mistaken and make a habit of cross-checking your judgements.

A particular point to note about testing is that there is a difference between testing for mastery and testing for other purposes. When you give a test of something children have learned in order to see how well they know it, you should expect to get a high proportion of good answers from everyone if the learning has been adequate. If you are testing to discover where each child stands relative to his or her peers or in order to help you to make decisions about grouping children you should have a spread of scores with some children getting very high scores and others very low scores, because the purpose of the exercise is to differentiate among the children. A diagnostic test, particularly if it is standardised and planned to discover problems, may have any kind of score for any child, because it is designed to discover difficulties. The SATs are mainly designed as mastery tests although it will obviously be possible to identify children who have problems whose difficulties need to be explored further.

It is particularly important to distinguish between testing for mastery and testing for discrimination among the group of children, since the over-use of discriminatory tests is very discouraging for children who do badly. Generally speaking success leads to success and the teacher's task is to organise so that every child is able to succeed at some level.

The use of observation and testing

Teachers normally use tests and observations to find answers to the following questions:

1 Is this child ready for the next stage or for a particular form of learning or teaching?
 In this context you might use a test to discover what a child can do and what he or she already knows. You might also be interested in how the child sets about the task. Intelligence tests of various kinds might be said to come into this category, which may include some developmental and diagnostic tests. The assessment required by the National Curriculum and the SATs are intended to serve this purpose among others.

2 Has this child learned what I wanted him or her to learn?

This is probably the most common reason for testing in school and teachers usually make their own tests for this purpose. It may be a good idea gradually to develop a set of test material for work in specific Statements of Attainment, so that you have tests easily available or even on tape, which can be given to individuals as you feel they are ready to have their work checked. This material would also be useful for testing children who come new to your class in mid-year or children who have long absences.

If you regard each test you give as feeding into a test system over a period and code and store it carefully, you will in due course build up a body of material to use in this way. This also means that time spent on devising tests is used to full advantage.

3 How does this child perform relative to others of his age?

Most primary teachers like to encourage children to work to improve their own performance and discourage too much rivalry. There is, nevertheless, a need to know how a child is doing relative to norms of some kind and you may want to make this clear to parents in a tactful way. This will emerge clearly from the assessment for National Curriculum, but will make it evident to parents and others that the relationship is a complex one with children doing well in one aspect of curriculum and less well in others. This should help to make results more acceptable to children and their parents and make it clear to them the areas in which they must work to improve.

There may be a case for occasional use of a standardised test which gives national norms, to check whether there are children who are under-performing. It is very easy to regard the group you teach as the norm and accept some under-achievement without realising it.

4 What particular difficulties is this child experiencing?

When a child fails to make normal progress, you need to discover why. You also need to discover just what it is the child doesn't understand or can't do. You may therefore need diagnostic test material as well as your own observation.

There is some published diagnostic test material, but you really need to develop your own alongside. You need spelling tests which identify gaps in phonic knowledge and lack of knowledge of spelling rules. *Framework for reading* (1986) by Joan Dean and Ruth Nichols gives this kind of test and a number of others, together with suggestions for ways of teaching the skills and knowledge identified. You also need tests of mathematics which include knowledge of number bonds and tables and identify difficulties with particular operations. Such tests may be used by individuals or by the whole class if you are sorting out what they know at the beginning of the year.

Here again, if you work over a period in developing test material, you gradually build a kit of diagnostic material. It is also helpful, not only to collect material for diagnosis, but also material for teaching and practising the learning which the diagnosis identifies as being necessary.

Some forms of assessment

There are a number of ways of using observation and testing to make assessments:

1 A child's written work, drawing, diagrams, plans, models, graphs, etc. may show whether he or she has achieved what is required for a particular Statement of Attainment

You may be able to check some statements from the normal work of the class or by asking a child to show you a given number of examples of correct work. For example, the science statements in Attainment Target 1, level 2, say that a child should be able to 'record findings in charts, drawings and other appropriate forms'. You could ask a child to show you a given number of examples of recording in different ways. The English statements in Attainment Target 3, level 3, say that a child should be able to 'produce, independently, pieces of writing using complete sentences, mainly demarcated with capital letters and full stops or question marks'. You might say to the children that they will have achieved this statement if they can show you four pieces of work in which there are sentences with full stops and capital letters correctly used.

2 A child may show that he or she has achieved a particular statement as an integral part of another piece of work

A number of the statements are of this kind. For example, Attainment Statement 12, level 2 in the mathematics programme asks that a child should be able to 'choose criteria to sort and classify objects; record results of observations or outcomes of events'. This activity may be part of an environmental study or work in science.

3 A child may check his or her attainments using test material, possibly recorded on a tape recorder

Some of the mathematics statements lend themselves particularly to this form of checking. For example 'know and use addition and subtraction facts up to 10' or 'know and use multiplication facts up to 5×5 and all those in the 2, 5 and 10 multiplication tables'.

4 The teacher may need to check a child's knowledge and understanding by observation and questioning

Some statements can be checked only in this way, although this might well be done as part of on-going work. For example, in Science, one of the statements at level 2 says that a child should be able to 'understand how living things are looked after and be able to treat them with care and consideration'.

5 Children can sometimes be asked to note the Statement of Attainment related to a particular piece of written work
  This makes it easier for you to note the work which gives you specific information. It may also help to clarify for the child the particular goals of the work.

RECORD-KEEPING

Record-keeping has always been an important part of the teacher's work, but the National Curriculum makes new demands on teachers. It would be easy, in concern about recording each child's progress in the National Curriculum, to forget the need for long-term records and for records which give your own input to work and the corresponding output from the children.

Purposes of record-keeping

There are many reasons for keeping records besides those of recording progress in the National Curriculum. An important reason for record-keeping is continuity. If you should happen to have a long illness or leave your present school in mid-year, all that you have learned about your children will be lost, and appropriate records are needed so that someone else can take up where you left off.

Records may help you to match work to individual children and help them to overcome learning problems. Something a child does once may not appear to be significant, but if it happens several times, it may give you important clues to the nature of a difficulty. You may not notice this if you do not keep appropriate records. It would be difficult to keep this kind of record for every child all the time, but you can do it for a small number who have problems.

Important items from a child's background noted over a period may help you to understand his or her difficulties and put you in a better position to help. For example, a child who has changed schools a number of times may be insecure and need help in filling gaps in learning. A child who has a handicapped sibling may find it difficult to cope with the extra attention that the sibling needs from his or her parents. Background information of this kind is sensitive and you or your head may need to ask the parent concerned if he or she minds having it recorded so that teachers are aware of any difficulties the child may have. There is much to be said for background records being jointly compiled with the parents.

You also need to keep records which show what worked and what didn't work with individuals and the group. This means keeping records of what you have tried and with what success. Such information is important for your own development as a teacher as well as that of the children.

The list of people who need informative assessment given in *A framework for the primary curriculum* (NCC 1989a) does not include the next teacher although it stresses the value of records for continuity. Your records are also of value to your headteacher and possibly to a year leader or coordinator who may be relying on you for information about children and the success of the programme planned. You may also need to provide information for other services, such as the school psychological service or the health service.

Assessing the National Curriculum (SEAC 1990c) makes the following points about the records of children's progress. They should:

- be simple to complete so that they do not cause too much interference in classroom activities and practice
- include all the relevant information so that they may readily inform decisions about future action
- be meaningful to others who may have access to them
- be accessible to pupils so that they can enhance pupils' understanding of the teaching, learning and assessment process

What needs to be recorded

Every school should keep long-term records giving relevant information about each child's background and you should be able to turn to such records to discover what you need to know about your children. Background records ought also to give some health information. You need to know about disabilities and defects, particularly when they are not very obvious. You need to be aware of children who should wear glasses, children who have inadequate hearing, children who are colour blind and so on. You also need to know of any children with defects such as a weak heart or asthma or epilepsy which could affect what you do with them in school or any children who have had long absences through illness. You also need the kind of background information about the child's family which was mentioned above.

If you are to take on where the previous teacher left off, you need to know the facts about the work covered in the previous year. The National Curriculum makes this easier in some ways even though it demands a

Name..Year.......................................

Pupils should be able to:		Date checked and notes		
AT1 spkg and listening	participate as speakers and listeners in group activities, including imaginative play			
	listen attentively, and respond, to stories and poems			
	respond appropriately to simple instructions given by the teacher			
AT2 Reading	recognise that print is used to carry meaning, in books and in other forms in the everyday world			
	begin to recognise individual words or letters in familiar contexts			
	show signs of a developing interest in reading			
	talk in simple terms about the content of stories, or information in non-fiction books			
AT3 Writing	use pictures, symbols or isolated letters or phrases to communicate meaning			
AT4 Spelling	show an understanding of the difference between drawing and writing, and between numbers and letters			
	write some letter shapes in response to speech sounds and letter names			
	use at least single letters or groups of letters to represent whole words or parts of words			
AT5 Handwriting	begin to form letters with some control over the size, shape and orientation of letters of lines of writing			

Figure 13.1 English record, level 1

Date checked and notes							

great deal from teachers by way of recording. It should be possible to review a child's progress right the way through schooling.

School records or records to be passed on need to contain only what might be described as *considered records*. Your own day-to-day notes may contain comments about individual children and the success or otherwise of particular pieces of work, recorded for your benefit alone. These notes will form the basis of your final records.

You will also need records of each individual child. It is helpful to keep these records in a loose leaf file with a page for each child. You can then add material and put this into a longer term record when each page is full. Your file should include a check list for each child of the Attainment Statements from the National Curriculum arranged so that you can tick off items as they are achieved. The list on pages 244 and 245 suggests a way of setting this out.

There is much to be said, if you can find the time and especially with older children, for talking with each child about his or her overall progress and what you are recording. At this stage also, the child could add comments.

TYPES OF RECORD

Recording is a time-consuming process and it is therefore important to find forms of record which can be completed easily. Records can be classified as follows:

Notes of observations and check lists

These can be notes of things which occur which you feel are of interest, made day-by-day as things happen. You can make this kind of observation more systematic by observing a few children very closely each week and recording these observations in greater detail. This is a good way of tackling the observation needed to assess children's progress towards the Statements of Attainment. Notes of this kind, kept over a period, can provide insight into a child's development. The record on the next page suggests a way of recording which allows you to make a brief note about your observations each time you check a child's progress. This may be better than using a highlighter or crossing off a section because it gives you information about how far the child has gone towards achieving the Statement of Attainment. The continuation sheet follows this record and could, if necessary, be cut so that the statements are still visible, allowing you at least four sides for checks and notes. This is only likely to be needed where you are dealing with children with special needs.

Collection of specific information about each child's work and behaviour

A teacher may make observations against a check list of specific goals. These might be the Statements of Attainment or they might be such things as the development of independence in study or the ability to work with others. It is useful to identify a series of items and look for different things weekly, monthly or termly. This can be done by the individual teacher, a year group of classes or the whole school.

Collection of errors made by an individual

Errors in reading, writing and number work provide the teacher with important clues to a child's thinking. These become increasingly evident if lists are kept over a period. Children can help by doing some of this for themselves.

Records of achievement

Primary schools are also expected to keep records of achievement for children. *Assessing the National Curriculum* (SEAC 1990c) describes them as follows:

A record of achievement is:
- a cumulative record of an individual child's achievements in school
- compiled by the pupils, the teacher and others who are involved in the learning process
- usually confined to positive achievement
- the place to note personal and social attributes and a wider range of activities and experiences

The booklet goes on to state the purposes which records of achievement might serve:

- to involve the child and parents more closely in planning and reviewing the child's progress
- to enable teachers and parents to help pupils to develop as individuals
- to ensure planned continuity and learning development across points of transition in the child's school career
- to identify with parental help a child's strengths and weaknesses

It is easy to see the benefits that might result from this kind of record. It encourages the child to develop the habit of self-assessment and involves child and parents in considering development. Parents thus become more involved in what is happening to the child in school and aware also of the value of some of the child's out of school activities. It also involves the teachers in considering how best to carry out this work which will add to their understanding of each individual child.

Part of the record might include some form of profile. A profile has been described as a competency map which shows areas of weakness or strength, as can be seen from the examples below. Profile recording is particularly useful for the non-measurable aspects of development. When a profile is used for personal characteristics, it is important to see it as a starting point for development and improvement rather than as a description of inborn characteristics. The example in Figure 13.2 below would be useful to discuss with a child and consider his or her view of how it should be completed

	++	+	av	- -	-	
Imaginative		x				Lacks imagination
Persevering				x		Gives up easily
Well organised			x			Disorganised
Confident	x					Lacks confidence
Persistent					x	Distractible
Cooperative				x		Uncooperative

Figure 13.2 A personal profile

Another example was given in the chapter on parents. This was suggested by the School Examinations and Assessment Council for recording a seven year old pupil's achievement in mathematics. It shows the areas in which the pupil is doing well (Attainment Targets 2 and 3) and the areas in which he or she is doing less well (Attainment Target 6). It gives the teacher a picture of the areas on which the child needs to concentrate.

Tests and assessments

Test scores and teacher assessments are part of the process of implement-
ing the National Curriculum and over a period they will show patterns
which will be of interest. You need to be systematic in reviewing this kind
of information for all children. One way of doing this is to look
particularly at a small group of children each week so that over the term
you look carefully at all the children's work.

A collection of samples of a child's work over a period

The collection of samples of each child's work term by term is a good way
of giving a picture of his or her progress. The child can learn from being
involved in the selection of work for the record folder and this will
provide both child and parents with interesting evidence of progress.

Another way of doing this is to keep a set of exercise books in which a
week's work is done each term.

The collection of samples of work is not very time-consuming, is
helpful in establishing standards in the children's minds, and is a valuable
complement to the information collected by observation.

A record of progress through schemes with clear stages

A scheme which has clear stages, whether a published scheme or the
teacher's own, provides a record of the stage each child has reached in the
particular work concerned. It may be simply a matter of noting the page or
chapter a child has reached or the books a child has read and children can
very often keep this kind of record for themselves.

Lists of work covered or attempted

This is another record which children can keep themselves. It may also be
useful to make a duplicated sheet of work done by the class over a term or
year and then add a note of individual variations. These lists can then go
into the children's individual record folders.

Organisation statements for daily work

If you give children work in writing, the statements you make can form part
of your record of work if you think out carefully the best way to do this.

Notes made by children of work done

It will depend to some extent on the way you work how you use this kind of record. It is helpful on completing a project for each child to note the things he or she did as part of the work. It can also be useful if you work an integrated day of some kind to ask children to record what they have done at the end of each session. If you review these notes they give you some idea of how much work individuals are actually doing. They may also give you information relevant to learning within the National Curriculum. It is also useful to ask children to label some work with the number of the Statement of Attainment to which it relates.

Notes of discussions held with children and their parents and with other teachers

There is a case for reviewing each child's progress with someone else in the course of the year in order to check your own conclusions. In some schools, the head, the deputy or the year leader may do this with each teacher.

Regular meetings with each child's parents will now become a feature of work in all schools and it will be important to make a note of what was said at each meeting.

You may also want to review work with each child in the course of the year and this meeting too should be recorded since such a meeting should result in agreement with the child about the particular aspects of his or her work which need extra effort and a plan to improve in particular areas.

General points

In deciding what records to keep, bear in mind that you want records that are not only easy to maintain but also easy to use. Records which give you information at a glance are more likely to be used than long pieces of writing. Look, too, to see how much recording the children might do for themselves. Any factual record can be kept by children in some simple form from the earliest stages. Even five year olds can make a mark in a large box when they finish something.

A school needs to decide who has access to the records of an individual teacher. Ideally as many records as possible need to be kept in a form which can be shared with children, parents and other teachers. This avoids having to make additional records for discussion with others or for passing on to the next teacher. The next teacher may need something of a summary, however, as will the next school and there needs to be agreement about how this should be made. It will also be necessary to decide how much of a child's record should be passed on the the next school.

There must also be a decision about for how long records which are not passed on should be kept. There may be queries long after a child has left the school and this suggests that the records of an individual should be kept until that child reaches school leaving age. There may be local or national decisions about this.

COMMUNICATION AND CONTINUITY

The National Curriculum requires that teachers should communicate the outcomes of assessment to a variety of audiences which have rather different requirements. *Assessing the National Curriculum* (SEAC 1990c) suggests that the requirements are as follows:

- the pupil needs feedback on current activity as evidence of progress
- parents need periodic checks on progress in sufficient detail for them to work in partnership with the school
- the next teacher needs to know what has been done and how far each individual pupil has progressed to ensure continuity between years
- the headteacher needs to monitor and evaluate progress throughout the school to make sound management decisions on human and material resource allocations
- prospective parents need an indication of what the school sets out to achieve and how well their child's needs may be met
- the LEA will need year group aggregates in sufficient detail to plan INSET programmes to support the National Curriculum

One might also add to this the need for the next school to have information about the progress of individual pupils whom it will be receiving.

Teachers, records should now provide for much better continuity both within schools and between schools. Teachers receiving new children will have information from the previous teacher which will help them to decide where to start work with a new group. If this is to happen, teachers within a school and teachers in linked schools will need to decide on the meanings of their records. *Teacher assessment in the school* (SEAC 1990b) suggests that teachers attempt to use each other's records for planning purposes and discuss which parts of the record were essential and which parts were not really needed. *Assessing the National Curriculum* (SEAC 1990b) suggests that there should be a summary document passed on from teacher to teacher and that this should contain:

- details of levels in Attainment Targets that have been attained
- for levels towards which the pupil is currently working – the Statements of Attainment that have been attained in the level
- information about context and difficulties of Statements of Attainment assessed but not attained.

PROBLEMS ABOUT ASSESSMENT

Time

Every primary school teacher will be aware that the major problem about assessment is finding time to do it. This will gradually be resolved as teachers seek out ways of assessing which are part of their normal work. It will be particularly important to look for forms of assessment which do not require any special activity. The time problem looms less large when one breaks it down to the number of children whose work must be checked each day and each week if you are going to get round the entire class. For example, at level 2 in English, mathematics and science, there are eighty Statements of Attainment. For a class of thirty children this means 240 assessments. Put like this the number sounds alarming, but if one thinks of it as two assessments a day it becomes something much more manageable, especially as some of the assessments will simply be a matter of checking written work or noting what a child does in the course of ordinary work. In English, for example, there would seem to be about ten statements at level 2 which will need special checking. The rest could be checked as part of ordinary work.

It will also help, particularly with older children, if you explain what you are doing and invite children's cooperation in not interrupting you when you are trying to make checks on other children's progress.

Variety of levels

The National Curriculum requires that each child works at his or her own level and this does not make classroom organisation easy. However, primary teachers normally provide work at a variety of levels and the National Curriculum is making this more necessary. Suggestions in other chapters should help you with this problem.

Need for smaller steps

Children with special needs in particular will need work broken down into smaller steps than other children. They will probably need a number of lesser statements building up to the Statements of Attainment. It may be worth while contacting teachers in a special school, many of whom are in the process of doing this for their children. For example, the science statement 'be able to describe familiar and unfamiliar objects in terms of simple properties, for example, *shape, colour, texture,* and describe how they behave when they are, for example, *squashed, stretched* and *dropped* may need to be broken down into the following statements, each of which will need to be assessed:

- be able to describe familiar and unfamiliar objects in terms of their shape
- be able to describe familiar and unfamiliar objects in terms of their colour
- be able to describe familiar and unfamiliar objects in terms of their texture
- say what happens when objects are squashed
- say what happens when objects are stretched
- say what happens when objects are dropped from a height

Children whose home language is not English

It will obviously depend a good deal on how good a child's English is whether this poses a problem or not. There are likely to be some problems. It may be possible for the teacher to re-word what is being asked in a way that the child understands. Bi-lingual adults may help and it may be necessary to enlist the help of a parent to translate questions to a particular child or group of children. Other children may also be able to help in translating. It may also be possible to make judgements from what the child does rather than what he or she says.

Children may be intimidated by having their work checked

This may happen initially but children will gradually get used to the idea that careful checks are being made of how they are doing and that this is for their benefit. It will help to tell them as much as possible about what is happening. It may also be necessary to try not to be too obvious about checking. A teacher walking round with a clipboard may be more intimidating than a teacher coming round in the normal way to help and comment on work and ask questions about how well it is being understood.

Children may be upset by not attaining as well as others

This is undoubtedly a danger but it is helped by the complexity of the system, because children will in general be working towards a variety of different statements and this will make comparison more difficult. It could have the reverse effect in giving every child something to aim for which is within his or her grasp. A great deal will depend on how you present reports on progress to children. A child who is progressing slowly may be encouraged by your praise for the progress he or she has made in achieving level 1 statements in a group where most children are achieving statements in level 3.

Language

In communicating with parents in particular it will be important to select appropriate language. It will be necessary to explain to them the language describing the Statements of Attainment and the levels, but apart from them it will be important to avoid anything which could be considered to be jargon.

SELF-EVALUATION AND THE TEACHER

This book has included a number of analyses to help you to determine your style and preferences and to assess your own performance. The analysis charts include the following:

- Profile of organisational preferences
- Assessing a new class
- New children
- Classroom visit
- Effective teaching and learning
- Preferred teaching style
- The teacher's skill and knowledge
- Teaching skills: observation
- Teaching skills: organisation and control
- Teaching skills: communication
- Teaching skills: planning
- Teaching methods
- Themes, skills and dimensions
- Grouping for learning
- Group composition
- Classroom organisation
- Teacher's time log
- Children's time log
- Where the time goes
- The use of time, space and resources
- Individual children
- Working with parents

If you have already used some of these ideas, you will have done something to answer the question 'How am I doing?'. You may also like to look back at the aims and objectives you started with at the beginning of the school year and ask yourself how far you have achieved them. It is helpful to discuss this with another teacher or with your children.

Your development as a teacher depends very much on your ability to be self-critical, to look at your own achievements and build on them. This is not something you do in your early years of teaching only. You need to go on assessing and evaluating your work year by year throughout your teaching career. The good teacher is always learning.

14 Conclusion

We have now looked at all the main aspects of teaching and learning which are part of the difficult professional task of educating children. We have discussed all the factors involved in teaching a group of children and you should now be in a position to make decisions about all the issues involved in organisation. You may like to turn back to the analysis on pages 3–8 and look again at your answers to see if they would still be the same in the light of your consideration of the issues involved.

Each decision you make has implications for how you set about your task and for your long-term plans. You will also need to consider how you will work towards the organisation you want and what you will do to train your children to work in the way you choose. If this is very different from their previous experience it may take time and you would be wise to introduce changes very gradually and one at a time. If the change you envisage is very dramatic, it may take half a term before you begin to see results. Be prepared for this and be prepared also to stop and consolidate or even go back if something isn't working.

A particular picture of the well-organised classroom has been implicit in much that has been said in this book. It would therefore seem appropriate to end with a description of what such a classroom might look like.

The well-organised classroom is attractive and welcoming. There is colour and interest and it makes a visual impact on the visitor. At the same time it is clear that it is a workshop in which many activities take place. It is therefore functional with materials and tools carefully arranged so that they are easy to find, use and keep in good order.

Children are comfortable and at home in this classroom and it is easy to see that it is as much their base as the teacher's. Their work is much in evidence. It is carefully and attractively displayed, often by the children themselves, who are encouraged to think about the way things can be mounted and shown. There is never too much on display at the same time, however, and there is discussion of what is shown and it is frequently changed. Display is also used by the teacher as a starting point for work.

Children in this classroom feel secure in knowing what they may and may not do and this means that the day runs easily with children moving from one task to the next, sometimes because the next task is part of the programme, sometimes on the instruction of the teacher and sometimes because the child chooses it. They start work as soon as they come into the classroom and it is unusual to see a queue of children waiting for attention from the teacher. There are very few enquiries to the teacher about minor matters of organisation because they are largely taken care of by arrangements within the classroom. Children talk sensibly about what they are doing and learn from one another.

There is always a sense of purpose in this classroom. Children have been trained to do a good deal of planning and organising of their own work and are well on the way to becoming independent learners. Many children become so absorbed in what they are doing that they are prepared to continue with it at home and would choose to work through breaks in the day. They are confident in their ability to learn and do things and have many ideas which they are well able to follow up. They have also become self-critical in a way which helps them to further their own learning. In consequence the standards of work achieved by all the children are extremely high.

The curriculum followed by the class is broad, with many opportunities for using learning in the core subjects and the needs of children of differing abilities have been carefully considered. The teacher is very conscious of the need for first-hand experience and frequently takes the children out of school and brings objects and materials and people into school to extend their experience. The teacher also listens to children and encourages discussion and considers carefully how best to develop skills of all kinds, seeking out situations in which children can communicate for a genuine purpose rather than as an exercise.

The work of the classroom is planned to include class work, group work and individual work and these approaches are chosen very carefully so that they match the teacher's intentions and the needs of the children. The teacher is skilled at holding the interest of the whole class and at the kind of questioning which makes them all think deeply, from the most to the least able.

Work in groups is well used. It is sometimes a matter of a number of children at the same stage being given similar work and sometimes a matter of a group working together to agreed ends. The ability to work with a group has been carefully nurtured by the teacher and many children are now competent group leaders as well as being able to contribute to the work in hand, sharing and taking turns and trying hard to further agreed goals.

The teacher is also well-organised with work that is carefully planned, but at the same time provides flexibility and the opportunity to pick up children's questions or interests if they look as if they would be valuable to follow up. The teacher has clear aims and regularly reviews work in the light of them, demonstrating an enjoyment of learning which is communicated to the children in many areas of work and seeking new ways of stimulating and interesting them.

It is evident that the teacher likes children and enjoys their company, respecting them as individuals without dominating them. The ideas and suggestions they offer are received in a positive and encouraging way because the teacher has the ability to see things from the point of view of each individual child and is thus able to motivate children and match work to each one. Each child has the opportunity to enjoy the challenge of work which is just within his or her capacity but at the same time is able to succeed.

The teacher in this classroom uses time to good advantage and is relaxed. As children have become more independent it has become possible to turn attention to longer discussion and work with individuals and small groups, making them think through ideas and helping them to plan work and evaluate.

The teacher is involved in the wider professional setting of the school and also more generally as a professional educator. This means working to keep up with what is happening in education and seeing whether research findings and knowledge of how children develop and learn have any relevance to the classroom situation.

The relationships between the teacher and the children are reflected in the relationships of the children with one another. There is always a sense of caring in this class and it is evident in many of the day-to-day activities.

Few of us may feel that we can aspire to this picture, yet it is greatly to the credit of teachers in British primary schools that so many achieve something near it.

Bibliography

Association for Science Education; Association of Teachers of Mathematics; Mathematical Association; National Association for the Teaching of English (1989) *The National Curriculum – making it work for the primary school.* Association for Science Education.

Atkin, Janet, Bastiani, John and Goode, Jackie (1988) *Listening to parents,* Croom Helm.

Barker-Lunn, Joan (1970) *Streaming in the primary school,* NFER.

Bassey, Michael (1978) *Nine hundred primary school teachers,* NFER.

Bennett, Neville (1976) *Teaching styles and pupil progress,* Open Books.

—— and Kell, Joy (1989) *A good start? Four year olds in infant schools,* Basil Blackwell.

—— and Dunne, Elizabeth (1990) *Talking and learning in groups,* Macmillan.

——, Desforges, Charles, Cockburn, Anne and Wilkinson, Betty (1984) *The quality of pupil learning experiences,* Lawrence Erlbaum Associates.

Brennan, W. K. (1979) *Curricular needs of slow learners,* Schools Council Working Paper no. 63, Evans/Methuen Educational.

Bruner, J. S. (1985) 'Vygotsky: a historical and conceptual perspective' in J. V. Wertsch (ed.) *Culture, communication and cognition: Vygotskian perspectives,* Cambridge University Press.

—— and Kenney, H. K. (1974) 'Representation and mathematics learning' in J. S. Bruner *Beyond the information given: studies in psychology of knowing,* Allen and Unwin.

Bullock (1975) *A language for life (The Bullock Report),* HMSO.

Button, Jenny (ed.) (1989) *The primary school in a changing world: a handbook for teachers,* Centre for World Development Education.

Carrington, Bruce and Short, Geoffrey (1989) *Race and the primary school,* NFER-Nelson.

Cleave, S., Jewett, J. and Bate, M. (1982) 'Local education authority policy on admission to infant/first school' *Educational Research* 27, 40–3.

Cockcroft Committee (1982) *Mathematics counts (The Cockcroft Report),* HMSO.

Corner, Colin (1990) 'Assessment and the primary school' *The Curriculum Journal* 1, 2, 139–53, Routledge.

Crane, W. D. and Mellon, D. M. (1978) 'Causal influences of teachers' expectations on children's academic performance: a cross lagged panel analysis' *Journal of Education Psychology* 70, 1, 39–49.

Davie, Ronald, Butler, Neville and Goldstein, Harvey (1972) *From birth to seven,* Longman.

Dean, Joan (1977) *The literacy schedule*, Reading and Language Information Centre, Reading University.

—— and Nichols, Ruth (1972), (1986) *Framework for reading*, Bell and Hyman.

Denham, C. and Leiberman, A. (1980) *Time to learn*, National Institute of Education.

Department of Education and Science (DES) (1988) *Task group on assessment and testing – report*, DES and the Welsh Office.

—— (1989a) *English in the National Curriculum, Mathematics in the National Curriculum*, HMSO.

—— (1989b) *English programme of study*, HMSO.

—— (1989c) *Science programme of study*, HMSO.

—— (1990a) *Technology in the National Curriculum*, HMSO.

—— (1990b) *Technology programme of study*, HMSO.

Douglas, J. B. (1964) *The home and the school*, MacGibbon and Kee.

Education Act 1981, HMSO.

Education Reform Act 1988, HMSO.

Edwards, Derek and Mercer, Neil (1987) *Common knowledge*, Methuen.

Evans, Mary and Wilson, Mary (1980) *Education of disturbed pupils*, Schools Council Working Paper no. 56, Methuen Educational.

Galton, Maurice (1989) *Teaching in the primary school*, David Fulton.

—— and Simon, B. (1980) *Progress and performance in the primary school classroom (The Oracle study)*, Routledge and Kegan Paul.

—— and Willcocks, John (eds) (1983) *Moving from the primary classroom (The Oracle study)*, Routledge and Kegan Paul.

—— and Delafield, A. (1981) 'Expectancy effects in primary classrooms' in B. Simon and J. Willcocks (eds) *Research and practice on the primary classroom*, Routledge and Kegan Paul.

—— and Willcocks, John (eds) (1983) *Moving from the primary classroom*, Routledge and Kegan Paul.

—— Simon, Brian and Croll, Paul (1980) *Inside the primary classroom (The Oracle study)*, Routledge and Kegan Paul.

Giaconia, R. M. and Hedges, L. (1982) 'Identifying features of effective open education' *Review of Educational Research* 52, 579–602.

Goodacre, Elizabeth (1972) *Hearing children read*, Reading and Language Information Centre, Reading University.

Harlen, W. (ed.) (1983) *New trends in primary school science education*, UNESCO.

—— (1985) *Teaching and learning primary science*, Paul Chapman Publishing Ltd.

Heibert, J. (1984) 'Children's mathematics learning: the struggle to link form and understanding' *The Elementary School Journal* 84, 5, 497–513.

HMI (1978) *Primary education in England (The Primary Survey)*, HMSO.

—— (1982) *Education 5 to 9: an illustrative survey of 80 first schools in England (The First School Survey)*, HMSO.

—— (1985) *Education 8–12 in combined and middle schools*, HMSO.

—— (1989) *The implementation of the National Curriculum in primary schools*, DES.

Holt, John (1964) *How children fail*, Penguin Books.

Hughes, Martin (1986) *Children and number: difficulties in learning mathematics*, Basil Blackwell.

Jackson, K. F. (1975) *The art of solving problems,* Heinemann.
Kelly, A. (1989) *Gender differences in teacher–pupil interaction: a meta-analytic review,* Research papers in education.
Kerry, Trevor (1980) *Effective questioning,* Teacher Education Project, University of Nottingham School of Education.
Kirkman, Susannah (1990) 'What makes a good teacher?' *Times Educational Supplement* 7 September 1990.
Lewin, K. (1951) *Field theory and social science,* Harper.
Lynch, J. (1987) *Prejudice reduction and the schools,* Cassell.
Mortimore, Peter, Simmons, Pamela, Stoll, Louise, Lewis, David and Ecob, Russell (1988) *School matters,* Open Books.
National Curriculum Council (NCC) (1989a) *A framework for the primary curriculum.*
—— (1989b) *Non-statutory guidance in English.*
—— (1989c) *Non-statutory guidance in mathematics.*
—— (1989d) *Non-statutory guidance in science.*
—— (1989e) *A curriculum for all.*
—— (1990a) *The whole curriculum.*
—— (1990b) *Non-statutory guidance in technology.*
—— (1990c) *Environmental education.*
Parsons, J. E., Ruble, d. N., Hodges, K. L. and Small. A. V. (1976) 'Cognitive-developmental factors in emerging sex differences in achievement-related expectancies' *Journal of Social Issues* 32, 3, 47–61.
Plowden Committee (1967) *Children and their primary schools (The Plowden Report),* HMSO.
Rosenthal, R. and Jacobson, L. (1968) *Pygmalion in the classroom,* Holt, Rinehart and Winston.
Rutter, Michael, Maughan, Barbara, Mortimore, Peter and Ouston, Janet (1979) *Fifteen thousand hours,* Open Books.
Schools Council (1977) *Match and mismatch: Raising questions; Teacher's guide; Finding answers,* Oliver and Boyd.
School Examinations and Assessment Council (SEAC) (1990a) *Teacher assessment in the classroom.*
—— (1990b) *Teacher assessment in the school.*
—— (1990c) *Assessing the National Curriculum.*
Sherif, M., Harvey, O. J., White, B. J., Hood, W. R. and Sherif, C. (1954) *Experimental study of positive and negative intergroup attitudes between experimentally produced groups: robbers cave study,* University of Oklahoma Press.
Southgate, Vera, Arnold, Helen and Johnson, Sarah (1981) *Extending beginning reading,* Heinemann Educational Books for the Schools Council.
Sylva, K., Roy, C. and Painter, M. (1980) *Child watching at playgroup and nursery school,* Grant McIntyre.
Tizard, Barbara, Blatchford, Peter, Burke, Jessica, Farquhar, Clare and Lewis, Ian (1988) *Young children at school in the inner city,* Lawrence Erlbaum Associates.
Tyler, R. W. (1979) *Basic principles of curriculum and instruction,* University of Chicago Press.
Vygotsky, L. S. (1978) *Mind in society: the development of higher psychological processes,* Harvard University Press.
Warnock Committee (1978) *Special educational needs (The Warnock Report),* HMSO.

Wells, C. G. (1985) *Language, learning and education: selected papers from the Bristol study: language at home and at school,* NFER-Nelson.

Wheldall, Kevin and Merritt, Frank (1984) *Positive teaching: the behavioural approach,* Unwin Educational Books.

Wragg, E. C. (1984) *Classroom teaching skills,* Croom Helm.

Index